BECOMING THELMA LOU

My Journey to Hollywood, Mayberry, and Beyond

By
Betty Lynn

With Jim Clark
and Tim McAbee

Becoming Thelma Lou
My Journey to Hollywood, Mayberry, and Beyond
By Betty Lynn with Jim Clark and Tim McAbee
Copyright © 2022 Jim Clark and Tim McAbee. All rights reserved.

Published in the USA by:
BearManor Media
1317 Edgewater Dr #110
Orlando, FL 32804
www.bearmanormedia.com

Perfect ISBN 978-1-62933-974-0
Case ISBN 978-1-62933-975-7

BearManor Media, Orlando, Florida
Printed in the United States of America
Book design by Robbie Adkins, www.adkinsconsult.com

Front cover photographs: TAGSRWC Archives (main image and bottom inset), Surry Arts Council (top inset). Back cover photographs: Hobart Jones (top left), Author collection (middle left), TAGSRWC Archives (bottom left and right).

Contents

Foreword by Tanya Jones v

Preface ix

Chapter 1: A Kansas City Start 1

Chapter 2: Call of Duty. 37

Chapter 3: Taking a Bite of the Big Apple—And It Bites Back! . 66

Chapter 4: Off to Hollywood. 81

Chapter 5: After the Fall of the Studios, Humpty Dumpty,

   and the Rise of Television 135

Chapter 6: Finding My Place in Mayberry 178

Chapter 7: Leaving Mayberry 207

Chapter 8: After Mayberry 213

Chapter 9: *Return to Mayberry* and Elsewhere. 235

Chapter 10: Further Returns to Mayberry. 249

Chapter 11: Ties that Bind—Mayberry and Mount Airy 283

Chapter 12: Positive Signs 288

Epilogue. 306

Acknowledgments 308

Foreword

My friend, my Mayberry mentor, my adopted family, my counselor—Betty Lynn was all of these things and much more to me.

My first encounters with Betty included working out the logistics of getting her from Los Angeles to Mount Airy. For her first trip to Mayberry Days in 2001, Betty was on the same flight from Los Angeles to Charlotte as Howard Morris. She was seated in coach, while Howard had booked himself for a seat in first class. Howard purposely misbehaved so much that the flight attendants moved Betty to first class to help with him—Howard's intent all along.

Another year, Betty called me from an LAX ticket counter to let me know that she had missed her flight. She immediately handed the phone to the ticket agent, who worked with me to find a way to get "Thelma Lou" to Mayberry Days.

After her appearances each year at "Colonel Tim's Talent Time," the big closing show at Mayberry Days, I would take Betty back to her hotel (or to her apartment after she moved to Mount Airy). She and I would sit in my car and talk for hours. Betty would describe all the things she loved about Mayberry Days, as well as Mayberry in general, and confide about all the things that she didn't particularly like and thought should be changed. I would express my views and confess to her in return. Each of us knew that we could confide with confidence.

Betty loved being in Mount Airy and spending time with her fans. She remembered their names, and she remembered their joys and their sorrows. Betty had a sincere empathy for others. A few years after she began coming to Mayberry Days, Betty started talking about making Mount Airy her home. Talk became reality when she moved to Mount Airy on January 17, 2007. Hobart and I picked Betty up at the Charlotte airport. Prior to her arrival, I had directed the placement of the many, *many* boxes that were packed by movers in Los Angeles and sent to Mount Airy.

Betty moved into her new "nest" with a gorgeous view of the Blue Ridge Mountains. She loved watching the changes of the seasons. Her new hometown welcomed her with lots of burgers, fans, and, most of all, love. Taxi drivers, in awe that they were helping "Thelma Lou," carried her groceries to her apartment. She got special treatment in all aspects of her life.

I would hear about Betty's activities from others in town before Betty herself had a chance to tell me. Mount Airy is definitely a small town. People keep an eye on each other. They observed Betty's every move with both goodwill and curiosity. Betty adjusted quickly to Mount Airy. She was every bit as attuned an observer as those who were observing her.

Her visits to the Andy Griffith Museum remain memorable for thousands upon thousands of fans. She loved telling fans that I was her agent and arranged her schedule. The reality was that I simply did whatever she instructed me to do.

Betty was a part of my family and my daily life. She called Hobart "our husband." She attended my children's out-of-town weddings, and she was at all of our family holiday and other gatherings. My grandchildren thought she was magical. She told Ryan and Skyler that fairies were real, and that became a matter of fact in their lives. Parker loved taking flowers to her and getting her wonderful hugs. They all just simply couldn't believe that they knew "Thelma Lou."

Betty always knew that I was there for her when she needed me. From time to time, she had challenges. Betty had a major surgical procedure shortly after she moved to Mount Airy. Hobart and I sat in the waiting room at a Winston-Salem hospital for hours as the surgeon worked miracles. Betty became so close to the surgeon that, when, after a few years of follow-up, he told her that he was considering releasing her from his care, Betty asked him to please keep her as a patient. She told him that she loved seeing him and also that she really enjoyed eating at Village Tavern during her trips to Winston-Salem to see him. Like the taxi drivers and the rest of us, the surgeon simply couldn't say no to Betty. He agreed to see her for a few more visits, and Village Tavern sold a few more of their signature hot fudge sundaes.

Everyone who met Betty loved her. Betty told more stories about her life than I could ever imagine one person could possibly have experienced. You'll find many of her favorites in this book. What an amazing time to be in Hollywood. What a remarkable and talented lady. What incredible memories each of us has of her. I can't wait to read and relive her special moments and stories.

I think about Betty every day when I pass her ninetieth-birthday exhibit outside my Arts Council office. She is forever a special part of my life and my memories. During Betty's last days, her apartment was filled with hundreds of cards sent by adoring fans for her ninety-fifth birthday. Throughout her time in Mount Airy, Betty was always surrounded with love, and she responded with the same love in return.

Thank you, Betty, for all the memories, all the smiles, a few shared tears, and all the love!

Tanya Jones

Preface

This book's journey to publication has been like a visit to Mayberry. That is to say that our work on the book has pleasantly strolled along and spent a lot of time simply rocking in chairs on front porches. Bursts of activity have often been followed by lengthy periods of more strolling and more rocking. Our taped interviews for this project with Betty began in 2004. The last recordings were completed in September 2021. Betty was making final revisions to the manuscript just a few weeks prior to her death in October 2021.

We have strived to preserve Betty's voice throughout the pages ahead. We have made modifications only as much as was needed to enable the smooth transition of spoken words to the printed page. Our mission was simply to be Betty's typists and transcribers. We hear Betty's voice speaking to us in these pages, and we hope that you will as well.

The only parts of this book that were written after Betty died are the Foreword by Tanya Jones, this Preface, the Epilogue, the Acknowledgments, and the captions for photographs. We have tried our best to represent Betty's vision for this book in those passages.

Betty lived a truly remarkable life and was a marvelous, natural storyteller. She was also blessed with an extraordinarily sharp memory of events from throughout her long, adventure-filled life. You might expect during a lifetime spanning ninety-five years that there would be many forgotten details and confused or conflated memories. Not so in Betty's case. Our fact-checking found only a handful of minor details that needed slight tweaking. Our own, somewhat younger brains probably have far more memory errors about events that have happened to us in any given recent week, not to mention a lifetime.

Countless millions of us continue to be entertained by Betty's performances, most notably, of course, as Thelma Lou on *The Andy Griffith Show*. Even folks fortunate enough to have met Betty and perhaps to call her a friend likely will be surprised by some of the experiences that she shares in this book.

Surprises notwithstanding, Betty was a joy and a light in this world. We hope you find a corresponding delight in reading her story in her own words.

Jim Clark and Tim McAbee
April 2022

Chapter 1: A Kansas City Start

TODDLER IN THE GRASS: About one year old and not much taller than knee-high to a grasshopper. Photo courtesy of Surry Arts Council.

"Take it from the top" is a familiar refrain in music and theater rehearsals. I'll follow that cue and do the same as I share my story with you here.

I was born at Research Hospital in Kansas City, Missouri, on August 29, 1926. Former President Harry Truman died at the same hospital the day after Christmas in 1972. I was baptized as a baby as Elizabeth Ann, a good, solid Irish Catholic name. When

I was confirmed at age seven, I added Theresa, so I was Elizabeth Ann Theresa.

My birth was several weeks earlier than my mother's expected due date of late September to early October because my deranged father, in a violent rage, had beaten my mother so badly that she went into early labor. The truth is that my mother almost lost me before my birth.

I never knew my father. I probably rarely even saw him. After being married for about two years, my mother left him in the summer of 1927, when I was ten months old. We went to live with her parents, George and Johanna (aka Josie) Lynn, who also lived in Kansas City. My mother, grandmother, and grandfather were the people who raised me. My Aunt Mary was still at home at that time as well, because she did not get married until she was forty-six.

My father must have been quite mentally ill. Prior to his beating of my mother that caused my early birth, my father had pressed the barrel of a loaded rifle against my mother's pregnant belly with me inside and had threatened to blow her to pieces. Later, when I was a newborn, my father put Mother and me in a closet and started lighting matches and stuffing them under the locked door while threatening to burn down our house.

Mother finally got up the courage to leave. While my father was away from the house one day, Mother ran to a neighbor's house and called her parents. At that time, my mother and her parents were somewhat estranged. Her parents had been against the marriage. I know it must have been difficult for my mother to admit that she had made such a big mistake by marrying my father. She chose our safety and our future over her pride.

After Mother left my father, it took almost five years to get the divorce finalized because my father's family had political influence in Kansas City. Mother eventually hired a hard-nosed criminal attorney. He was finally able to expedite the matter.

Once the divorce was official, Mother got full custody of me. My father was supposed to pay child support, which would have allowed him some visitation. He never paid a dime. I therefore had no contact with him. Even after the divorce, my father continued to make lots of threats. One such threat was to kidnap me, but not

GOT YOUR GOAT?: Just kidding around. Giddy-up! Photo courtesy of Surry Arts Council.

because he really wanted me or cared about me. My mother said he just wanted to cause problems and to be an irritation—in other words, purely for spite.

My family's concerns about my father were so great that I had to be walked to and from school by a family member. The school was informed that I was never to leave with anyone other than my mother, my grandparents, or my Aunt Mary, no matter what another person might say to try to convince the school staff. Even though I was young, I was aware of a lot of things and I was careful. I used to have a recurring dream in which I was in the school yard and there would be a big navy blue car that would slowly drive by. I think I had actually seen that car at some point, and then started dreaming about it.

My father worked for the city in some capacity. I never knew what he did. Whenever Mother started to tell me something about him, I would say, "I don't want to hear it." And so it was that I never had a relationship with my father at all. My poor mother would try to tell me things about him, but I would stop her.

It bothered me whenever anyone asked me about my father. I finally asked Mother what I should say when I was asked about him. She suggested that I say that he is dead in order to stop the questions. I told people my father was dead for so many years that, in my mind, he really was dead. That avoidance of confronting the truth about my father would come back to haunt me.

In September 1948, while I was filming *Mother Is a Freshman* for Twentieth Century-Fox, I was interviewed by Edwin Schallert, the drama editor for the *Los Angeles Times* and also the father of actor William Schallert. During the interview, Edwin Schallert asked about my father. I replied that he was dead. It never occurred to me that anything would come of it. The profile was published by the *Times* and then picked up by news services all across the country.

Mr. Schallert later called executives at Fox and screamed and yelled at them about how I had lied to him. He thought if I would lie about my father, then I had probably lied throughout the interview. I felt terrible about it and was in tears. I explained the situation to the Fox executives and, fortunately for me, a gentleman in the publicity department had a similar family situation and completely understood my dilemma. He came to my defense, called Mr. Schallert, and explained things. He went on to say that I should not be condemned for saying my father was dead. This was simply what I had said all my life to protect myself. I then had to go down to the *Times* offices and apologize to Mr. Schallert in person.

After some years of my having a successful career, Mother received a letter from my father. He had since remarried, but he wrote in the letter that he would leave his wife and move out to California to live with Mother and me. He felt that, in the eyes of God, they were still husband and wife and that he would be happy to come and live with us. She wrote back and made it clear that she had absolutely no interest in anything of the kind. My mother, grandparents, and I were resolute that they and I should never have any further relationship with him.

When Harry Truman became president, Mother told me that one of my relatives was in his cabinet. I told her I did not want to know about it. I now wish I had let her tell me.

One morning after breakfast, I happened to look at the obituaries in the *Los Angeles Times*. I thought I recognized my father's name. I asked Mother if I was correct in thinking the man listed in the obituary was my father. She said that indeed he was. We were not

SAY "CHEESE": A formal portrait when just a kid. Photo courtesy of Surry Arts Council.

surprised that, as he had indicated he would do, my father had actually been living in the Los Angeles area, probably for years, when he died.

Around 2003, long after my father, as well as my mother and grand-parents, had died, my friend Joan Leslie called me and explained that a lady she had been talking to wanted to contact me. The lady claimed to be a relative. I declined. Then about a month later, Eli-nor Donahue called me with a similar story. She had met a lady who claimed to be my cousin and wanted to get in touch with me. Again, I declined. I had absolutely no desire to be in touch with my father's family.

I said at the outset that I would "take it from the top." I should've instead said "take it from the beginning," because my father was anything but the top. He was the rock bottom. It often worried me that his evil blood was part of me. I choose to believe that the love from the rest of my family, a strong faith, and the grace of God conquered that evil.

At first, I was reluctant even to mention my father in this book. I spent much of my life trying to avoid even the thought of him. As I was working on this book, I came to realize that his harmful actions and also his absence had set the course for my formative years—everything from my mother's trauma and my premature birth to our living with my grandparents and living with a fear of him.

My father was both a painful void and a menacing shadow loom-ing over my family's life. The negativity that my father represented required the creation of a lot of counteracting positives in order for my family and me to survive and ultimately thrive. And that we did.

That's enough about my twisted father. As the song says, "You've got to accentuate the positive—eliminate the negative." So, let's go back and take it from the top, or at least near it.

Finding a Rhythm

When I was five, I started taking piano and ballet and tap lessons at the Kansas City Conservatory of Music. I will always be grateful for the scholarship that allowed me to attend. There was no way my family could have otherwise afforded the classes. I attended once a week. I continued the piano lessons for just a short time, and then decided to focus on dance. I later wished that I had kept up with the piano.

SACRED MOMENT: It's apparent that no one said, "Say 'cheese'" for this confirmation portrait taken at age seven. Photo courtesy of Surry Arts Council.

I did stick with dancing and later singing lessons, both of which I loved. Helen Burwell, a beautiful lady, was the dance teacher. She would go away in the summer and study in New York or Los Angeles, and then return to teach. She was a marvelous teacher.

When I was six years old, I was in a talent contest. I won the first-prize of twenty dollars for my imitations of Lon Chaney, Mae West, and ZaSu Pitts. I also remember a recital when I was about twelve years old. My mother made me a short apple-green raincoat of oil cloth. I wore a little hat and my tap shoes and had an umbrella. I sang "One Rainy Afternoon," which Ida Lupino had sung in the popular 1936 musical comedy film of the same name. I danced with the umbrella, which was my mother's idea. I won a ten-dollar prize for that performance.

We had a recital every year at the conservatory. I was grateful that I always got to do a solo. I would sing and dance. I maintained the scholarship until I was sixteen. I was also an assistant to the instructor for my last few years, until I was seventeen. Helen would choose a number for me to sing, and my mother would make a costume for me. Mother not only made my costumes, but she also made many of my everyday clothes. She was capable of doing almost anything. She was incredibly artistic and very talented.

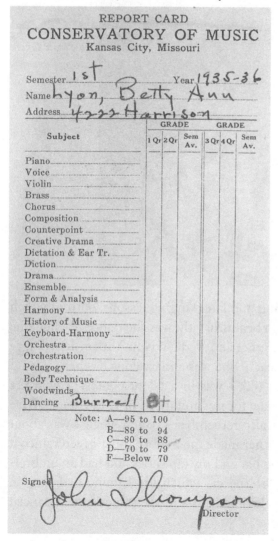

MAKING THE GRADE: We're not lyin' when we say that a nine-year-old student was clearly a better dancer than Conservatory Director John Thompson was a speller of last names. Photo courtesy of Surry Arts Council.

GOIN' WITH THE FLOW: This is probably not a dance move that Helen Burwell taught at the conservatory, but when you're feelin' groovy, you just make up your own moves. Photo courtesy of Surry Arts Council.

A BIRD? A PLANE?: No need for a cape. A gleeful young lady spreads her wings and is ready to soar. Photo courtesy of Surry Arts Council.

*HELLO, DOLL!: The best Christmas gift ever, a Shirley Temple doll in
1935. Photo courtesy of Surry Arts Council.*

When I was in the fourth grade, I got very sick. The doctors
thought I might have polio. Fortunately, it turned out that I didn't.
The doctors never did determine exactly what I had, but they at
least confirmed that it wasn't polio.

Maybe because I had been so sick, for Christmas that year, I received
an extra special gift, a Shirley Temple doll. It was the biggest thing I

ever got for Christmas. I just loved it. My mother took my picture with the doll, which I have kept all through the years.

After I recovered from that illness, the doctor advised my mother that, if I were to get very sick again, she might not be able to cover the expenses. He suggested that she take out a five-hundred-dollar life insurance policy on me in order to make sure that, if I died, she would at least have enough money to bury me. I never knew about that policy until I was in my late fifties and Mother was in the hospital and dying.

I told her, "Oh, Mother, I don't want to talk about that now." *For heaven's sake*, I thought. After all those years, of all the times for her to bring that up—she was the one dying, not me.

For all I know, that life insurance policy is still in force out there somewhere. When I die, maybe something will get triggered in some computer somewhere and, out of the clear blue sky, my estate will miraculously receive a five-hundred-dollar windfall. Just in case, "Thanks in advance, Mother!"

My Mother

Like me, my mother's name was Elizabeth. She helped me so much in every way. Mother would play the piano for me when I was singing and help me with interpretation. She would say, "Well, Betty, it's like telling a story. You just have a little more breath behind it." I didn't have the voice she had. She had a naturally wonderful mezzo-soprano voice. She had gone to Catholic school, and the nun who taught voice had been an opera star. Mother said her real training came from that nun. Later, at sixteen, Mother was given a scholarship to go to Chicago and study with a nationally respected voice coach of that era.

I remember Mother talking about performing in a production of *Hansel and Gretel* with the opera company in Chicago. She also performed in New York at one point. Mother even had her own radio show. It was called *Memories*. It was on WHB, Kansas City's second-oldest radio station. Mother would sing pop classics and would either play piano or have an accompanist, sometimes a harpist. When I was very little, maybe two or three years old, I would occasionally get to go with her when she did her radio show. I would just sit there and listen to her sing. I was spellbound by the whole experience.

My Aunt Mary, my mother's eldest sister, who also lived with us until she got married, would sometimes go with Mother and me to Mother's performances. By the time I was born, most of Mother's performances were in Kansas City, but every once in a while, she accepted jobs in Chicago and elsewhere. Aunt Mary would usually travel with us.

Aunt Mary was actually my mother's half-sister. My grandmother had been married before she married my grandfather. Aunt Mary had the most beautiful blond hair and bright blue eyes. I remember Mary saying that, when my grandmother was pregnant with her son, George, Mary prayed hard that George would have blond hair and blue eyes because everyone else in the family had brown hair and brown eyes. She wanted someone who looked like her. She prayed and prayed, and, lo and behold, George did have blond hair and blue eyes.

Mother told me that when she was appearing onstage one night, Mary was seated in the front row with me on her lap. As Mother was singing, she looked down and I had both of my hands over my

ALL DECKED OUT AT THE DOCK: With the fabled SS Catalina *ferry as a backdrop, young Betty is seated next to grandfather George Lynn during a 1930s visit to Southern California. Perched below (left to right) are Betty's mother, grandmother, and Aunt Mary. Photo courtesy of Surry Arts Council.*

ERIE TIME: A lakeside visit to Cleveland, Ohio, for ten-year-old Betty and mother, grandmother, and Aunt Mary. Photo courtesy of Surry Arts Council.

ears. Mother said that critique was really tough to take. She never let me forget that.

My mother played both the piano and the organ very well. In fact, her last job in Kansas City was for five years as the organist and choir director at St. John the Evangelist Church. The church had an old-fashioned organ that she had to pump with her feet while her hands were on the keyboard. She nodded her cues to the choir. She was in constant, seemingly twitchy motion, but she got the job done. She was fun to watch.

Mother also did concert work, and one of her jobs was singing for a "lightning artist"—sort of a Bob Ross of the time, but about five times faster. The lightning artist would produce an entire painting as my mother sang a song. Granted, it would generally be a long song, but the painter still had to be really fast to complete the painting before the end of the song. I wonder whether the clouds and trees painted by the lightning artist could ever be as happy as the ones Bob Ross painted.

A not-so-happy event was the time my Mother became ill with rheumatic fever and had to stay in bed for about a year when I was twelve. Extended periods of convalescence from occasional serious ailments would be something of a pattern among members of my family through the years, but overall I think we were a pretty hardy bunch.

WELCOME TO CHECKPOINT CHICKIE: Check out those hot wheels!
Photo courtesy of Surry Arts Council.

A Beautiful Neighborhood

I attended grade school at E.C. White Elementary School, near 49th Street, at the corner of Brookside and Main Street. My old school was torn down in 1965 to make way for the new Plaza branch of the Kansas City Public Library. That building in turn was overhauled into an even spiffier library branch in 2005.

Even as that location and the Country Club Plaza neighborhood have evolved over many decades—basically most of my lifetime— that area continues to have some of the old charm. We lived in the neighborhood surrounding The Plaza. It was a beautiful area. I truly loved The Plaza. Through the years, the city has incorporated more modern buildings, but when I was young, it was mostly Spanish style, inspired by Seville, Spain, and simply gorgeous.

The Plaza was decorated for every major holiday—no matter what. At Easter, there were big Easter bunnies on the street corners and big eggs that you could sit on. The Plaza Easter bunnies are a cherished tradition that continues to this day.

Around Thanksgiving, city crews and businesses put up an enormous number of lights throughout The Plaza. The Plaza Lights, as they not surprisingly have officially become known, are mostly amber and white with a few dramatic splashes of color. There's a big lighting ceremony, and some lucky dignitary gets to throw the switch to turn on all the lights. What a thrill that would be. The whole area becomes a dazzling light display, and it stays that way until mid-January.

Through the years The Plaza Lights have become a tradition not just for Kansas City residents, but also for tourists. For me, as a kid, The Plaza seemed to be gorgeous all the time. A specific memory I have is that there was a family that would come up from Mexico every summer to perform music at The Plaza. The adults and the older children would play instruments and sing, and the younger children would dance. It seemed that each year there was a new baby to celebrate. It was a festive tradition. We anticipated their arrival every summer. Their arrival at The Plaza wasn't just their family tradition, but ours as well.

Though Missouri native son Walt Disney had left the Kansas City area for California just before the initial Plaza was built, I've often wondered if The Plaza Lights weren't at least part of his inspiration for his use of lights to such great effect at Disneyland. I like to think so.

Now, with all the modern buildings, the look of The Plaza has changed. When I went back for my fiftieth high school reunion in the 1990s, I still enjoyed seeing The Plaza, but I loved it the way it was when I was growing up even more.

The Kansas City stockyards were about five miles due north of the neighborhood where I grew up, but if the winds blew strongly north to south, as seemed to happen at least once a year, we would smell them. It was awful. But we couldn't complain. It was worse for the people who lived or worked downtown. The odor for them was probably inescapable, because the stockyards were just west of the downtown business district, and the winds generally blew west to east.

A DAY ON THE TOWN: The odds are good that this young shopper is coming from or going to a Katz Drug Store, a beloved Kansas City institution for many decades. Photo courtesy of Surry Arts Council.

Speaking of the stockyards, I remember a traumatic incident that happened when I was in the third grade. Somebody at our school had the brilliant idea of taking us kids to the stockyards on a field trip. The odor was virtually unbearable. It made our eyes water. We had to watch the poor cows go across this big bridge-like structure. The workers would then hit the cows in the head. After that, I didn't eat meat for many months. I had been so sickened by what I had experienced that just the thought of eating meat made me feel sick all over again. Why somebody would think it was a good idea to take little kids to see something like that is a mystery to me. It was the only field trip I ever took.

My grandmother would send me down to a Safeway store, about a block and a half away from our house, to get some meat. I would stand outside the store for the longest time as I tried to get my courage up to go in. Once inside, I tried not to look at the raw meat. I would practically keep my eyes shut as I told the butcher what I wanted. It took a while for me to get over my revulsion at the sight of meat, but I eventually got to where I could once again enjoy a good hamburger or steak.

My Grandparents

It was a couple of years before the Great Depression that my mother and I moved into her parents' house. Unfortunately, once the full effects of the Great Depression kicked in, my grandparents were unable to make their mortgage payments and they lost that house. It broke my grandmother's heart.

For a long time after that, we lived in apartments. I remember hearing my grandparents talk about things they had done to help people. When my grandparents started having hard times of their own, no one was there to help them. Maybe it was just that everyone was experiencing similar difficulties and couldn't help. My grandparents had been only two payments behind. The builder was their neighbor. He lived right across the street from them. That didn't matter. It was every family for themselves.

That experience with my family haunted me through all the years I lived in Los Angeles. In the back of my mind, I always had this nagging worry that, with just one or two bad breaks or unfortunate events, I could end up being a bag lady with a shopping cart and wandering the streets. They call it the "Depression Era mentality." Once you've been through that, you're always aware that it could happen to you again. It's hard to ever let yourself feel totally secure. That's one way that my Christian faith has been such a source of reassurance for me. My relationship with God has always blessed me and helped me find peace of mind.

My grandfather was George Andrew Lynn. I called him Dad because he was the only real father I ever had. He was a locomotive engineer for the Missouri Pacific Railroad. He drove passenger trains for decades, including during World War II. His regular run was from Kansas City to Omaha and back. He would go to Omaha, spend the night, and then drive the train back the next day.

My grandmother's maiden name was Johanna Hill. She was also known as Josie. In fact, her gravestone reads, *Josie Lynn.* I used to plant Joanna Hill roses in California. They are beautiful yellow tea roses.

On April 26, 1943, my grandmother got a phone call from a man at Missouri Pacific. He told her that my grandfather would not be coming home at his usual time. The man wouldn't say why. She became worried because my grandfather had some close calls over the years, including a head-on collision with another train. Fortunately, he and the fireman were able to jump off the train once they realized they were on the same track as the oncoming train. In my grandfather's nearly fifty-year career with the railroad, he had—unfortunately and, for his part, unavoidably—hit seven vehicles stopped on the tracks. It's a miracle that only one resulted in a fatality. Dear reader, please don't ever take chances at railroad crossings!

When my grandmother got the call about my grandfather being late, she became frantic with worry as she imagined all of the bad things that could have happened to him to cause the delay. Somebody from the railroad eventually called back and told my grandmother that my grandfather would be returning that night, but at a different time. That relieved her mind a little, but the man who called still wouldn't say why my grandfather's return was being delayed.

A wonderful woman named Carrie Tinnell had worked for our family since the time my grandmother's children were teenagers— for over thirty years at that point, including as much as possible during the Great Depression—and she continued to work for our family until 1947, the year she got married, at age 74! Carrie, who was African American, was also a poet who once even wrote a poem for the governor of Kansas. Carrie lived on Nebraska Avenue near the railroad line that was part of my grandfather's regular route.

When my grandfather would pass the point closest to Carrie's house, he would give a special toot on the horn to say hello to Carrie. She would sometimes call our house to let us know that my grandfather had just passed by. But on this particular night, Carrie telephoned to say that she didn't know what was going on, but there were soldiers with rifles all along the track. This information only increased our curiosity and concern all the more.

As we would learn later that evening, the railroad had held my grandfather over in order to put President Roosevelt's car on his train. Because of my grandfather's reputation for overall competence and reliability, the railroad and government officials had chosen him to be the engineer for the president. As my grandfather passed Carrie's place that day, he gave his usual "toot," which no doubt caused the Secret Service agents to have a collective heart attack. Carrie called us to let us know that my grandfather had just passed by.

Because of heightened security concerns during the war, the president had to travel without the public knowing where he was. Later, there was a story in *The Kansas City Star* about Dad being the engineer for the president. I was so proud.

I would love to travel by train again. I think passenger trains are something our country should have kept going better than we have. We subsidize everything else, but complain about the railroads. Maybe it's my upbringing among train people, but for me, trains were always the best way to travel. Train trips were filled with scenery, the food was wonderful, and the crews were dedicated and expert. It's hard to get an experience that fulfilling from up in the clouds. It would break my grandfather's heart to know what has happened to the railroads. Maybe trains will make a comeback. President Biden seems to love trains. Maybe part of his legacy will be to revitalize passenger trains in America.

My grandfather started out with steam engines when he was twenty years old. He was a fireman and shoveled coal. He ended up being an engineer. Around the railroad, his nicknames were Pop and Skyball. He operated Missouri Pacific's No. 157 steam engine for five years. Beginning in 1940, his last engine was a beautiful new *Eagle* diesel, No. 7001, the second *Eagle* made as Missouri Pacific began its full-fledged transition to diesel engines.

During the years that the 7001 operated on the route between Kansas City and Omaha, the engine was known as the *Missouri River Eagle*. The *Eagle* engines were a gorgeous blue with a stylish silver eagle on the front. My grandfather's jumpsuit and cap were designed to coordinate with the scheme of the engine. He was a handsome man to begin with, and I always thought his official train attire made him all the more dashing.

I was thrilled to be able to travel with my grandfather for his last run before he retired on November 30, 1947, after nearly fifty years of working for the railroad. To think about that experience now still makes me very emotional. I was at Fox studios. I had just finished filming my part in my first movie, *Sitting Pretty*. Fox let me fly back home to go on the final run with my grandfather.

THE FINAL RIDE: In the cab with grandfather George Lynn for his last train run from Omaha to Kansas City in 1947. Photo courtesy of Surry Arts Council.

I rode up to Omaha as a passenger and stayed overnight. For the ride back to Kansas City, the railroad let me be in the cab with my grandfather and his fireman, G.W. Stabler. Missouri Pacific had never before allowed a woman to ride in the cab, but, because of their deep respect and gratitude for my grandfather, they made an exception for me. I dressed for the occasion as if it were a red-carpet premiere in Hollywood. I wore a green dress with a matching hat and a muskrat fur coat that was dyed white.

At station platforms all along my grandfather's route that day, there were dozens to sometimes over a hundred people waiting to say goodbye. The men my grandfather had worked with all through the years were choked up. He was choked up, too. Many of the men were so filled with emotion that they could barely speak. They just shook my grandfather's hand. It was very moving. Between stations, people were standing and waving. We passed several trains along the way, and their entire crews would be at the windows on the side facing us as they waved and cheered. My grandfather was

TRACKS OF YEARS: Wearing a dyed muskrat coat and holding a large bouquet of flowers, a proud granddaughter joins family, friends, and Missouri Pacific officials in celebrating George Lynn's retirement after decades of service. The beloved railroad man holds the heart-shaped flower arrangement sent by wife Johanna. The wrapped package on the ground is the fine leather suitcase that the railroad gave as a retirement gift. Photo courtesy of Surry Arts Council.

overjoyed by the send-off he received. My grandmother always said that her only rival was that locomotive. They spoke of the train as a "she." My grandfather loved his trains. He truly did.

When we pulled into Union Station in Kansas City, there must have been two to three hundred people waiting to greet us, including several members of our family. There was a ceremony on the platform with remarks of congratulations from top railroad officials. The president of the railroad had sent a telegram, which was read to the crowd. My grandmother, who had recently made the move to Los Angeles to live with my mother and me, was too infirm to travel unless absolutely necessary. She sent a heart-shaped bouquet of red carnations with gold ribbons that read, "Love, Josie."

I don't believe that my grandfather received a gold watch for his retirement. After all, any good railroad man would already have his trusty watch. Instead, he was presented with a leather suitcase. The whole day had been the perfect cap to a distinguished career that my grandfather loved. I was incredibly honored to be able to share that special day with him.

My grandfather would have immediate use for his new suitcase. In time for Christmas, he joined my mother, grandmother, and me in Los Angeles. The four of us were together once again, living in one house. The only difference was that we weren't in Kansas City anymore. My grandparents spent their last years in California. Grandma lived in Los Angeles for only a year and a half before she passed away in 1948 at age seventy-three. My grandfather lived eleven years beyond her, passing away at age eighty-one in 1959.

Feathers and Fur the More

One Easter when I was very young, my grandparents got me a little baby chicken. We called him Chicky. One day Chicky was walking around the house, and I couldn't find him. Or maybe Chicky was a she—who knows? As I went into the kitchen, my grandmother was standing there with a broom in front of her. I said, "Where's Chicky? I can't find Chicky."

She said, "Oh, I think Chicky went to look for its mother."

That answer kind of satisfied me, and I went back to playing. It turned out that my grandmother had accidentally stepped on

Chicky and killed him. She didn't know he was there. She had mashed him, and she was trying to scoop up his body with a broom. She had the broom in front of Chicky's remains. I can still see her looking at me so straight and serious. But I never forgot, because I wanted Chicky. Where's Chicky? Poor Grandma. After I was grown, she told me what had happened. She said she didn't want me to see the smooshed chick.

Another time, my grandfather had brought home a full-grown chicken. I don't know what he named it. That chicken went missing, and then one night we had chicken for dinner. My grandfather thought Grandma had cooked it. She said she never would have done that. Even so, my grandfather would never eat chicken ever again. We couldn't believe that his aversion to eating chicken would last that long. Whenever a chicken came out of the oven and was served, he wouldn't eat it. My grandfather always maintained that the missing chicken wasn't the reason, but I don't know what else the reason could have been. It must have been either his attachment to that chicken or something similar.

PORCHSIDE PALS: Favorite dog Bob stands guard over Betty and cousin Jack O'Brien, who was just under three weeks younger than Betty. Jack was Aunt Loretta's son and Cousin Joan's brother. Photo courtesy of Surry Arts Council.

We also had a dog. His name was Bob. He had a bobbed-tail—
thus the name. He was a border collie, black with a big white collar.
He was the most wonderful dog. When my grandmother's father
died in October 1919, my grandmother went down to Vernon
County and brought home this puppy for her children. He was a
pup from her father's dog. Bob was still living when I was seven or
eight years old and my mother and I were living with my grandparents. He was about fifteen years old by that time.

After our family moved to an apartment on Harrison Street, we
were on the second floor. Poor Bob was in pain from arthritis and
other ailments of age. I know going up and down those apartment
steps was hard for him. I haven't quite reached Bob's final age in
dog years, but I think I already understand how he felt about stairs.

Sometimes I had to take Bob on a leash for a walk. Even as an old
and infirm dog, Bob was still strong enough that he could almost
drag me down the steps. I remember lying on the kitchen floor with
him and putting my head on his stomach. He was moaning, and I
would pet him. It was a terrible loss for our family when Bob died.
I know for a fact that he was the smartest dog in the world. Our
whole family loved that dog. He was like a member of the family.
Because we lived in an apartment and had no land of our own, my
grandfather took Bob's body out in the country somewhere and
buried him.

Years later in Los Angeles, though my grandfather discouraged
me from doing so, I got a black cocker spaniel. I named him Topper.
He didn't like me at all. He even bit me in the face one time. Topper had a ferocious bark and often scared visitors. He would "tree
them," as my grandfather would say. I would have to go outside and
grab his collar to hold him back in order to allow visitors safe pas-
sage into our house. He was a good guard dog—probably too good.

Topper adored my grandfather. They were almost inseparable.
Topper liked to ride in our car. He would sit behind the back seat on
the ledge next to the rear window. When I was driving, my grandfather would sit in the back seat with Topper. One day, as I looked in
the rearview mirror, my grandfather had slouched down in the back
seat, and Topper was resting his head on my grandfather's head with
those long ears hanging down and making it look like my grandfa-

DOGGIE LIKES FROGGY: Holding a frog toy, grandfather George Lynn has the full attention of family dog Topper. Aunt Mary is seated in the middle. Photo courtesy of Surry Arts Council.

ther was wearing earmuffs or a fur hat with flaps. It cracked me up. I still laugh when I picture the two of them doing that.

Topper was trained to go get my grandfather's house slippers out of the closet in his bedroom, bring the slippers to him, and then take my grandfather's street shoes to the closet. Our bedrooms were in the back of the house, so Topper had to go through the whole house in order to perform this ritual. It was a wonderful routine.

Beginning to Do a Few Tricks of My Own

While I was attending Southwest High School, I got my first job working in local radio. It was called *The Jo Ann Taylor Show* and was broadcast Saturday mornings on KMBC from the John Taylor Department Store in downtown Kansas City. My roles varied

A MOTHER'S HANDIWORK: This costume, created in 1940, is one of many sewn by Elizabeth Lynn's loving hands. The custard-colored costume is part of the permanent Betty Lynn Exhibit at the Andy Griffith Museum in Mount Airy, North Carolina. Photo courtesy of Surry Arts Council.

depending on which items the store was featuring that week. Various ladies portrayed the character of Jo Ann Taylor. The advertisements were done as little dramas. For example, one week I might play the part of a girl getting ready to go to summer camp, and perhaps there would be a cute little blouse on sale for $4.95. I would tell about it. Another time I might play a bride who was planning her wedding, and on this broadcast I would talk about whatever wedding-related items the department store wanted to advertise.

I don't remember exactly how I got into radio, but it was likely through some combination of my mother's initiative and Helen Burwell's connections. By that time, I was not just a student at the Kansas City Conservatory of Music. I had helped with instructing the younger students for a number of years. The conservatory was a logical place for a local radio show to seek new—that is to say, inexpensive—performers. Given my long tenure at the conservatory, I would have been an obvious prospect.

I find it interesting how sometimes significant things have happened in my life and either I never knew or no longer recall how they came to be. That's the case with my start in radio. But what I do know is that I was very glad to get the job. I loved doing it. I was

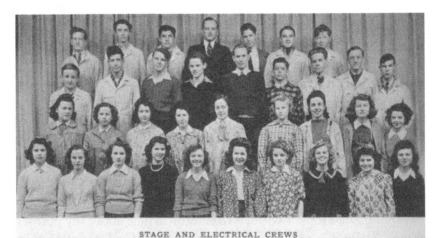

STAGE AND ELECTRICAL CREWS

Top Row: Kennard, Benton, Williams, Mr. Smith, Zoglin, stage manager, Plagmann, Barney. *Third Row:* Young, Fogel, Hurst, chief electrician, Higdon, O'Meara, Kirkwood, Baumgartner, Stooker, Parry. *Second Row:* Cunningham, Smith, Kaufmann, Matthews, Kaufmann, O'Brien, Cusick, Hazlett, Jackson. *Bottom Row:* A. Mantz, Winchell, Carswell, M. Mantz, Lynn, Robinson, Arnold, Gay, Helman, Bono.

HIGH SCHOOL CREW: Front and center but still behind the scenes with fellow stage crew members in this junior-year photograph from the 1942 edition of Sachem, *the yearbook for Southwest High School. Photo courtesy of TAGSRWC Archives.*

paid $7.50 per show and was thrilled about that. Those radio shows were my first paid jobs.

I also became a featured speaker at school. My teachers often asked me to read to the class. I'm not sure why they selected me as often as they did, but I was always glad to do it. I wasn't shy about getting up in front of a group to speak.

All kinds of random seeds were planted during my school days, only to sprout years later. An English teacher once gave me some sheet music. It was just something she wanted me to have. Many years later, in August 1949, I had occasion to use that same sheet music while doing *Peg O' My Heart* at the Laguna Summer Playhouse. The words were a bit different, but the music used in the play was the same as the sheet music my teacher had given me.

Laurette Taylor, a well-known actress in the first half of the last century, had originated the role of Peg on Broadway in 1912. In fact, *Peg O' My Heart* was written by J. Hartley Manners, Laurette's second husband, with Laurette in mind for the role. Laurette's son, Dwight Taylor, was in Laguna at the time I was playing Peg in *Peg O' My Heart*. After seeing one of the performances, Dwight called society columnist Hedda Hopper and told her how wonderful he thought I was in the play. He told her that he couldn't believe how much like his mother I was in the role. I considered that to be a great compliment.

I had never seen Laurette Taylor in *Peg O' My Heart*, but I had stepped into a performance of *The Glass Menagerie* on Broadway in 1945 and caught a glimpse of her as Amanda Wingfield. She was absolutely stunning in that role and earned rave reviews. That's why I was so pleased by the comparison of me to her by Dwight Taylor. Hedda Hopper wrote a wonderful article about my performance. Sadly, due to a tornado, I lost that article, along with most everything of mine that was stored at the time in a family member's garage in Kansas City.

Say It Ain't Sew Business

Back to my high school days: I also did some acting. I was scheduled to play a lead role in our senior play, *What a Life*, which had been a hit on Broadway a few years earlier. Unfortunately, I was

BETTY ANN LYNN, major in *Redskin Revels;* member of courtesy committee, Glee Club, stage crew, and Scalpers.
GEORGE L. MacCURDY, staff sergeant and marksman in R O.T.C.; Honor Roll; member of tennis squad; junior critic of Ruskin; courtesy committee; Denver University speech scholarship; V .C.; Sachem business staff.
ROBERT H. MACKEY, captain in R.O.T.C.; member of rifle team; expert rifleman; Student Council representative; V. C.

SENIOR MOMENT: From the 1943 edition of Sachem. *Photo courtesy of Surry Arts Council.*

failing sewing class, and you couldn't be in the senior play if you were failing anything. (And yes, sewing was a regular class offered in high school at that time.)

From the get-go, it was obvious that the sewing teacher didn't like me. Maybe this teacher had a bad experience with a previous redhead in her class and was inflamed by even the sight of me. In any case, she gave me a hard time and constantly needled me. I may not have been the next Betsy Ross, but I didn't sew all that badly. I successfully made the items required of me in the class.

My mother and I went to see the sewing teacher. Mother explained that I did not intend to be a seamstress and that I was going into show business. We were not interested in whether I could sew. Mother further pointed out that she did not feel the teacher had the right to prevent me from being in the senior play. The teacher finally relented and gave me an "I" (Inferior), rather than an "F" (Failing), so I got to be in the play. One of my best friends, Mary Eileen O'Brien, was also in the play. We played the same part. The play ran only two nights. She played the role one night and I played it the other.

I also performed at some of the assemblies in high school. I remember reciting "Nancy Hanks," a popular poem of the time. It was about Abraham Lincoln's mother. It started, "If Nancy Hanks came back as a ghost / seeking news of what she loved most." That was killer stuff in high school in the early1940s.

On another occasion, I had to climb a shaky ladder and get onto an even shakier platform to sing a song. Another girl and I were dressed as bluebirds up in a nest. We sang "The Love Nest," which was used as the theme song, only without the lyrics, for George Burns and Gracie Allen's radio show, and later for their television show. I was just glad to get through that without needing to discover whether I could fly.

I turned seventeen the following August, and enrolled for the fall semester at Junior and Teachers College of Kansas City, which is now Kansas City University. Because my mind just was not on school at all, I failed almost everything. My real focus was working as a singer at the Town Royale supper club in the Biltmore Hotel in downtown Kansas City. I performed there six weeks, and then

ROYALE TREATMENT: A vintage postcard advertising two of Kansas City's top spots for savoring music by talented entertainers while enjoying "fine foods and charcoal-broiled steaks." Photo courtesy of TAGSRWC Archives.

went to the Plaza Royale, the owners' other nightclub in town. It was located near where I lived in the Country Club Plaza area. I would then perform there for six weeks. I worked from 5:30 p.m. to 1:30 a.m., and then went home. I was paid about thirty-five dollars a week.

During that time and for the rest of her life, my grandmother was in nearly constant pain and often thought she was dying. When I got home from my supper-club gigs, my grandmother was usually still awake. My mother or I, or my grandfather if he happened to be home from a Missouri Pacific run, would stay up with Grandma. I tried to comfort her by getting her to take deep breaths and exhale slowly. Doing that seemed to help her relax.

By about four o'clock in the morning, the nitroglycerin or the little bit of codeine we gave Grandma would take effect, and whoever had been sitting up with her could finally go to bed as well. Because I had to be up early for school, I got very little sleep. The subjects I passed were generally art and drama.

One history teacher in particular did not care for me. This time I couldn't blame his disdain for me on a hypothetical vendetta against redheads. I knew the reason he didn't like me. It was because I argued with him about Catholicism. He regularly had mean things to say about my faith. I finally stood up one day and confronted him. I told him that I was tired of hearing him say such things.

The dean called our house and told my mother that she should not have me singing in these clubs, and that I was failing my courses. This was upsetting to me, because Mother did not "have me singing" in the clubs. I had an agent who sent me to auditions, and I got the jobs. I was an entertainer and it never occurred to me that it was wrong to be in the clubs. I wasn't going there to drink. I was there to sing. The dean maintained that I should be studying instead of singing.

Because the dean was so upset, Mother and I went to see him. Luckily, Mother had known the dean's daughter, who was studying to be a concert pianist. The daughter had gone to New York, hoping to get into Juilliard. Mother explained that she knew his daughter and knew how talented she was. Mother further explained that she understood his daughter wanted to be a great concert pianist and that I wanted to be in show business as well. She told him that it frankly didn't matter to her or to me whether I passed my history class. I continued to sing in clubs, and my college days soon became history.

For my club work, I was billed as "Betty Lynn—Song Stylist— The Red-Haired Angel." The pianist at the Town Royale supper club, a lady named Zina, accompanied me. On my first night, I wore a formal gown with my hair up. I sang a wide selection of the popular songs of that time, as well as standards and show tunes. We also took requests. I noticed throughout the evening that patrons would come up and request a song or two, and then put money in a

ARMED FORCE: All dressed up and ready either to carry the weight of the world or to reach for the stars. Photo courtesy of Surry Arts Council.

big bowl on the piano. I would say, "Oh, you don't have to do that. That's all right. I'll be happy to sing it."

On our first break of the evening, Zina was quick to reprimand me for discouraging tips. She explained that the two of us would split the tip money at the end of the night. Obviously, I had no idea about the tip jar, but the working relationship with Zina improved. Later, there was another lady who occasionally played in the club. She brought her own organ and played it, as well as the piano. She also sang. Her name was Zora.

Time at Ease

I met a lot of nice people during my time singing at the supper clubs. Many of them were young men in the military. Two nice guys who often visited the club were Pete and Eddie. They were buddies, and the three of us had interesting conversations and innocent, fun times out on the town together. They even came over to our house for home-cooked meals on a few occasions.

Another young man I enjoyed spending time with was Edgar Dalton. His preferred nickname was Duke. He was a lieutenant in the Army Air Corps. He was a handsome, sweet, wonderful young man. He was a navigator and was eventually shipped out to a base in England. While he was away, we kept in touch as best we could by writing letters.

By the time Duke returned to America, I was in New York and getting ready to go overseas with the USO Camp Shows. My grandmother told Duke where I was, and he navigated his way to New York to find me. He asked me to marry him. I was flattered and thought Duke was adorable, but I was not thinking of marriage at that time. Not only was I about to be going overseas for an extended time, but I was also focused on my career as an entertainer. Duke and I eventually lost touch. He moved on with his life, and I pursued my career. I have no doubt that he made a great husband to someone else. For better or for worse, it just wasn't meant to be me.

Marriage apparently wasn't in God's plan for me. I dated a lot of very nice gentlemen over the years. Especially when I was in New York and later in Los Angeles, I always seemed to be able to have a date for a premiere or other social engagement. Sometimes the men were more like escorts. Sometimes those pairings would be arranged by a studio publicist for the benefit of either me or my escort, but most were real dates.

My most serious romantic relationship was with a man named Bill. He was a widower and an attorney in Los Angeles. We were engaged three times. Each time he proposed, he presented me with a gold necklace. He broke the engagement the first two times. He was conflicted. He also had feelings for a woman named Marilyn. He apparently would think he had finally decided that I was the one, propose, give me the gold necklace, and I would accept. Then he would become wrapped up in thoughts of Marilyn—I might just as well call her Juanita—and get cold feet. The engagement would be off and I would return the gold necklace.

That happened the first two times. By the time of our third engagement in 1974, my suitor was so confident that I was definitely the one for him that he proclaimed that if we didn't get married, I could just keep the necklace anyway. All the arrangements were made for our wedding at my church, St. Timothy Catholic Church in West Los Angeles.

My fiancé came by my house one night and informed me that Marilyn was back in town, and he was once again having feelings for her. That was it. Three strikes and this marriage dodger was out. I picked up the phone and called the Bishop at St. Timothy's and told him that the wedding was canceled.

The Bishop told me how sorry he was to hear this news. I replied, "Well, I'm not. It's better to find out now than after the ceremony." I had loved my confused beau, but I wasn't about to continue down this loopy path, much less down the aisle.

And you can bet that I did indeed keep the gold necklace. After all the heartache, I had earned it! I loved Bill and I know he loved me, too. He was just torn when it came to decisions of the heart. The rest of the story is that Bill did in fact eventually marry Marilyn a few years later. I believe they lived happily ever after. I hope they did. Both are deceased now.

So much for romance. Back to the nightclubs decades earlier in Kansas City: Two gentlemen, Dr. Deming and Mr. Newstreet, owned both the Town Royale and the Plaza Royale. My arrangement of alternating six-week stints at each location was working out nicely for all of us. However, my employment abruptly ended when a new twenty-percent entertainment tax was imposed by the government during World War II. The owners were concerned that their clientele would balk at the increase in prices, so they avoided the new tax by doing away with some of the entertainment, which unfortunately included me.

A Singer in Woolf's Clothing

With my Kansas City nightclub career kaput, I went to work for Woolf Brothers, which was a beautiful department store right across Main Street from the Town Royale. At the time I started working there, Woolf Brothers primarily carried menswear, except for a few ladies accessories. I got a job behind the counter selling

PORTRAIT OF A YOUNG LADY: A studio photograph taken at about age seventeen. Photo courtesy of Surry Arts Council.

accessories. I was regularly recognized as the former singer from across the street at the Town Royale.

The lady in charge of my department called my mother and told her that Woolf Brothers was interested in sending me to New York to train as a buyer. She also told her that I had sold some purses and other merchandise that had been just sitting on the shelves for years. I wasn't a pushy salesperson and was surprised when Mother told me what the lady had said. Mother explained to the lady that I would be thrilled at their interest, but that I planned to go into show business. However, Mother told the lady she was welcome to discuss the offer with me.

In the meantime, twin girls who were friends of mine from school had noticed in the newspaper that USO Camp Shows was coming to Kansas City to hold auditions. They told me about the ad and encouraged me to audition. I auditioned for a man named Saul Turek and a couple of other men with the USO. Mr. Turek told me to contact him when I turned eighteen.

Chapter 2: Call of Duty

In September 1944 and now eighteen years old, I followed through and contacted Saul Turek. He arranged for the USO Camp Shows to bring me to New York. My mother just needed to sign some paperwork giving permission for me to join the USO, and I would be all set. At that time, anyone under twenty-one needed written permission from a parent or guardian to sign up with the organization. Mother couldn't believe that I was interested in being a part of the USO—especially if it meant touring overseas to God only knew where. She kept asking me whether I was sure about my decision. I said to her, "If I were a boy, they would make me go."

Mother replied, "But you're not a boy. You're a girl." I was very patriotic, as most people were in those days, and I wanted to do something for the war effort. I convinced Mother that this was what I wanted to do. Even though Mother was very scared for me, she and I took a train to New York, and she signed the papers allowing me to join the USO.

The USO sent me to Saks Fifth Avenue for my uniform. It was all wool, including a wool-lined raincoat and hat. Mother paid for pictures to be taken of me in my uniform. She had her copies tinted. She kept one of her prints on the piano at our house for years. I didn't know where the USO was planning to send me in that uniform. Given all that wool, I assumed I might be going to Europe. I assumed wrong.

As all of us new USO recruits honed our acts, we initially performed primarily at military bases along the East Coast. For more than three months, we developed our shows by doing these performances. I received ninety-six dollars per month for incidentals.

Various people performed in these shows. I remember one guy was a golf pro. He wanted me to join his act. He explained that I would simply lie on my back on the stage and he would put a golf ball on my forehead and then knock it off. He promised that he

WOOL'S WORTH: Tailored at Saks Fifth Avenue, but soon to be closer to Kathmandu. The shoulder patch bears the USO Camp Shows insignia. Photo courtesy of Surry Arts Council.

would not hurt me. Despite his assurances, I declined. I had a drive for show business, but not that kind. It did not suit me to a T to be a tee. I chose to stick to my singing and dancing.

One night stands out in my mind. I performed at Fort Dix in New Jersey. My mother had made me a beautiful costume of white satin with iridescent sequins that she had sewn by hand. The top had straps and there was a short flared skirt. Over the short skirt, there was a long skirt which hooked in the back. That design allowed me to sing, then unhook the longer skirt, toss it aside, and dance. That night I sang "I'll Be Seeing You." It was outdoors and there was a large crowd. It was dark, so I couldn't see how big the crowd was, but I knew there were a lot of people. I had already done a song and dance number and then I came back out for this one.

At that time, "I'll Be Seeing You" had just come out and was very popular. Before 1944 was over, Bing Crosby, Frank Sinatra, and Billie Holliday each would have a big hit with it. When I finished singing the song that night, there was dead silence. I was stupefied. I had never performed when the audience didn't applaud or react in some way. Thinking that I must have done a terrible job, I just stood there for a while and smiled meekly.

After what seemed like an endless pause, there suddenly was a burst of applause. As I walked off the stage, the director of entertainment was standing in the wings. I asked him what had happened out there. He informed me that the men in the audience had just received their orders. They were shipping out at midnight. The song had deeply touched them. I cried that night and still get emotional telling this story. In fact, it is hard to sing that song and not think of those guys and wonder about their fates.

One night, Candy Jones, the beautiful fashion model who was already quite well known, was also in the show. Like me, she ended up touring extensively in Asia with the USO. At well over six-feet tall, Candy was a favorite pin-up model with the servicemen. She suggested that I meet with Harry Conover, who was her modeling agent and future first husband.

I went to Mr. Conover's office in Manhattan. As I entered the office, I began taking off my gloves. I didn't get the first glove completely removed before Mr. Conover reached for my right hand and grabbed an empty glove. We visited a bit and then he gently informed me that he did not represent junior models. Even though I was eighteen, I photographed younger. He was kind, but my career as a fashion model never made it to the runway.

That was just as well because I was about to be unavailable for any modeling for a while, at least in New York. A man from USO

STEPPING UP: Eager for the chance to serve and to raise the spirits of others. The shoulder insignia represents the China–Burma–India theater of war. Photo courtesy of Surry Arts Council.

Camp Shows called me in and told me that the organization would like for me to tour overseas as part of what was known as the Foxhole Circuit. He said that Tommy Decker, a twenty-one-year-old guitarist from Chicago, would accompany me. Tommy had recently been playing electric guitar with the Slatz Houseman Trio on the jazz circuit in the Midwest.

The USO man explained that Tommy and I would visit general hospitals, station hospitals, and field hospitals. I was to be "the girl next door" and go from ward to ward, singing, taking requests, and visiting with the servicemen. I told the man that sounded like something I would like to do.

In preparation for traveling overseas, I received an enormous number of vaccines. I think I got a shot for every known communicable disease for which a vaccine had been developed. I promptly got a high fever from my body's reaction to all of the shots. I was hallucinating. I remember being in a hotel room with no clothes on, walking around, and talking to myself out loud. In a panic, I called Mother and told her that I thought I was dying. She caught the next train headed for New York. By the time she arrived, I was feeling much better, but it was still a comfort to have her with me.

The timing of the vaccines and my mother's coming to New York meant that she was also there when I got the call one day that December notifying me to be ready to ship out. I can still remember going to Union Station to catch the train. All I knew was that I was going on a train to Florida. My mother tried to hold back tears and once again tried to persuade me not to go through with leaving. I have to admit that it crossed my mind that I might never see her again. By that point, however, not only did I feel duty bound to go, but I also really wanted to go and be part of the war effort. I knew there was potential for danger, but I also had the sense that it could be an unforgettable adventure. I was both apprehensive and excited about the experiences that lay ahead for me.

Off We Go with the USO Camp Shows

Our group was at a base in Florida for about a week as USO officials briefed us about the basics of our "special mission," as it was called, and its purposes and protocols. When I got on the airplane, I still didn't know where I would end up. On top of that, it was the first time I had ever flown in a plane!

We sat in bucket seats on either side of the plane with our cargo in the middle. It turned out that we were going to the China-Burma-

India theater of war (the CBI), but no one yet had told us that. I had wool clothes and other cold-weather gear. I never understood why nobody would tell us where we were going. It wasn't as though we were on a top-secret mission. At least, I don't think we were. In any case, we weren't clued in about the secret destination until later on.

Our trip across the Atlantic included a stop in Bermuda, followed by the Azores, and finally Casablanca. As we learned along the way, these were basically just stopovers as we headed to our final destination. We put on a show for the servicemen who were stationed at each of the locations.

Tommy Decker was from a Greek family in Chicago. He didn't like me very much, but I thought that was actually a good thing, because if he had liked me a lot, that could have been a problem. He played guitar pretty well, and his playing got better as the tour went along. He occasionally even did an instrumental. He was dedicated to the mission and had a strong work ethic. There was also a group of concert artists on this tour. There was a soprano, a tenor, a contralto, a violinist, and a pianist. They were operatic and quite grand. They traveled alongside us.

Our lodging, if you can call it that, while in Casablanca was horrible. They put us in a rundown hotel that had been taken over by the American soldiers. I shared a dingy room with the violin player. My bed was just a tattered mattress on the floor. It was partially stuffed with straw and smelled of urine. I would've been better off in a stable. I kept my coat and hat on, and turned my coat collar up and pulled it as tightly as possible around my neck. Unfortunately, my mouth was exposed. Any insect that bites will fly or crawl for miles to get to me. Whatever it was that bit me that night caused my lower lip to swell up really big. It was also very painful. I went to a medic, and he gave me some camphor, which did little to help my pain. I was unable to sleep and had a dreadful introduction to Casablanca. It was not the beginning of a beautiful friendship.

After we left Casablanca, we made stops in Cairo and then Tehran, where we arrived on Christmas Eve. A very nice young man with the USO named Neal Savage was in charge of our traveling group of entertainers. I have often wondered what happened to him. He was Catholic, as I am.

Neal told me there was going to be a midnight Mass led by Father John Tackney, an especially devoted Maryknoll priest, who spent much of his life serving in some of the harshest and most far-flung locations, especially in Asia. That level of devotion to missionary work is a hallmark of the Maryknollers, and Father Tackney was an exemplary example.

Neal invited me to go to the Mass, and I accepted. After the service, we stayed to have coffee and talk with Father Tackney. I didn't get back to the barracks until about two in the morning. The snooty ladies from the concert group were also staying in this barracks. They reported me for being out so late. Neal let them know I was with him and that we were both with a Catholic priest.

After this incident, I requested that I not be scheduled to perform with or travel with that group anymore. Today they might be called "mean girls." I heard later that the group was reprimanded for numerous incidents of misconduct, and some were even kicked out of the USO.

After Tehran, we flew to Karachi, which at that time was still part of India. This was a couple of years before Pakistan was created in the separation from India, which was still under British rule. Besides India, I spent most of my time in Burma, which is now Myanmar, but it will always be Burma to me.

At this point in our touring, we were not just visiting hospitals. Wherever there were even a couple of servicemen, we would be sent to visit. In part because everything was so unpredictable from day to day, our itinerary was not very organized. It was a matter of performing wherever we were needed or wherever we happened to be at the time.

On one expedition, our little group got lost and had quite a scare. Tommy and I were heading to Bhamo in the Kachin region of far-north Burma. A young sergeant was driving our command car. Tommy was in the back with his guitar, and I was in the front next to the driver. We went through areas that had been bombed out. Even though it was supposed to be the dry season, it started raining—and not just a shower, but a monsoon-like downpour. Some of the bridges were washed out, and we had to travel over makeshift bamboo and rope bridges that had been placed for crossing.

COMMAND PERFORMANCE: With Tommy Decker and a Dodge command car, one of several vehicles used for travels throughout Burma and India. Photo courtesy of Surry Arts Council.

As it was getting dark, the driver finally admitted that he was lost. We would find out later that we had somehow managed to drive about ten miles into China, which was an ally, but we were surrounded by pockets of territory held by Japanese soldiers. Our driver said that we needed to turn around and try to go back the way we had come. As he started to back up, we heard someone shout at us. We looked down into a ravine to the front and left of our vehicle. There was a little man with long black hair. He was dressed in yellow and carrying a machine gun. The sergeant backed up quickly and then suddenly stopped. He realized the guy had on GI boots. The driver yelled at the man. He was an American—a Greek from Chicago, in fact. Tommy was thrilled to see him.

The man was with an Office of Strategic Services (OSS) group that had people from Burma's Kachin region fighting with them. One of the Kachin people was a little boy of ten who had killed a lot of people. The OSS group invited us to visit with them. They said that the Kachins were fighting in areas they were not used to and that they wanted to go back to the hills where they lived.

I sang and Tommy played for the group, and they shared with us some of what they had to eat. We also learned the reason that the man we first saw was dressed in yellow. He was wearing a parachute. Supplies were dropped to fighters by parachute, and the man had fashioned clothes from one. (I'll bet *he* didn't get an "Inferior" in his sewing class!)

The OSS group decided to send someone back with us to see if they could get through the Chinese checkpoints. The Chinese were protective of their border and tended to be rather trigger happy. The OSS men didn't know if the Chinese would allow Americans through, and there was no way to send communication to them to let them know ahead of time that the OSS wanted to get through. It was apparently harder to get through Chinese defenses on purpose rather than by accident, as we had done earlier.

As we prepared to depart, a Marine captain got in our command car with a young man and a local interpreter. They sat opposite me in the back. All three had guns, and the captain also gave Tommy a rifle, as he was now in the front with the driver. The captain then gave me a blue steel .32 automatic pistol and a shoulder holster. He also gave me instructions that, if anything happened, I was to use it. I didn't know whether he meant that I was to shoot somebody or myself.

It was pitch black and we had to travel without lights. We were all quiet as mice, and I was praying, because we knew the Japanese were sprinkled all around. We came upon an improvised roadblock that had been made by laying several cut trees across the road. Several Chinese Nationalist soldiers came out toward us with bayonets. The sergeant turned on our vehicle's headlights and the interpreter called out to the soldiers at the roadblock.

Whatever the interpreter said to them must've been satisfactory, because the Chinese soldiers didn't shoot at us. I was told to stay in the vehicle while the men walked toward the Chinese soldiers. The Americans explained that we needed to get through. The soldiers agreed to allow us to proceed. They moved the trees to the side of the road so that we could get through.

We later stopped at a place that we had been through earlier. It looked deserted. Tanks had been left behind and buildings were bombed out. In the bottom of one of the buildings were two American soldiers. Their communications equipment was damaged. They couldn't receive messages, but they could still send messages. That was sufficient for what the Marine captain needed to do. We stayed there just long enough to have a coffee break with the two soldiers. The Marine captain stayed behind, and the rest of us went on our

WINGING IT: A performance, with Tommy Decker accompanying on his trusty Gibson jazz guitar, for a live audience and for an Armed Forces Radio Service broadcast over Station WOTO (Wings Over the Orient) in Bhamo, Burma, on February 12, 1945. Photo courtesy of Surry Arts Council.

way. The sergeant, who had gotten totally lost driving our vehicle, later told me that his job for the Army was drawing maps. In fairness, where we were was extremely difficult terrain. With or without a good map, anyone could easily get lost.

We eventually made our way to our intended destination, the American outpost in the city of Bhamo. Because we hadn't arrived when expected and no one had heard from us, the commander of the outpost had scrambled search planes and helicopters to look for us. The commander was furious with us for getting lost and worrying everybody. It wasn't like we had tried to get lost or hadn't done our very best to get there as soon as we could. Maybe he thought we got lost on purpose. I guess his anger showed that he cared. The base's bishop came to speak with me and said that they had been praying for our safety. I thanked him and told him that I had been praying, too.

Of Wings and Prayers

One day in the spring of 1945, I was scheduled to go entertain in Mandalay, which would have been more than a day's drive on extremely difficult roads, which, as I had already found out, were sometimes not much more than beaten paths. Instead of traveling by road, I was to make this trip by air. The plane was a little Stinson L-5. They were known as the "flying jeep," and that was about right. It was a two-seater with an open cockpit. The L-5 was an unarmed plane, a liaison aircraft. It was used for surveillance and mapping, and for transporting commanding officers, and sometimes commanding singers, from place to place.

The pilot for my flight was from Chillicothe, Missouri, less than a hundred miles, as the crow flies, northeast of my hometown of Kansas City. Ordinarily, I would have been delighted to meet someone from so close to home. But I think I would've preferred to fly on an actual crow rather than with the pilot of the L-5 that day. He was a hot-shot pilot and wanted to do aerial tricks for me. I was terrified. At one point, he turned off the engine and showed me how the plane could glide. I begged him to please start the engine again. He thought this was terribly funny. I was not amused. At all.

NOT EXACTLY THE ORIENT EXPRESS: *Or even a Missouri Pacific* Eagle, *but still on a good track with Tommy Decker (far right) and some other entertainers. The location in this photo is not known, but the eventual destination was Burma and India. Photo courtesy of Surry Arts Council.*

After we landed near Mandalay, I was met by members of a unit called the Mars Task Force. They were a multinational outfit, including Kachin guerillas, that was similar to the more famous Merrill's Marauders. In fact, some of the fighters from Merrill's Marauders were part of the Mars Task Force. Each of these special groups had endured tremendous fighting in extremely harsh conditions in order to reopen the Burma Road to Kunming in China, a mission that they had accomplished shortly before I arrived in the region, and to establish the Ledo Road from India.

I was later told that I was the first female American to travel the Burma Road during wartime. I don't know whether that is true, but I do know that I never saw any other American women while I was there. The GIs were very protective of me and really looked after me. As others had before and later would as well, they noted my red hair and freckles. They said I was their "female Huckleberry Finn."

Both the Burma Road and the Ledo Road were key overland supply routes to China for the Allies. When the Japanese had taken control of the Burma Road in 1942, the Allies had to maintain supply routes by dangerous airlifts over the mountains between Burma and China, a region nicknamed The Hump.

I would later ride over The Hump to visit and entertain troops, including members of the Mars Task Force, in China. On this particular day, I was put on the back of a big, black mule, accompanied by task force members on horseback, for part of the ride into Mandalay. The mule's name was McDonald. He was from Missouri and apparently was quite legendary among the troops. Mules were a vital part of operations in the rugged terrain of northern Burma. There were lots of mules that were part of the Mars Task Force. A few of them were for riding, but most were pack mules. McDonald was a

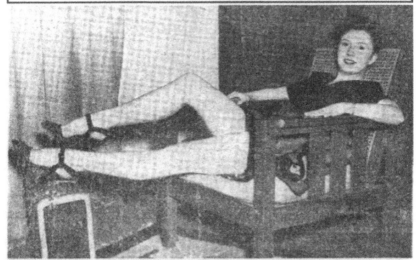

Words Seem So Futile at Times

There are occasions when Ye Chicken Eds feel that they are wasting time and space in writing descriptive matter, and this is one. The speechless-leaving creature is Betty Lynn, of the USO camp show called "Smoke Rings," which has been over here for a couple of months.

COVER GIRL: Front page above the fold of the March 8 edition of the Hump Express, *the official weekly newspaper published in 1945 by the India-China Division of the Air Transport Command of the U.S. Army Air Corps. Photo courtesy of Surry Arts Council.*

mule for riding. It was a rough ride, but still better than parts of my recent plane ride with the mule-headed Missouri pilot!

I don't remember how Tommy Decker got to Mandalay that time, but he soon joined us there. After our performances and visits with wounded servicemen in Mandalay, I flew back to Bhamo and prepared to ride in a command car on the Ledo Road to visit servicemen over The Hump in China.

A wiry little fellow named Doc rode with me. He had been assigned the job of giving booster shots for various diseases, including smallpox, to the men who were building a pipeline to provide one-hundred octane gas for aircraft. In some regions of the China-Burma-India theater, various tropical and waterborne diseases accounted for more casualties than actual combat.

Every so many miles along the Ledo Road, we would stop and I would sing for the servicemen and construction crews. They would

A FACE IN THE CROWD: It's tight quarters at this standing-room-only stop with the USO. The exact location is not known, but it's somewhere that's very hot, very humid, and an especially tough room if you're the trombone player—or the person standing in front of him. Photo courtesy of Surry Arts Council.

feed us, and sometimes we would spend the night. Throughout my time in India and Burma, the food was often barely edible. I no longer wondered why food in the military was called mess. I ate a lot of bread and apple butter with coffee. Grain weevils and other insects and vermin would get into the bread. Every now and then, we could get oranges and bananas, which were safer. Their skins provided some protection from insects and pathogens. It was at least easier to tell if they were infested or had been contaminated.

I swam in the Salween River. Actually, I didn't exactly swim in it per se, because I can't swim, but I bathed in the river while wearing my clothes. If I had to go to the bathroom, somebody would have to check out the latrine, and then let me in and stand guard to ensure my privacy. To give me a shower, the men poured buckets of water over me, but I was dressed.

BAND OF BROTHERS: With Tommy Decker (back left) and some of the ever-protective troops who watched out for the small USO Camp Shows troupe. Photo courtesy of Surry Arts Council.

Sometimes while driving over the mountains, we could see planes flying below us. These were very narrow roads, and we were occasionally met by Chinese tanks. It often felt as though we were barely staying on the road. At one point, we looked down below us and saw an armored vehicle that had just gone off the road and over the side of the mountain. It was upside down with the wheels still turning.

There was another occasion when we were in the border region. We stopped in a village to rest and get fuel. A local Chinese woman was sitting outside the building where we stopped. When she saw me, she held her baby out for me to hold. Not knowing what else to do, I accepted. I held the baby for a short time and then handed the baby back to the woman.

The woman kept handing the baby to me to hold. I assumed it was her baby. I could tell it had a fever. I would hold the baby awhile and then hand the child back to the woman and nod my thanks for her letting me hold the baby. She continued handing the baby back to me to hold. I didn't speak Chinese and she didn't speak English.

I AM WOMAN—HEAR ME ROAR: Armed and ready for tiger patrol with local villagers in India. (Hey Barney, check out all the bullets!) Photo courtesy of Surry Arts Council.

I didn't know what she wanted me to do. Maybe she thought I was a doctor or nurse.

I asked the men with me what they thought I was supposed to do. They didn't have any more of a clue than I did. I said to anyone around who might understand English, "I'm sorry. I'm eighteen years old. I can't take this baby." I wasn't a mother. I didn't know what to do. I handed the baby back to the woman one last time. Our group continued on our way. I couldn't bear to look back to see how our departure, without having done more to help the baby, had been received.

As we were heading back toward Burma, we saw an American flag at half-mast at a military post. We knew someone important had died, but did not know who. It was not until we arrived in Calcutta (modern-day Kolkata) several days later that I learned it was President Roosevelt who had died.

When I first arrived in Calcutta, USO Camp Shows officials took me to an outdoor stage where a large crowd was gathered. It turned out that Anglo-Indian young ladies were vying for Miss

ALL THE WORLD'S A STAGE: Whether in 1945 or any time, the Taj Mahal is an especially beautiful backdrop for jubilant song and dance. Photo courtesy of Surry Arts Council.

Calcutta. The officials persuaded me that it would be good public relations for me to participate. That was the only beauty contest I ever entered—and I actually won! They put this big sash across me that said Miss Calcutta 1945. I believe I was the sole redhead in the contest, so maybe I cornered the ginger vote with the judges.

The frivolity of a beauty contest was a welcome respite from the horrible realities, which were never far from us. We sometimes visited a patient one day and returned the next day to find he had died. This was extremely tough for me to deal with. I remember spending time with burn victims, paraplegics, and amputees—many were only eighteen years old, my age. It was so sad.

While I was based in Calcutta, USO Camp Shows would fly me out just about every day to a different location to sing—sometimes in India, sometimes in Burma. I would go sing and then come back. There was a smallpox epidemic at the time. I was regularly vaccinated at the airport before flying out.

One of my trips from Calcutta was to Ceylon, which is now Sri Lanka, off the southeastern coast of India. An English couple had a tea plantation. The USO had asked the couple if they would put me up for a few nights. It was obvious that the couple had a bad impression of people in show business. They refused to let me in their home. They instead allowed me to stay in a bombed-out building on their property. Even though I slept with my gun under my head, I was still very scared. When the man brought tea early one morning, he startled me, and I screamed bloody murder. He probably thought that was just the overly dramatic behavior of showfolk. I was there for a couple of days, and they seemed to warm up to me by the time I left, but I don't think I was ever exactly their cup of tea. I must say, though, that their tea was quite good.

After the Allies recaptured Rangoon from Japanese occupation with Operation Dracula in 1945, many of the POWs came to hospitals in Calcutta. I was among the first Americans to see them. Virtually all of the men were dehydrated and emaciated, and many were in desperate need of medical care and even just adequate food and water.

All these years later, it is hard for me to think about those men and the suffering they endured. Even after they were rescued, I'm sure many never recovered and never made it back home alive. Many others suffered severe injuries and death before they even had the chance to get medical care. I'm embarrassed to think that just months earlier I had griped about the insect bite on my lip in Casablanca. Little did I know then of the true horrors of war.

At the end of our tour, Tommy and I were asked if we would rather fly home or take a ship. Both of us decided to make the trip by ship because we had flown a lot and had some close calls. On one flight in Burma, I was invited to come up to the cockpit. As I was talking to the pilot and copilot, I looked out the windshield and saw that we were heading directly toward a mountain. I yelled, "Oh, look!"

The copilot nonchalantly put both feet up on the control panel and said to the pilot, "You take it from here." The pilot quickly turned the plane left on its side and then steered to what felt to me like straight up. I was thrown against the side of the plane and a sergeant sitting behind us held me tightly in place until we leveled out and I could regain my balance. I could see trees very close out the window as we banked away from the mountain. Then, once we gained enough altitude, the pilot turned back and went over the mountain.

Another time, a pilot let me sit in the copilot's seat. He wanted me to take the controls. I told him I couldn't even drive a car. He insisted that I try and told me just to keep the steering wheel level. I reluctantly agreed and took over, but then almost immediately asked that he retake the controls. He did so and then put the plane on autopilot. He was talking to me when, all of a sudden, the plane began to make funny noises and was bouncing up and down.

An officer came into the cockpit and was checking the equipment. Things leveled out and we soon landed. There happened to be a major onboard, and he just assumed that I had been at the controls and had caused the problem. He read me the riot act. I let him know that things went wrong while the plane was on autopilot. I felt terrible, but I knew I hadn't caused the problem. We switched to another plane and continued on our way. I didn't go anywhere near the cockpit on that flight.

Homeward Bound

After experiences like those and just a lot of rough flights in general, Tommy and I felt traveling home by sea was appealing. Our vessel was the transport ship USS *General A. W. Greely*. The *Greely* was a brand new ship that had been commissioned just a few months earlier. Its first voyages were for transporting troops, as well as people like Tommy and me, back home from India. On May 28, 1945, Tommy and I boarded the *Greely* in Calcutta and set sail

SQUARED AWAY: The official inventory of items that were shipped home in a trunk after the stint in the China-Burma-India theater. Photo courtesy of Surry Arts Council.

homeward from the China-Burma-India theater with our special mission accomplished.

We had some really bad storms during the voyage. A lot of people aboard the ship got extremely seasick, but I never did. I was lucky. I didn't feel ill at all. Maybe that's because, when I got on the ship, I was already exhausted. I was simply too tired to get sick.

I was assigned a lower bunk in a cabin with seventeen other women, most of whom were Red Cross workers. As soon as I got to my bunk, I collapsed into it with my back to everybody. I just stayed right there. I didn't stir at all. I simply wanted to stay there, rest, and forget everything. My time in Burma and India had been exhilarating and fulfilling in many ways. I was proud to have served my country and the war effort, but it also had been an arduous and draining experience.

Some of the Red Cross girls remembered me from my visits to hospitals. They were worried about me because I was hardly moving at all. After about four days of my just lying there, they sent for a man to come talk to me. I think he was a medic, but he might even have been the ship's captain. I was in such a fog that I was never sure who he was, but he was very nice. He said, "Now, I want you to promise me that you'll get out and walk on the deck and that you'll go into the mess and eat."

I said, "All right."

I finally did get up and show some signs of vitality again. After months of demanding travel through India and Burma, I was just dead tired. More than that, as I would later come to understand, I was emotionally spent as well. My wartime service had been a strenuous, often gut-wrenching experience. It was that way for all of us, no matter whether you were a battle-hardened soldier or an eighteen-year-old entertainer from Missouri.

On an Even Keel with Peggy Neel

Among those onboard the *Greely* with us was a lovely young woman named Margarete "Peggy" Neel from Arkansas. Peggy had been involved with the USO at Fort Chaffee in Arkansas before starting her work with the Red Cross during and after the war. She had been working with the Red Cross at a hospital in Australia when a famous photograph was taken of her pushing a wounded soldier, Private Gordon Pyle, in a wheelchair. That photograph later appeared on the cover of magazines and at least one book. After the war, the photo was used on a poster as a fundraiser for the Red Cross. Well over a million copies of the poster were distributed around the world.

Peggy and I had met in Burma, and I had seen her one other time. She had come to India and Burma with the Red Cross right after her stint in Australia. She was a convert to Catholicism. She had a little-bitty organ that she played. Aboard the *Greely*, we would go below deck. She would play her little organ, and we would sing and say the Rosary.

Peggy and I stayed in touch after the war. One time in the early 1950s, she came out to Los Angeles and spent the night with me, my mother, and my grandfather. Another thing that she and I had in common was that Peggy's father was a dispatcher and depot agent for the Missouri Pacific Railroad. That was an instant bond with my grandfather, who worked his entire career with the Missouri Pacific. Peggy was a wonderful friend and a remarkable person. After her service with the Red Cross, Peggy became an elementary schoolteacher. She died far too young, just in her mid-fifties, in 1971, but even so, she had lived an extraordinarily full and giving life of service. I was blessed to have known her.

Back to my sea story. Some of the crude conversations I heard among the ladies upset me. I really wanted out of that cabin. The crew later announced that we could sleep on the top deck at night. I couldn't get up there fast enough. Once I got out and walked around a little and started eating a little bit of food, I was fine.

My favorite spot to sleep was up on the platform with the gun turret. It would be just me and whoever was manning the antiaircraft gun that night. I had a specific corner I slept in. It was also a great spot for stargazing. Being so far out at sea and looking up at the night sky was simply breathtaking. The sky looked as though it was covered with diamonds. Especially when living in a big city like New York or, later on, Los Angeles with all the light pollution that washes out the night sky, I sometimes forgot how beautiful the stars are, but then I would just think about the night skies at sea.

THE NEEL DEAL: The famous photograph of Peggy Neel and Private Gordon Pyle that was used for promotional purposes by the Red Cross. Photo courtesy of TAGSRWC Archives.

It's still a vivid memory. It was the most beautiful sight. I never saw anything like that before and never will again.

After our ship left Calcutta, we sailed south in the Sea of Bengal, around the tip of India, then north through the Arabian Sea and the Red Sea and then through the Suez Canal and into the Mediterranean, past Gibraltar, and finally out into the Atlantic.

The war in Europe was officially over, but we were still at war with Japan. We were therefore in blackout and under escort with a convoy of gunships for much of the voyage. Once we were through the Suez, the convoy left us and we were all alone. We still had to operate in blackout mode with lights off and black material covering things, all of which not only made our journey safer, but also made my stargazing even better.

One safety measure aboard ship was decidedly grimmer. Onboard with us were several traumatized servicemen who had been declared "mentally unfit to serve," or Section 8, as it was then known. Ropes had been put up as a makeshift barrier around the perimeters of the decks to keep the men from jumping overboard. Some of the men paid attention to the barrier and some, tragically, did not. Long after the fighting stopped, the horrors of the war raged on.

After we had been sailing in the Atlantic for a while, the crew discovered that the ship's gyroscope wasn't working. We were unintentionally heading toward South America, when our actual destination was the port at Newport News, Virginia. I don't know if the crew got the gyro fixed or just navigated by other means, but after four weeks at sea, we finally arrived at Newport News on June 28, 1945. Even the crews on the first ships that reached nearby Jamestown in 1607 could not have been happier to be in Virginia than I was on that day.

As soon as I could get to a telephone, I called my family and told them that I was safely back in the United States and would be home soon. My mother told me, "Oh, Betty Ann, I kept praying to Saint Anthony that you would stay safe and be respected while you were overseas." She needn't have worried. No girl in history ever had more big brothers looking out for her than I did with the servicemen overseas.

The USO had arranged for me to stay at a boardinghouse in New-port News. I must say that it felt good just being back on American soil and in a bed in an actual home.

Tommy didn't want to linger in Newport News any longer than he had to, and I didn't have any reason to do so either. He suggested that we take a Greyhound bus and go to the USO in New York the next day, which is what we did. My first sight of Washington, D.C., was through the window of a Greyhound bus at night. I saw all the monuments glowing in the night. It was a glorious sight. Especially after where we had been overseas for all those months, seeing Washington, D.C., was both beautiful and reassuring. We truly were back home.

The USO tour had been the experience of a lifetime for me. Even so, I never forgot that the war had been a far more gruesome and harrowing experience for those who were in the military, not to mention all of the innocent civilians who had been devastated by the war. For so many, it had been not just the experience of a life-time, but also the end of life as they had known it or even the end of their lives altogether. I can never forget that.

When Tommy and I arrived in New York City early in the morn-ing after our overnight bus ride, we went to the offices of the USO to let them know that we were back and to officially sign out from our tour of duty with a little bit of paperwork. There wasn't much to it. Of course, I was just one of many thousands of people returning home from overseas during that time. Just to be efficient, the pro-cessing of all of us through the system had to be somewhat stan-dardized and impersonal to a degree.

My hooded raincoat had been stolen early in my tour, but I wore my gun under my blouse, so it had not been taken. The USO kept my dog tags, my passport with all the rubber stamps of my trav-els, and everything except my uniform, my other clothes, personal items that were in my duffel bag and trunk, and my gun.

After all I had been through, signing out with the USO felt anti-climactic. Everything else would feel that way for a while, too. I intuitively understood that the physical demands and the emotion-al intensity of those previous months, especially with the horrific things I had seen, had left some emotional scars that would take some time to heal.

At the same time, I also felt—and still feel—tremendous pride in having done my small part in helping my country during a time when even the nation's way of life and the world as we knew it were at stake. All that said, I was really elated to be back home. What I didn't know at that time was that, within just the next few weeks, Japan would surrender, the whole awful war would finally be over, and the entire world could rejoice.

There's No Place Like Home

Eager to get back home to my family, I boarded the first train I could get that was headed toward Kansas City. After about a day and a half on the train, I arrived at Union Station in Kansas City and then took a cab to my family's new apartment. My family unfortunately had to move to a different apartment while I was away. A man had bought their apartment building and he was converting the units to condominiums. So, the home I was returning to wasn't the same home I left. Then again, I wasn't the same either.

I had just the duffel bag, trunk, and the twenty pounds I had gained while overseas. You wouldn't think a young girl could gain weight like that during the war in Burma and India when so many others were starving. I think I gained weight in part because I could never comfortably go to the bathroom. Someone always had to take me to the latrine or bathroom and stand guard while I did my business. It took me about three months to lose those twenty pounds.

I surprised my family when I arrived at their front door. I rang the doorbell. Mother opened the door, and there I was. I had never seen her so happy. I was overjoyed to see her as well. Both of us broke down in tears of joy as we hugged.

Mother later told me that, when she looked at me that day, my face was purple and my freckles were black. My fair complexion had been burned many times from being in the sun with no protection. This was partially due to the fact that, while I was in India and Burma, we sometimes traveled on the railroad sitting in box cars with the doors open. We were also out in the open when we traveled on railroad hand cars that were pumped by hand. Sometimes

STILL SQUARED AWAY: Back on the home front in Kansas City with Cousin Jack. Photo courtesy of Surry Arts Council.

we were exposed to the sun while on planes and ships. Even the wind would blister me. At times, the temperature had been over 115°.

After I settled in and got some rest, Mother showed me a stack of letters that she had received from servicemen who had written to thank her for letting me perform with the USO. They were very touching to read. Even though I was sometimes invited to socialize with the colonels, captains, and other officers, I usually declined and chose instead to visit with the GIs. Whether officers or rank-and-file servicemen, they were always very protective of me. I was treated very well. I truly appreciated that many of them took the time to write letters to my family.

A few weeks after I returned home, I received a letter from the U.S. Department of State that said I had performed above and beyond the call of duty. I was later made an Honorary Colonel of the American Legion. I also received a service ribbon that I could wear. The ribbon was accompanied by a letter from the USO Camp Shows signed by Abe Lastfogel, who was chairman of the William Morris Agency as well as president of USO Camp Shows during the war.

I would later meet Mr. Lastfogel on the set one day in 1953 when I was doing *Where's Raymond?* with Ray Bolger. I started to mention the letter to him, but decided not to. I was just one of several thousand performers who had done the USO shows. As head of the William Morris Agency, Mr. Lastfogel later played a key role in putting together the deal to create *The Andy Griffith Show*.

I stayed in Kansas City for a little over six months. It took that long to fully recuperate mentally and physically from my time overseas.

A Japanese Boomerang

As it turned out, maybe I hadn't recuperated as fully as I had thought. Years after I thought I had successfully dealt with all my wartime experiences, I had a surprising reaction to an encounter.

In all the months that I had traveled through India, Burma, and China, I never directly encountered any Japanese soldiers. They were reportedly in the areas around us many times. For all I know, they may have been hiding in the jungle as we passed, but I never saw them.

Flash forward to more than a decade after the war. I was at home in Los Angeles. One of our neighbors was a Japanese-American man. His great-uncle had just arrived from Japan for a visit. My mother was outside in the yard visiting with our neighbor and his great-uncle. I happened to look out our breakfast-room window and see this head with a Japanese military cap bobbing back and forth in the bottom row of panes. The next thing I knew—I was face down on the linoleum floor. That was my instant reaction to seeing that man's cap. I was totally surprised by my response.

Here it was more than ten years since the war in which I had never even seen a Japanese soldier, much less had an encounter with one or engaged in combat. Yet, hitting the floor was still my automatic reflex to seeing that Japanese military cap. I thought to myself, *If this is how I react, what must it be like for all those servicemen who had endured the atrocities and horrors of actual combat?* I couldn't imagine it. It was a time before anybody had begun understanding things like post-traumatic stress. The closest term we had to describing it back then was "shell-shocked."

In the meantime, before that long-delayed realization about myself, I felt revitalized after my time at home in Kansas City. Even my freckles had healed. Fully energized, I decided to go back to New York City to see if I could get a job as an entertainer. I packed a bag and traveled by train back to New York. I was anxious, but also eager and full of hope that I could make it there.

Chapter 3: Taking a Bite of the Big Apple—And It Bites Back!

When I was first at Twentieth Century-Fox in 1948, the studio's publicity department spun an official biography that claimed that I had spent virtually all of my savings to get to New York back in February 1946 and that I arrived with just thirty-five cents and a shoebox with five cream cheese sandwiches on raisin bread. It went on to state that a bottle of nail polish had leaked onto the sandwiches but that I had eaten them anyway. That was Hollywood's version, but in fact, it wasn't far from the truth. It wasn't just the sandwiches that were as tough as nails in New York.

Prior to my heading back to New York, an acquaintance in Kansas City had recommended that I contact her cousin, who was an entertainment agent in New York. My mother thought this was a wonderful idea and that perhaps this lady would look after me a little. I went to her office down around 32nd Street and introduced myself. She was wearing a man's hat, and I think she was in a man's suit. She told me that her husband had died the previous year. She invited me to stay at her home, which was a short train ride away in the New York suburbs.

Ahead of my arrival, my mother had sent a big box of my things to the woman's home. When we walked into her house, I noticed that there was just one bed. As it turned out, she was an agent for carnival workers. She asked if I could cook. I told her that I could cook a little. She asked if I could paint. At first, I didn't know what she meant. I thought she meant paint pictures. Wrong. She actually wanted me to paint the inside of the house. The lady then asked if I could drive. When I told her I could not drive, she said she would teach me. She wanted me to take her to the train station each morning and then pick her up at night.

I thought to myself, *I'll never get out of here. I'll be her slave and I'll never get to Manhattan. What will I do? What have I gotten myself into?*

That first night, I slept on the edge of the bed. The lady was probably as good as gold, but I was scared to death. The situation was awful. When she went to work the next morning, I took my suitcase, and got on a train to Manhattan. I just left the box with my music and personal items that my mother had sent.

When I arrived back in the city, I was unable to find a hotel room. After walking all over Manhattan, I returned to Grand Central Station where I had left my luggage in a locker. I decided to spend the night there on a bench. After a while, I was approached by a police officer who explained that, if I didn't move along, he would have to arrest me for vagrancy. I explained my situation to him, and he compassionately directed me to Travelers Aid.

The Travelers Aid staff found a room for me at The Gregorian, a hotel on West 35th Street. In the taxi on the way to the hotel, I asked the driver if The Gregorian was a nice hotel. He said, "They're all the same, lady. Whether it's The Waldorf or The Gregorian, the same thing goes on in all of them."

As I would soon learn, The Gregorian had seen better days, as had its neighborhood. The Gregorian had once been an elegant hotel, but it was over forty years old by the time I arrived and it had not maintained its former glory. But it was a family-owned hotel, and they treated me well.

The Rehearsal Club

Though I was grateful to have found The Gregorian when I did, I nevertheless immediately started looking for a more permanent place to live. I had heard about The Rehearsal Club, a boardinghouse exclusively for women working in the performing arts, especially the theater. It had inspired the 1936 Broadway show *Stage Door*, which the following year RKO adapted for an Oscar-nominated movie starring Katharine Hepburn, Adolphe Menjou, Ginger Rogers, and Lucille Ball in one of her first credited roles in a feature film.

The Rehearsal Club consisted of two brownstones located side by side on West 53rd Street. It was handy to the Theater District. John D. Rockefeller, Jr., owned the buildings and arranged for their use as lodging for women in the arts. The lease was reportedly for a dollar per year.

Some of The Rehearsal Club's residents were Rockettes who had jobs, while others were hoping to get into show business. Carol Burnett is probably the best-known former resident. She lived there a few years after I did.

At the time I was there, a charming Canadian lady named Kay Carlton was in charge. She interviewed me and listened sympathetically as I told her about my situation and explained that there was no way I could be a maid, painter, and chauffeur for the carny lady. She told me that it might take a while, but I would hear from her.

Two days later, Ms. Carlton called me at The Gregorian and said I could come to stay at The Rehearsal Club. I was thrilled that I got in. I felt very lucky to live in this legendary boarding facility. Residents had their choice of brunch or lunch, and dinner was also served. I was put in a room with another girl who was very sweet. We shared a bathroom. When she left, I had another roommate for a while.

Many of the ladies living at The Rehearsal Club went on to have a lot of success. One was Jo Van Fleet. She had arrived in New York just before I had. While she was still living at The Rehearsal Club, she made her Broadway debut in *The Winter's Tale* in early 1946. Not long after that, she married William Bales, the show's choreographer. They were married until he died in 1990.

During her marvelous career, Jo won a Tony Award for her role in *The Trip to Bountiful* in 1953, and, just a couple of years later, she won an Academy Award for Best Supporting Actress in *East of Eden*, which was also her first film. Not too shabby! Many more accolades would follow. In the early 1990s, a few years before she died, I ran into Jo in Los Angeles. She said to me, "Betty, you did so well." I appreciated her thoughtful compliment, and I thought to myself, *Not as well as you, my friend.* She had such a fine career. Even better, she had lived a splendid life. But Jo was right. We two old pals from The Rehearsal Club could look back at our careers with pride for having done all right for ourselves.

Another friend I made while living at The Rehearsal Club was Lenka Peterson, a beautiful, talented actress from Omaha. At the end of 1950, both of us had roles in *Take Care of My Little Girl,* a film about sorority life, starring Jeanne Crain and Dale Robertson, that was released by Twentieth Century-Fox in 1951. Jean Peters and Mitzi Gaynor also were featured. Natalie Schafer (Lovey Howell on *Gilligan's Island*) played our sorority's house mother.

Like me, Lenka's birth name was Betty Ann. Her stage name of Lenka was inspired by her mother's first name of Lenke, and she changed her last name from Isacson to Peterson. Another thing that we had in common was our performing with the USO during World War II. While I was in the China-Burma-India theater, Lenka was in the Pacific theater.

When Lenka came out to Los Angeles to shoot the movie, she brought her baby and her mother with her. I picked them up at the airport, and we went to the studio together. Lenka was terrific in the movie. She was a rarity in Hollywood—she had naturally blond hair! When we finished filming a few weeks later, I took Lenka, her baby, and her mother back to the airport. We never worked together again, but we stayed in touch.

Making the Rounds

Back to my early days in New York: Living at The Rehearsal Club gave me great peace of mind. Having a comfortable and secure place to stay, I could now focus on finding an agent who didn't just want me to paint walls and run errands. I went to the Actors' Chapel at St. Malachy's Church, which was just a few blocks away on West 49th Street. I spoke with the monsignor there and shared with him that I had been overseas and was now living at The Rehearsal Club. I told him that I needed to get an agent.

Through the monsignor's theater connections among the parishioners at St. Malachy's, I was given the names of three agents. I visited all three, but Louis Shurr was the only one who followed through and got back in touch with me. I was delighted to sign with him. I figured if he was good enough for Bob Hope and Ginger Rogers, he should be good enough for me.

Louis Shurr's office was in a prime location, the Paramount Building on Broadway between 43rd and 44th. Between his office, The Rehearsal Club, and the Actors' Chapel, I pretty well had the Theater District surrounded. Or at least Times Square. That was now my neighborhood.

Louis got me a few auditions right away, but nothing came of them. On one occasion, I remember trying out for the part of a woman in her twenties. They were also casting for a supporting role that required a younger-looking woman. After the initial audition, I returned later the same day in different clothes and no makeup hoping to try for the other role. The director did a double-take, but he still let me read for the second role. Unfortunately, I didn't land either role, but you couldn't blame a girl for trying out—twice.

I was scared to death that I would never be able to find work and that the USO shows would end up being my career peak. This is a terrible thing to tell about myself, but I have always had a lot of fear. I would just have to make myself go ahead and try things anyway. Fear doesn't actually go away, but you find ways to manage it. Some people turn to alcohol or drugs to "settle their nerves." Those things obviously have a downside and, at best, mixed results. In my case, I prayed a lot and would just grit my teeth with determination to power through the fear.

On the first day of filming the *Return to Mayberry* reunion movie in 1986, we were getting ready to do a scene with Don Knotts and me. I had cottonmouth due to nerves. Bob Sweeney, our director, was drinking some coffee. I asked him if he had any left. He gave his cup to me and I drank it. I explained to him that I had cottonmouth. It was just fear. In this instance, I think part of my fear was that I had qualms about doing the movie so many years after the television show and having it come off well.

When I told Don Knotts about my concerns and fears, he said, "You're kidding me." He couldn't believe I felt that way at that point in my career and knowing how we had always clicked so well.

I said, "No, I'm not kidding. I'm scared that this won't work." As soon as we started filming, though, the old chemistry kicked in, and my saliva glands started working again. I think, at least to some degree, a certain amount of fear is healthy. It keeps you on your toes and helps you focus on the task at hand. Even so, I've never stopped praying.

Of course, Don Knotts was the consummate prepared actor. I think maybe he didn't have fear so much as worries about getting things exactly right. He knew that, for him, being prepared was the best remedy for his worries. He never stopped worrying, and he never stopped being prepared.

Back in my early months in New York, my auditions were resulting in virtually no good prospects. I had done just a few odd jobs, including working as a junior-size model for a St. Louis clothing manufacturer who had come to New York to show his line. I was getting very discouraged. What savings I had left were rapidly dwindling. The message that New York seemed to be trying to convey to me was that I did not in fact have what it took to make it there.

Rejected and dejected and in tears, I went downstairs to the lobby at The Rehearsal Club to use the house phone to call my mother. I told her that I wanted to come home because nothing was happening for me. I didn't feel that I was meant to stay in New York.

Always my rock, my mother responded, "No, honey, God has something in store for you. He's just not ready to give it to you yet." She added, "You can't get what you want by turning around and running."

Being the devout Catholic that she was, Mother then said, "Betty, the fifteenth of August is the Assumption of the Blessed Mother. Let's make a novena around that. If you're meant to stay there, something will happen. If you're not, you can come home."

For those not familiar, a novena is a tradition in the Catholic Church where you pray about a certain thing for nine days, usually at exactly the same time every day. People looking for jobs often direct their novenas to Cajetan, the patron saint of job seekers. The novenas done for the Assumption of the Blessed Mother are traditionally more general, but throwing in a specific request for career guidance is perfectly fine.

I agreed to do the novena with my mother. I started praying every day that, if it were God's will that I do something, it would happen in the next nine days. If nothing happened during that time, then it must be God's will for me to go back to Kansas City.

Answered Prayers

Within a week of starting the novena, I got a call back for *Park Avenue*. The play with music was a satire about divorce. It had a strong pedigree with Nunnally Johnson and George S. Kaufman writing the play and Kaufman also directing and with Ira Gershwin writing the lyrics to the music by Arthur Schwartz.

I had first auditioned for *Park Avenue* back in June. Not knowing Ira Gershwin was in the audience that day, I sang "Embraceable You." Had I known Gershwin was there, I would not have done a number he had written. At the time, I thought that blunder had killed my chances. The casting director told me that my singing voice wasn't strong enough for a lead in a Broadway musical. He said that they might have something for me in the chorus and that they might get back in touch later. In other words, "Don't call us. We'll call you."

Years later, I often heard Andy Griffith tell the story about how he felt discouraged from pursuing a professional singing career because someone had told him that his voice was "overly brilliant." In my case, I could have used some of Andy's extra vocal brilliance. Because of the disheartening advice he received, Andy pursued a career in comedy and then acting instead of singing. Along the way, of course, Andy proved he could sing just fine—and he had a Grammy on his mantel to prove it.

For my long-delayed second audition for *Park Avenue*, I had selected my best black dress and chose to sing Noel Coward's "I'll See You Again." It was a popular song, and I thought it might also plant a subliminal seed that the director and producer should want to "see me again."

Maybe that worked, because George Kaufman asked me to come back the next day, but to have my hairdo up—more in the fashion of the sophisticated ladies on Park Avenue. He also asked me to bring a bathing suit for my callback. Because I didn't swim, I didn't

SINK OR SWIM: A swimsuit shot from another time, but likely feeling no more comfortable than for the Park Avenue *audition in 1946. Photo courtesy of Surry Arts Council.*

own a bathing suit. One of the Rockettes at The Rehearsal Club was kind enough to lend me her Catalina blue one-piece suit.

There were six of us at the second callback the next day, August 15th, the date of the Assumption of the Blessed Mother. I wore the bathing suit but was very uncomfortable because I had never appeared in a bathing suit. Those auditioning us called out, "Smile,

Betty!" It was obvious I was uncomfortable. On top of that, we also had to sing.

In his office immediately after that day's audition, Max Gordon, the show's producer, offered me a contract for *Park Avenue*. I just as immediately signed the contract to be a singer and dancer. There were six of us who played bridesmaids. This was the only actual performing job I had gotten in about a year. Talk about miracles—I was relieved and thrilled! I later learned that it was Ira Gershwin's wife, Leonore, who had suggested that it might be a good idea to have one of the girls in the chorus not be so matchy-matchy glamorous and sophisticated. Freckled, red-headed, and distinctly Midwestern, I fit the bill.

The play had a solid cast. Mary Wickes was one of the principals in the play. Leonora Corbett and Arthur Margetson, both older and British, were the leads. Six dancers were brought in from California. All six had been in movies and were well known.

We began rehearsals and, not long after that, started doing tryout performances in New England for about six weeks. For my part, I sang with the other girls and also had a little pantomime that was separate from them. For that scene, I was alone onstage as a bridesmaid. I walked downstage toward the audience. The storyline called for my character to be entranced by a wedding. To accomplish that effect, each night I focused on the balcony and envisioned the Blessed Mother sitting up there.

The play's original choreographer was Eugene Loring, but he was replaced by Helen Tamiris. She found out that I could also dance, so I did that in addition to singing in the chorus and doing my little pantomime. I was onstage more than the ensemble of female singers. I got notices. Several reviews mentioned "the cute little redhead" or similar descriptions. Since there were three other redheads, we didn't know which of us the reviewers were referring to until one reviewer finally mentioned my name. The others were shocked that it was me. I was a little surprised, too, but also pleased.

We were on the road with *Park Avenue* for a long time before we opened on Broadway. The producers were having lots of trouble with the show, and the play didn't get the enthusiastic reception that they had expected. As a consequence of the show's needing

MOVIN' ON UP: The cover of the Broadway playbill for the 1946 production, starring Leonora Corbett and Arthur Margetson. Photo courtesy of TAGSRWC Archives.

work, our time on the road meant long hours of rehearsals in addition to the performances. It was exhausting. I got pneumonia and didn't even realize that was what it was until we got back to New York. The weather had been cold and rainy that October in New

England, and I didn't have a warm coat. All I had was an unlined raincoat. But I was in a show bound for Broadway and I simply didn't think about taking care of myself. I was completely focused on the work. The show must go on, and I must be in it!

On one occasion, during my stint with *Park Avenue,* illness worked in my favor. Martha Stewart—the actress and singer, not the "It's a good thing" lifestyle maven—got sick, and I was tapped to perform her featured role of Madge Bennett for three nights. That break was another of the "good things" that helped me stand out from the chorus at a time when several Hollywood scouts happened to be observing the show.

We were in Philadelphia when I received a call from the New York office of David O. Selznick, the legendary Hollywood producer. He wanted to see me when I came back to town. When we finally had our Broadway opening at the Shubert Theatre on November 4, 1946, the show itself didn't get great reviews, but I received a good amount of positive attention. As far as I was concerned, my just being in a Broadway show had been a miracle.

In addition to the Selznick Company, four other studios made offers to do screen tests: Twentieth Century-Fox, Universal-International, Warner Bros., and Paramount. It was yet another miracle that I received these offers from the studios.

Louis Shurr decided to go with Twentieth Century-Fox, which signed me to an option contract. Once the option was exercised, my contract was for $350 per week with performance options that could potentially increase the amount to $3,500 per week. For the record, those higher targets were never reached. Not even close.

In the meantime, I couldn't see Mr. Selznick until he came to town. Even though he knew Fox had the option but had not yet exercised it, Mr. Selznick still wanted to see me. He was a great big bear of a man. He was very kind and kissed me on the forehead. He told me that, if things didn't work out with Fox, I should contact him. I told him that I knew he was going to do *Little Women* and that I very much wanted to be a part of it. When I was first at Fox, I had Mr. Selznick's request in the back of my mind. It was a potential fallback plan. After I had been at Fox for a couple of years,

I never thought of contacting him anymore. I doubt he was still thinking about trying to sign me either.

After I signed the option contract, I did two screen tests for Twentieth Century-Fox in New York. Fox had an old studio on Eighth Avenue. It was rarely used and was filthy. I was scheduled to do a screen test there, but we rehearsed in the Twentieth Century-Fox offices. Frank Gregory, who was a writer for stage and film and was well known at the time, had written a skit that I was to perform with a male actor. I also had to sing a song and do an interview.

The Fox offices had a large room with two desks in it. One desk was occupied by Frank. Sitting at a desk in another corner was Lee Strasburg, who later became the director of the renowned Actors Studio in New York. Lee came to the office every day, sat at this desk, and read the newspaper. He had a contract with Fox, and things evidently didn't work out in Los Angeles, so he was sitting out his contract by coming to this office in New York every day.

As I was rehearsing the skit, Lee kept looking over his paper and observing me. I got very self-conscious as he watched me rehearse. I told Frank that I could not continue rehearsing in this manner. He laughed and encouraged me to continue. He explained that Lee just wanted to see how I was doing. Later, after Fox picked up my option and I was getting ready to move to California, I went to say goodbye to everyone at the Fox offices. Lee was there and he kissed me on the forehead and wished me well. He was very kind.

When I arrived for my first screen test at the Eighth Avenue studio, someone just slapped some pancake on me and put me in front of a camera. I was not given much attention at all. I then did an acting test with a young man. When I saw the test, I was shocked. I looked awful. I thought I looked like Mickey Mouse—only not cute like Mickey.

A makeup artist named Eddie Senz, who worked for Fox, had done makeup for Virginia Bruce's screen test. He was with Virginia when they played her test. Fox happened to play my original test at the same screening. Eddie explained to the Fox executives at the screening that he thought I had not been treated properly for that first test and that I deserved another test. He had his own salon and offered to do my makeup free of charge. The Fox executives agreed.

I went to Eddie's salon and he made me up for the second test. He also put my hair up and stuck a few red curls on top. He had just finished making up Lynn Fontanne, who was a Broadway legend as well as Oscar nominee. Eddie suggested that she come look at me. He introduced us. Lynn stood behind me as we looked into the dressing-table mirror. She said to Eddie, "She looks just like a Renoir." Eddie agreed. I then made it a point to check out some art galleries to see exactly what a Renoir looked like. I was content when I saw that the famed artist often painted redheads with bright, wide faces.

I did the second screen test. Then I waited. The studio had six months to decide whether they wanted to exercise their option and use me in a movie. Unfortunately, I was not paid during those six months. When I auditioned for other projects, my agent had to let producers know that Fox had an option on me. As a consequence, I lost some jobs even though there was interest in me. Due to the Fox option, producers were hesitant to hire me. They didn't know if I would be available for as long as they might need me.

A case in point was that hesitancy costing me a gig at the Copacabana. Monte Proser, who ran the fabled nightclub, wanted to hire me as a featured singer at the Copa. In referring to me he said, "She has class." When he found out about the option, he lost interest. Our paths would cross again down the line.

A Rose to the Occasion

From that second screen test, Fox finally, after six months, decided to exercise its option. As had been the case during our tryouts on the road, *Park Avenue* also did not go over very well on Broadway and had closed on January 4, 1947, after just two months. My reviews were, frankly, some of the bright spots for the production. Billy Rose, who wrote "Pitching Horseshoes," a widely read newspaper column about show business, had been to the play on opening night. He mentioned my name and used about half of his column to write nice things about me. He wrote that I was "the cutest thing on Broadway" and also wrote something to the effect of "Betty Ann Lynn was a strawberry sundae with a cherry on top."

When Fox decided to send me to Hollywood, Louis Shurr suggested that, before I left New York, I should go meet Billy and thank him for his kind words. I agreed and went to see him the day before I was to leave town. Billy had his own theater. One side of his office was all glass. He pulled back the curtains. The view from his office looked right down on the stage. When I went to visit him, *Brigadoon* was playing. Ironically, I had been to see *Brigadoon* with the guy who did my last screen test with me, along with his parents from Canada. I remember dancing all the way down Sixth Avenue. It was such fun.

Now, here I was—watching the same show from up in Billy Rose's office. I explained to him that I was leaving New York and that I wanted to thank him for the nice things he had written about me. As I started out, he asked, "Well, aren't you going to kiss me goodbye?"

These days, that might be considered a borderline #MeToo moment, but I agreed and kissed him. He then said, "You kiss like a little girl."

I replied, "Maybe that's because I am," and away I went.

After that, Billy mentioned me about ten different times in his column. In an installment of his column timed to coincide with the release of my first movie, *Sitting Pretty*, in March 1948, Billy described me as a "carrot-topped cutie" who had a "lace-curtain Irish face and the baby fat which, I thought, was becoming on her." In that same column, he wrote that I was "the only girl with exactly the right number of freckles." My freckles got a lot of ink in the newspapers. I think my favorite instance was one in 1948 in *The Mirror*, a short-lived Los Angeles newspaper, that said I was as "delightfully freckled as the finest turkey egg." I suppose that's at least better than being called a turkey.

At one point, Billy Rose wrote that I was third on his list of women that he most wanted to marry, a list that included Ingrid Bergman and several others. (At the time, he was in the second of five marriages to four different women, all actresses.)

When I came back to New York years later to audition for something after Fox dropped me, I arranged to stay at the Barbizon Hotel for Women, a residential hotel on East 63rd Street. Like The

Rehearsal Club, and as its name indicates, it was for female guests only. Just as I got to my room, the phone rang. It was Billy Rose. He somehow knew that I was there as soon as I walked in the door.

Some of my friends in New York discouraged me from going to Hollywood. They felt that I was getting recognition in the theater world. They were worried that I might get lost in the shuffle while trying to make it in the movie industry. Their concerns might have been justified, but I really wanted to give movies a try. Whether or not a pot of gold were waiting for me, this girl with the "lace-curtain Irish face" wanted to follow her rainbow to the west and see if, with a little luck, she could make her show-business dreams come true.

Chapter 4: Off to Hollywood

As I began making my way to Hollywood in June 1947, Fox allowed me to stop in Kansas City and pick up my mother. Because I was not quite twenty-one years old, my mother still had to sign any contracts on my behalf. She would move to California to live with me.

While I was in Kansas City, my cousin Patty, my Uncle Ralph's daughter, came over to see us and said, "Well, you don't look like a movie star." She probably wasn't wrong.

Because Mother was going to California with me, she needed to find someone to stay with my grandmother. My grandfather was still working for the railroad and would regularly be gone overnight. My cousin Joan, daughter of my Aunt Loretta (yes, that means her maiden name was Loretta Lynn, but she was not a coalminer's daughter!) was still just a teenager. Grandma paid Joan to come and stay with her.

Joan was a wonderful person and also quite beautiful. She had gorgeous thick red hair that was naturally curly. I can still remember Aunt Loretta brushing Joan's hair. Sometimes she was a bit rough and Joan would cry. Loretta could make curls by wrapping Joan's hair around her hand. I always wanted curls like that. My grandfather was planing some wood one time. I picked up the curled pieces of wood and stuck them in my hair. I was about nine and had a Dutch bob at the time. Hair extensions are popular now, but I had those years ago and mine were made of wood.

I remember one time when Joan took my grandmother to The Plaza in Kansas City. Grandma had not been down there for many years. With my grandmother's limited mobility, it was an ordeal for Joan to get her there, but she somehow managed it. They had their picture taken in a photo booth at the dime store. Grandma looked just as happy as she could be. But no matter how happy she looked about being at The Plaza, my grandmother was nevertheless determined to get to California to be with Mother and me just as soon as she possibly could. After his upcoming retirement, beginning in December, my grandfather would then join the three of us in California.

I was in Kansas City for only a few days that June—just along enough to make sure my grandmother would be well taken care of and to get my mother packed up for the move.

Westward Ho!

Mother and I caught the *Super Chief* train as it came through Kansas City from Chicago on its way to California. My exciting new adventure was literally on the fast track.

At one point during our journey west, I looked over in the club car and there was Copacabana owner Monte Proser, for whom I had auditioned a few months earlier. I went over and spoke to him. With Monte was Jule Styne, who was already a hit songwriter for bands and films and who would later collaborate on songs for hit Broadway musicals, including *Gypsy* and *Gentlemen Prefer Blondes.* It seemed that everybody was going to California, but on this train ride, I think Mother and I were likely the only ones who were actually moving to the Golden State.

On June 20, the day my contract with Fox became active, our train arrived in Pasadena, which was the West Coast terminus for the *Super Chief.* By not being in Los Angeles, the Pasadena train station had the advantage of helping well-known people avoid having to deal with as many paparazzi. Of course, Mother and I could have gotten off the train anywhere, and no one would have noticed or cared, but Pasadena it was.

We were picked up at the station by one of the agents from Louis Shurr's office. Louis had arranged for us to stay at the Hollywood Plaza Hotel on Vine Street, near Hollywood Boulevard. I had to pay for the room, so we could stay there only a week. I had very little money because, for the past six months, I had been under the option with Fox and therefore had not worked.

Mother and I fortunately soon found a room to rent in a couple's home in Beverly Hills. They had an apartment with an upstairs and a downstairs. The couple had two little kids. They rented a room across the hall from the kids' room to mother and me.

Once we got to Los Angeles, one of the first things Mother and I did was secure a ruling from Los Angeles Superior Court Judge Frank G. Swain that stated that I was mature enough to handle my own finances. That ruling meant that I didn't have to have any funds withheld from my paychecks as savings or in trust, as was required by law for juvenile actors. Because I was going to turn twenty-one in under two months, the issue soon would have been a moot point in my case, but those extra weeks of access to my full income were important as my mother and I got situated in Los Angeles.

We had been in Los Angeles for a short while when we came home after dinner and received a telegram. It was from my grandfather and it stated that he and my grandmother were on their way to L.A. by train from Hutchinson, Kansas. Especially since Joan was looking after them, we had thought and hoped my grandparents would wait at least a couple of months before coming to California. Despite my grandfather's assurances, my grandmother was scared to death that she would end up being left behind in Kansas City, so she convinced my grandfather that they needed to go ahead and move to L.A. right away.

The biggest problem with that insistence was that Mother and I simply had no room for them at the place where we were staying. We immediately started looking for a bigger place to rent. We had been walking daily to Mass at Church of the Good Shepherd in Beverly Hills. Mother said, "We are going to have to pray really hard to find a place for four people before they get here." As we walked up Rexford Drive, we looked over and saw a big, gray two-story house with a sign that read, *For Rent by Owner.*

We knocked on the front door, and a sweet lady named Mrs. Hanna opened the door. The lower floor of her home was for rent. She had blocked off the stairway and was living upstairs. She had put a stairway at the back of the house that allowed her to get in and not disturb the lower floor, which had a living room, dining area, kitchen, and one tiny bedroom with a tiny bathroom. This must have been the housekeeper's quarters. The rooms were completely empty—no curtains, no stove or refrigerator. Nothing. We were desperate, so I signed a lease. I rented the space for $175 a month. Then I went to Sears and got some things for the house. I also went to other stores and opened lines of credit, which I was able to do just because I was under contract with Fox.

For the first few months after my contract was activated, Fox paid me regularly. During that time, we shot my first film, *Sitting Pretty*. My pay had been bumped up by twenty-five dollars to $375 a week, but, after all the deductions, the check I got was more like $275. I used some of that pay to buy blankets and a small bed for my grandfather, and I arranged to rent a hospital bed to be delivered for Grandma for their little room. I got my grandfather a special foam mattress.

Mother and I went to an army-navy store in Santa Monica and bought two cots. They were very heavy. We put them on our shoulders and carried them on a bus from Pico Boulevard in Santa Monica to the stop nearest our new home and then hauled the cots the last three or four blocks. They were so heavy that it still hurts for me even to think about carrying them. We also bought sheets and pillows. We got a double burner and rented an icebox and had ice delivered.

It took two days after my grandfather's telegram for my grandparents to get to Los Angeles. Mother and I went down to Union Station to meet them. I can still see my grandfather pushing Grandma in a wheelchair. She was wearing a little hat with a feather on it. She was smiling, and her big brown eyes were bright with excitement. Mother and I were thrilled as well.

When we got to the house and went inside, my grandparents were shocked by how sparse the furnishings were. I don't know what they expected as they went into this empty house. My and Mother's cots were in the dining room. The hospital bed and my grandfather's bed were in the tiny bedroom. I suppose they expected something nicer. We weren't the Beverly Hillbillies, but we were close. On the plus side, my grandfather loved the foam mattress that I had bought for him. He said it was the best mattress that he ever had.

Comfortable mattress notwithstanding, shortly after bringing my grandmother to California, my grandfather returned to Kansas

ONE STEP AT A TIME: An early publicity photograph for Fox. Photo courtesy of Surry Arts Council.

City and continued working as an engineer on the *Eagle* passenger train for a few more months, until his retirement at the end of November.

We were in that house for a year. Mrs. Hanna wanted to sell the house to us, but I couldn't afford to buy it at that time. While living there, a transformer blew and we could smell smoke. Mother called the fire department. Mrs. Hanna came downstairs and pretended to be living in the lower level, as if we were just visitors. She then explained to us that it was illegal for her to rent the lower floor of her house to us. We had no idea. We also learned that Mrs. Hanna was widowed and had sold this house and then regretted selling. She bought the house back from the man, but he charged her more than he had paid her. She needed to rent the lower floor to help cover her mortgage.

When our lease was up with Mrs. Hanna, I rented a nice duplex with three bedrooms and two baths. My grandparents had a private bedroom and bath. Mother and I had twin beds and shared a bedroom. The third bedroom was used as a den. We rented the duplex for over a year. During her time living in Los Angeles, my grandmother's health continued to deteriorate, and, sadly, she would ultimately die while we still lived in that duplex.

Family Matters

I remember the first earthquake that my family and I experienced. Grandma's bed was on wheels. I stood on one side of the bed and mother stood on the other side. As the bed rolled back and forth with Grandma in it, we assured my grandmother that we were going to be all right. To think of how the bed rolled around the room is funny now, but it wasn't funny at all to Grandma.

I called the local American Medical Association office and got the names of a few heart specialists for Grandma. We had a phone installed in case of an emergency. We later had a few pieces of furniture shipped from Kansas City, including a grand piano. Over time, I continued to go to department stores and furniture stores to buy a piece at a time in an effort to make our home more comfortable.

My grandmother had a terrible heart condition and was basically bed-ridden for about the last dozen years of her life. There were times when she was in the hospital, and the doctors thought she would surely die. My mother would call the family to come in. Grandma would then rally and recover.

At other times, even though she was in bed, my grandmother enjoyed life. Grandma had those beautiful, big brown eyes, and they saw everything going on around her. She loved listening to the radio and reading daily newspapers. She was a real live wire. Especially at night, though, Grandma had great difficulty breathing, and she had a lot of anxiety. She said it felt as though the Empire State Building were sitting on her chest.

The entire time I was overseas, my mother had to take care of Grandma without my help. None of Mother's siblings helped out. There always seems to be one member in each family who tries to take care of everyone. In our family, that person was my mother.

A doctor finally told my mother that she had to occasionally have a break and get out of the house. I eventually became the primary caregiver for my grandmother and others, later including my mother. I wanted to take care of them. They were my family and I loved them dearly. My grandparents had stepped up to take Mother and me in when Mother left my father. Grandma was like another mother to me.

My grandparents were so good to me. I always hoped that someday I would be able to respond in kind and take care of them when they needed that help. Through God's grace, I was able to take care of all the hospital bills for Grandma, and I bought whatever my grandfather needed. I also ended up taking care of Aunt Mary, as well as Uncle Ralph, one of Mother's brothers.

Ralph was such a sweet person. Women at church would tell my mother how handsome her brother was. When Ralph came to California, he was in a wheelchair, but he eventually regained his strength to be able to walk. He started walking with a walker and then used a cane. Mother and I were in the breakfast room the first time we saw him walk. Like a child, he worked so hard at learning to walk. He bought himself a beautiful brown suit for Easter and walked to church. The church we attended was St. Timothy Catholic Church, which is at the corner of Pico and Beverly Glen, not far from our house. Even though there was a ramp on one side of the church, Ralph walked the steps.

Many years later Ralph started getting sick. After various tests, the doctors discovered colon cancer. After he performed surgery, the doctor said the cancer had spread into Ralph's bones. Ralph didn't live long after the surgery. He died on November 5, 1977. He was only 71.

When I first moved to Los Angeles, I bought four burial plots at Holy Cross Cemetery. Looking back, I suppose that purchase meant I intended to stay in L.A. awhile, if not permanently. Those graves were the first land I ever owned. Holy Cross is a Catholic cemetery located on the edge of Culver City, just a few miles south of where we lived. Holy Cross had been open for only about a decade when I bought the four plots. My plan was to have a grave for my grandfather, my grandmother, my mother, and me.

My grandmother died on December 20, 1948, and was buried on Christmas Eve. We buried Grandma in the second grave in order that my grandfather could later be buried beside her in the first one. He died on May 24, 1959. My mother died on January 27, 1984. Aunt Mary and Uncle Ralph are buried nearby in the same cemetery. My Aunt Loretta had stayed behind in Kansas City, where she was buried after she died in 1990.

After my mother passed away my Aunt Loretta came out to California to stay with me for a while. She answered the phone one day and I heard her say, "Who? Who? Who?"

Bette Davis, was on the other end of the line asking, "Boo? Boo? Boo?" (As I'll explain shortly, Boo is what Bette called me.) I thought this "Boo-Who" exchange was hilarious, but Bette didn't think it was funny. She had a sense of humor, but she wasn't as silly as I am. She thought I was silly because I found humor in a lot of things that she didn't.

After Bette moved away from Los Angeles, she would occasionally come back to town for a few days at a time. She would generally stay at the Hotel Bel-Air and usually in the same bungalow. If I wasn't working at the time, I would go stay with her. She always hated to be alone.

I actually got kind of lonely not hearing "Boo" anymore after Bette died. By that time, she was the only person who still called me that. I missed Boo just as I sometimes missed my middle name. I had been Betty Ann Lynn when I started my professional career. I dropped Ann after a while and professionally went by just Betty Lynn. I thought it would be simpler and easier, and it was. But I still kind of missed my middle name. I thought Betty Ann sounded prettier than just Betty.

Shortly after I moved to Mount Airy, North Carolina, in 2007, I told a friend that I had recently been to Moody's Funeral Service to make arrangements for my funeral and for sending my body to Los Angeles for burial at Holy Cross Cemetery, where I still had my plot. My friend seemed surprised that I didn't plan to be buried in Mount Airy. I thought to myself, *I can see my gravestone now—"HERE LIES THELMA LOU—SHE WAS THE CAT'S!"*

Actually, as I thought about it, being buried in Mount Airy made a lot of sense. It would certainly be a convenient choice. In the end, I decided that sticking to my original plan of being buried near my mother and grandparents at Holy Cross in California was the best choice. It feels right and it's also practical because my plot is already paid for.

Having Faith

It was yet another miracle that I ever even made it to California. In a sense, much of my life has been that way. I've had a lot of luck in a lot of ways. I also believe in divine intervention. The Lord truly does work in mysterious ways, and things have had a way of working out in my life.

I could not go out and look for work. I depended on my agents to send me. I prayed they would find work for me. The agents sometimes seemed to forget about me, or else simply couldn't have cared less. As my cousin Patty had said years earlier, I did not look like a movie star. A lot of people agreed, and they were right. They likely expected a beautiful, blond-haired bombshell, not a redhead with freckles. Considering that handicap of my not fitting the profile of the typical glamorous movie star, I suppose things worked out pretty well for me.

I had a lot of responsibilities at home. Over the years, I took care of several family members, and we always had a lot of bills that needed to be paid. Because I wasn't always under contract, I would become frightened when I thought of all of my family obligations.

On more than one occasion, especially after my years under contract with Fox came to an end, I started to look through the help-wanted ads in the newspaper, even as I prayed that another acting job would come up first. I would think, *Oh, Dear God, please help me get a job somewhere.* Fortunately, just as I was beginning to wonder what other kind of work I was capable of doing, another acting job or personal appearance always seemed to come up in the nick of time.

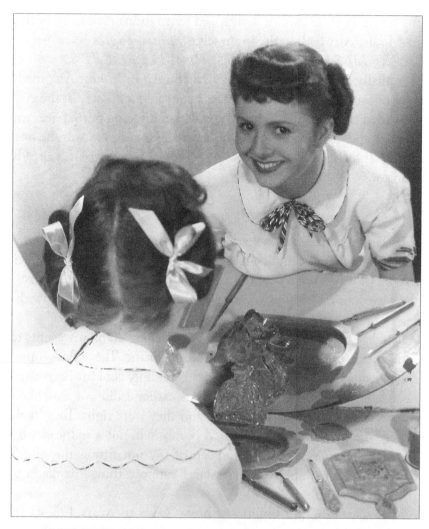

A MOMENT FOR REFLECTION: Another early studio shot for Twentieth Century-Fox in 1947. Photo courtesy of Surry Arts Council.

I have always relied on my faith and still do. I say a lot of prayers. God has been good to me. I had a good family and other people I love. Even though I took care of several family members and it was sometimes difficult to provide the best care possible and to see them suffer as they got older, I thank God that they had their minds. I loved them so very much, and they had great humor. Faith and humor get you through a lot. Even as we go through struggles, we need to have joy and laughter and not take ourselves too seriously.

I always think one thing young actors should realize when they get into the business is that they need to allow themselves some lightness, in addition to spending a lot of time on their knees, pleading, "God help me" as they wait for opportunities. Show business is different in that way. There are some jobs that you can initiate on your own. If you see a yard that needs to be mowed, you can contact the home owner and offer to mow it for a fee. With acting, you generally have to wait to be asked in order to work.

I remember hearing Willie Nelson say in an interview years ago that he spent a lot of his time just waiting for the phone to ring with somebody calling to ask him to come perform somewhere. He said it wasn't like he could just invite himself to come perform music for people any time he felt like it. I think Willie's phone has rung more than mine. These days, he's also more likely to be the one making calls asking others to come perform with him. But Willie's point is still valid. Singers and actors and all of us who have worked in the performing arts spend a lot of time waiting by the phone. These days, we can at least carry our phones with us.

Sitting Pretty

Once my mother, grandmother, and I were well settled in Los Angeles, it happily wasn't long before I started work on my first movie. We began filming *Sitting Pretty* at the Twentieth Century-Fox studios in late October 1947 and wrapped before the end of the year. *Sitting Pretty* was the first Mr. Belvedere movie. It starred Clifton Webb as the male lead, Robert Young, and Maureen O'Hara. Richard Haydn was also in it. He was terrific. It was a great cast and a funny movie. Clifton told me that Robert Young had thought he was to be playing the Mr. Belvedere part and was shocked when he found out that he was instead playing the husband.

I didn't have to audition for *Sitting Pretty*. I just got the part. I went in and spoke to Walter Lang, the director, for a minute. He just nodded his head. I think the studio basically told him that, unless he had a major objection, he needed to use me. I got the part of Ginger, the babysitter. I learned my lines and then went in and got into the bobbysoxer outfit that the wardrobe department had picked out for me. A man came into my little dressing room to see if I knew my

THE HOLLYWOOD RIDE BEGINS: The first movie scene ever for our ingénue, with Robert Young in Sitting Pretty *(1948). Photo courtesy of TAGSRWC Archives.*

lines. I knew them, and he told me I looked all right. It all may have been just routine stuff for him, but it was a big day for me.

My first scene was with Robert Young in a car that was just a mockup. When they called me, I walked onto the set. I had never seen a movie being made. There were two men rolling logs under this partial car. Robert Young was sitting in it with the cameras and the director just ahead of him. They put me next to him in the "car." The men got the mechanics of rolling the car worked out, and Walter Lang then told us to run the lines one time for him. As we ran the lines, I looked at Robert Young and could not believe I was there.

I had always seen Robert only on screen, and here I was trying to flirt with him, a major movie star. Walter Lang then said he was ready to do a take. We shot it, and they actually used that first take. The crew then sat the camera and lights for an over-the-shoulder shot for Robert's close-up, and then some other shots. Coming from a singing and live theater background, I was utterly fascinated that this was how movies were made. I was thrilled to be there.

After we had filmed that first scene, it finally occurred to Walter Lang to ask, "Have you two met?" referring to Robert Young and me. I told him that we had not. He introduced us, but there I had been already just flirting away with Robert during the entire scene.

Every now and then, I had a part like that where I hadn't even met my fellow actors. A similar incident to the one with Robert Young happened with Robert Taylor. After I was released from my contract with Fox, I had a small part in *Many Rivers to Cross,* a comedy Western for MGM that we filmed in 1954 and that was released the next year. In addition to Robert Taylor, the film starred Eleanor Parker and featured James Arness, Alan Hale, Jr., and Russell Johnson. (Yes, the future Marshal Matt Dillon of *Gunsmoke* and the future Skipper and Professor of *Gilligan's Island* were all saddled up for this picture!)

Eleanor Parker had dyed her hair red for the film. In order not to have too many redheads in the film, I wore a black wig. The opening

EVERYBODY JUST HOLD ON: A scene in Many Rivers to Cross *(1955), a frontier comedy starring Robert Taylor (with a feather in his cap) and including an uncredited Darryl Hickman (the shoulder-holder). Photo courtesy of Surry Arts Council.*

NOT ALL SMILES: Maureen O'Hara doesn't seem nearly as enthralled with Robert Young as their babysitter is in this scene from Sitting Pretty *(1948). Photo courtesy of Surry Arts Council.*

shot for me was to rush in and kiss Robert Taylor all over the face, without my ever being introduced to him or anything. I was so embarrassed that I didn't know if I could do it. But I had to. So, I ran in, grabbed him, and kissed him all over his face. Four years later, I worked with Robert again in *The Hangman*, a film for Paramount. I told him about our first encounter, how nervous I was, and how sweet he was. He was a darling.

My character once again flirted with Robert's character in *The Hangman*. I played a waitress at the hotel where he was staying. She had a crush on him. I was constantly having crushes on Robert Taylor. This was the first picture he had done away from MGM. He didn't know anyone at Paramount, so he was glad to see me, a familiar face. Between scenes, I sat and visited with him and with Fess Parker, who also starred in the movie. I liked both of them a great deal. What was not to like! They were two very talented and very nice people, and very easy on the eyes.

Meanwhile, back at *Sitting Pretty*, I had another sequence where I was in a bedroom. The scene was in the original movie, but was cut out later when they chopped it up and shortened it. In the scene, Robert's character called Ginger on the phone, even though Maureen O'Hara's character didn't want him to do so. Thinking back, I guess I can understand why they cut it. It was just a phone call. In another scene, they came home, and I had a bunch of teenagers there. They were all dancing and having a ball. All in all, it's a fun and funny movie.

Apartment for Peggy

After *Sitting Pretty* wrapped in December of 1947, I was in *Apartment for Peggy*. My part was small, but at least I was credited. I had a scene with Bob Patten, who wasn't credited for his role. Bob went on to have a nice career as a character actor, especially in television. *Apartment for Peggy* starred William Holden and Jeanne Crain. It also featured Edmund Gwenn. The producer, William Perlberg, wanted me to dye my hair. (This was my first film in color.) He did not want me to have red hair in the movie. I refused. I told him, "God gave me this hair, and I'm not going to do anything to it."

He just glared at me. I offered to wear a wig, or a hat or a scarf. I was adamant about not dying my hair. I wore a scarf the entire time. In the end, they didn't keep much that they filmed with me. I never worked for Mr. Perlberg again.

We shot most of my scenes in *Apartment for Peggy* in a tiny apartment. Bob Patten and I played a husband and wife who were parents of twins and living on a college campus. Bob's character was a GI who had come back home during World War II. It was a good movie, but not one that did much for my career other than keeping me busy for a few weeks.

Once I was done with my bit in *Apartment for Peggy* in early 1948, Fox had no new projects lined up for me on the immediate horizon, so the studio chose to put me on an unpaid layoff, which the standard studio contract allowed them to do. After doing my first couple of movies back to back, I enjoyed the break, but I missed the income.

My career—and income—had already been fallow for six months of the previous year when I was unable to do any extensive work in New York because of Fox's option. I now had a layoff for twelve more weeks. I knew I wasn't the "usual thing" for the studio. I felt everyone at Fox was beautiful—including Jeanne Crain, June Haver, Betty Grable, Maureen O'Hara, and Linda Darnell. All these ladies were gorgeous. I think Fox was a bit unsure about what to do with me.

It had been only a few months since Mother and I had moved to Los Angeles, and already Fox had put me on layoff for several weeks, basically the winter of 1948. People think that Hollywood is all glitz and glamour, and nowadays, actors do get paid better, largely thanks to a stronger union. But back in the Golden Age of Hollywood, the studios still had all of the power and most of the money. The biggest stars made enough to live very comfortably, but the majority of us were struggling. I was barely making a living, and I was the major earner for my family, including Mother and my grandfather. On top of that, I was caring for my sick grandmother. It could be hard at times.

Fox fortunately put me back on the payroll to do some general publicity work in March 1948 and for the *Sitting Pretty* premiere in April. Fox then lent me to Warner Bros. for *June Bride*. I would then be very busy for the next few years.

Staying Tuned with Radio

When not working on movies, I was often able to get jobs in live scripted shows for radio, which were still thriving even as television was becoming more popular. I did several installments of *Lux Radio Theatre*, which for many years was hosted by Cecil B. DeMille. The *Lux* show promoted Broadway shows and Hollywood movies, along with Lux soap. After the show moved from New York to Hollywood, most of the episodes were adaptations of movies—often with a movie's lead actors being paid handsomely to reprise their film roles.

One of the first *Lux Radio Theatre* episodes I did was *The Dark Corner*, a drama adapted from the popular 1946 movie starring Lucille Ball, Clifton Webb, William Bendix, and Mark Stevens. Our radio version was first broadcast in November 1947, when I had a window of free time during the *Sitting Pretty* shoot.

In those days, there was a live audience watching the radio show. We had a rehearsal before we did the live radio broadcast. The script called for me to mention Darryl F. Zanuck, the head of the studio. I repeatedly mispronounced his name. The room roared with laughter. Bill Smith, a gentleman from Fox who brought me to do the radio show, called me aside and admonished me, "You had better learn to say that name right, or else both of us will be fired." I kept repeating the name to myself, hoping to get it right.

Just before we went live, Lucille Ball walked up behind me and tapped me on the shoulder. She asked, "You got that name right yet?" We both laughed. Lucy then said, "You have the hair color I've always wanted." Lucy had started dyeing her hair red a few years earlier, but had not yet settled on the exact shade that would become her signature. As for Darryl Zanuck, I think I succeeded in pronouncing his name right during the actual performance. Or at least nobody got fired because of my pronunciation.

I recall another incident with Lucy. Both of our mothers belonged to The Motion Picture Mothers, a social and charitable organization. My mother was the president for a couple of years. I was also fond of Lucy's mother, DeDe. At a Christmas event one year, the actors were asked to sing Christmas carols to all the mothers, which was very sweet. Lucy and I both sang.

Fox ended my winter layoff in time to send me on a junket to Missouri in March 1948 with several other actors, including Lon McCallister, Randy Stuart, and Colleen Townsend. The junket was promoting a movie called *Scudda Hoo! Scudda Hay!* which starred Lon, June Haver, Anne Revere (who was on a streak of Oscar nominations, including a win for *National Velvet*), Walter Brennan, and Natalie Wood. Colleen Townsend had an uncredited role in the movie, but she wasn't alone. So did Marilyn Monroe.

Also on the junket was Louanne Hogan, a fabulous singer and fellow Midwesterner, who often dubbed the singing for actresses in films. Oscar-winning composer Mack Gordon also came along. He had an incredible string of hits—everything from "Chattanooga Choo" and "At Last" to "You'll Never Know."

We all went to the premiere in Sedalia, Missouri. The movie is set in the rural Midwest. Sedalia fit that description and made an appropriate setting for the world premiere. Other than Kansas City, I had never been anywhere in Missouri except to St. Louis by train. I knew nothing about the rest of Missouri. Sedalia is about a hundred miles east of Kansas City, but a world away from the life I had known.

The Fox publicity people knew that I was from Missouri and probably thought that connection might help with their publicity. Sending me on a publicity junket was also a good trial run for me because *Sitting Pretty* was set for wide release the next month. It was good to get my name and face familiar to the public ahead of that. We crowned the queen of a contest, perhaps the Queen of Sedalia, and made appearances around town to promote the movie. We then were onstage after the screening of the film.

We also did a publicity stop in Kansas City, and some of my relatives came to see us that night. We were so busy that I didn't even get to speak to them. While we were in Kansas City, Bill Winters, one of the publicity men, came to me and said that one of my former high school teachers was there, and she wanted to give me some flowers. When I went outside the dressing room, a woman walked up and gave me a big bouquet. She said, "These are from your father."

I immediately gave the flowers back to her and told her to tell my father I would get a restraining order if he ever tried in any way to reach me again. I assumed this lady might be his wife, so I went on to say that I hoped he was good to her, but that he had not been good to me and my mother. This encounter greatly upset me. I broke down and cried. I pulled myself together and went onstage. While I was being interviewed, someone yelled out that I was lying about something. I didn't know what I was supposed to be lying about. There was nothing brought up that I would be untruthful about. The only thing I had ever lied about was my father being dead, but that was not brought up. I was stunned. Everything was quiet. I stopped but then continued.

Many years later, when my Uncle Ralph came out to Los Angeles and stayed with us for three or four years until he died, he told us that it was his ex-wife, my Aunt Frances, who had stood up and yelled out. He said he just wanted to sink into the floor at the time and had never told us about it. He said he didn't know why Frances would do such a thing. She had always been nice to me, but jealousy can make people do terrible things. I don't know exactly what she yelled or why, and Uncle Ralph said he didn't understand it either. I was glad he finally told me.

Gratuitous family intrigue: Frances, was romantically involved with my Uncle Ralph's best friend. (It will be no surprise to Mayberry fans that Frances's middle name was Juanita, just like Thelma Lou's waitress nemesis!) Everyone knew about the affair except Ralph. He eventually found out, and then divorced Frances.

Anyway, there I was back in my hometown and, within just a few minutes, I had a couple of bad experiences. I thought, *What a homecoming!* It truly broke my heart.

On a positive publicity note, my role as Ginger in *Sitting Pretty* earned a Photoplay Gold Medal. The movie received a Gold Medal too. The Photoplay award was sort of the People's Choice Award of its day. It was a popularity contest based on polling of moviegoers by Gallup, rather than an award for an outstanding performance. Even so, I was happy, especially at that key early stage of my career, to receive that recognition. It was nice to know that audiences liked me and my movies.

That's Shoe Biz

I believe it was around that same time—maybe a year or two later, but fairly early in my tenure at Fox in any case—that the studio executives asked me to meet Marilyn Monroe and show her a little dance routine. Marilyn came into the studio at Fox one morning, and I was very happy to meet her. I thought she was a very good actress.

The Fox folks asked me to show her a few dance steps, specifically how to do the soft-shoe. I demonstrated it, and then she tried it. She caught on right away. I could tell she was very smart. Fox also asked me to teach Vanessa Brown that same morning. She arrived a little later than Marilyn did. When she got there, Marilyn and I both were able to show her what we had been working on. Vanessa didn't catch on instantly, but she picked up enough to be able to practice. I'm sure she eventually got it. Like Marilyn, Vanessa was a very smart lady.

What was fun about that experience was what Marilyn did with the man who was playing the piano for us. She was wearing this very low-cut blouse—*very* low-cut—and she leaned way over the piano and gazed flirtatiously at him with those sultry, half-closed eyes of hers. He was so thrilled by her flirtation that he practically forgot how to play the piano for a minute. We all had a good laugh about that. Marilyn was so playful and funny.

Aisle: Be There

I ran into my friend Jane Nigh one spring day in 1948, and she told me about this part at Warner Bros. that she had gone in to see about. She said, "There's a part at Warner Bros. in a picture with Bette Davis. It wasn't right for me, but you would be great for it. You should get your agent to take you."

I called Al Melnick at Louis Shurr's office and told him that I heard about this part and that I would like to read for it. He told me that the producers already had someone for the part.

I said, "Well, Jane Nigh told me that I'd be perfect for this part, and I would like to try for it."

Al kept hemming and hawing. I suddenly had more nerve than I had ever had before, or since, and said, "Well, if you don't want to take me, I'll get somebody who will."

Al said, "I'll tell you what's wrong, Betty. We have a girl under contract to Warner Bros., and we think she might have the part. That's why I didn't want to take you."

I said, "Well, evidently she doesn't have the part, or Jane wouldn't have been testing. They wouldn't have had her audition today. This other actress hasn't got it close at all. I want to go."

Al said, "Well, all right." He wasn't happy, but he took me over.

I went in and read for the title role, which was by no means the starring role (it was fourth billed), in *June Bride* for director Bretaigne Windust. Fox sent over a screen test that I had done with Tyrone Power the year before for *The Luck of the Irish*. I didn't get that part, although I always wished I could have done it. Anne Bax-

READY TO BE WED: A publicity photograph for June Bride *(1948).*
Photo courtesy of TAGSRWC Archives.

ter landed the role and, I must say, she did a fine job. Of course, she
was always great.

Back at Warner Bros., Bette Davis, Bretaigne Windust, and the
others saw my screen test and decided to let me have the part. That
really surprised Al Melnick.

The woman who Al assumed would do the part was indeed a wonderful actress. I often thought later that she probably would have been great in that role. But this time I got the part. I was going to be Barbara "Boo" Brinker in *June Bride*. It was my first chance to work with Bette Davis and Robert Montgomery. I was twenty-one years old, and I was ecstatic—both about getting the part and about the stars I was going to be working with.

I came home, and my mother said, "Oh, I always had a crush on Robert Montgomery."

My grandmother said, "I don't know about Bette Davis. She has those great big eyes. I don't know about her." Grandma was pretty smart.

In order for me to work on *June Bride*, Twentieth Century-Fox had to lend me to Warner Bros., which in turn reimbursed Fox for its continued contract payments to me during the time we filmed, which was from May to July 1948.

When I walked on the set for the first day of production, I met Barbara Bates, who was to play my sister. Raymond Roe was our young neighbor, who was crazy over my character. That's who she was going to marry. The story was that a fancy New York magazine was going to do a wedding story about this small-town family. Bette played the managing editor, and Bob Montgomery's character had been away for a long time. There obviously had been a prior romance with the two of them. She couldn't stand him anymore and was upset that he was back on the payroll. At first, she just put up with him. Naturally, they get back together in the story.

Bette Davis was great to work with. Mary Wickes, my fellow Missourian, was also in this movie, which was funny to her because I had made my Broadway debut in *Park Avenue*, which she was also in. Now we were in a movie together. Fay Bainter and Tom Tully were also in the film.

In one scene, I was supposed to run down the stairs. Bretaigne Windust wanted me to jump two or three steps at a time. Once the set was built, I went over and practiced running down the steps as he wanted. The steps were not built to the standard height of most steps, so this was quite a challenge, but I kept working at it. When the time came to do the first take, Bretaigne had Bette be just a few feet from the doorway. He would have a prop person ring the doorbell. That was Bette's cue to go toward the door, and it is was my cue to bound down the stairs and reach the door before Bette did. However, I had to be way off from the staircase because otherwise my shadow could be seen hovering in the shot. That left a lot of distance for me to cover.

On cue, I came bounding down the steps and ran to the door. Because she started from only a few feet away, Bette got to the door well before I did. We did the scene a few times, and each time Bette reached the door ahead of me. After one more take, Bette slapped me right in the face. Not too hard, but Fay Bainter and everyone watching were horrified that she had done it.

That prompted me to tell Bretaigne, "Keep Bette back from the door. Don't let her be that close and don't give her a cue until I'm getting closer." I told him that there was simply no way I could make it to the door before she did if we started on the same cue. He agreed.

For the next take, Bretaigne held Bette back by giving her a light to watch for her cue instead of listening for the doorbell. The change worked. It was a simple fix. It shouldn't have taken my speaking up in order for others to figure that one out.

When Bette slapped me, it was as if she was letting me know that I was unnecessarily holding things up. I think she enjoyed doing it. That is one reason it didn't upset me. When I looked in her eyes, it was like she was amused more than anything. Even at the time, I had the feeling that she was doing the slap, at least in part, for show. It didn't bother me that she hit me as much as it seemed to bother others who witnessed the slap.

Fay was especially upset and told me, "That's a terrible thing that she did." She had worked with Bette through the years, including on *Jezebel*, for which both had won Oscars—Bette for Best Actress and Fay for Best Supporting Actress.

I said, "Oh, it's all right." I think if Bette had slapped her, Fay would have punched her right back. Fay had been around Hollywood a long time and didn't take any guff from anybody.

Starting with *June Bride*, Bette and I became good friends. I think she noticed when she slapped me that I didn't have a fit, but

MORAL SUPPORT: With Bette Davis in June Bride. *Photo courtesy of Surry Arts Council.*

instead I used the slap as motivation to help solve the problem. That slap also helped put everyone in the production on alert that Bette would not tolerate having her time wasted. Not that everyone in Hollywood didn't already know that, but it didn't hurt to remind folks every once in a while. At least it didn't hurt much.

As shooting progressed, I felt pretty good about what I was doing. I felt in sync with the film's rhythm and pace, which most film productions naturally develop when things are going well. I was quite comfortable. There was one little hitch, though. The crew would call, "Bette to the set," and every time Bette would come in, I'd run in, too. Bette finally asked me, "Would you mind if we call you 'Boo'?"

I replied, reassuringly, "I don't care what you call me."

She told me I could call her Bette, and she would call me Boo, my character's name. From then on, everyone working on the picture called me Boo. And everybody Bette met or knew or introduced me to also now called me Boo. They didn't know who Betty Lynn was ever again.

OH, NO YOU DON'T!: Cease and desist, Mr. Makeup Man. Don't you dare cover up those trademark freckles, not even for June Bride *(1948). Photo courtesy of Gilmore-Schwenke Archives.*

Even after the production and outside of Hollywood, Betty introduced me to people as Boo Lynn. Rupert Allan, Bette's legendary publicist, was with Bette and B.D., Bette's daughter, in Europe doing some publicity one time. Bette and B.D. kept mentioning Boo Lynn. Even though Rupert had known me for years and even had dinner at my home, he didn't realize Bette and B.D. were referring to me when they talked about Boo. I think it wasn't until 1963, when Rupert and I both attended B.D.'s wedding and B.D. said something about Boo that he finally made the connection.

For *June Bride*, there wasn't much fuss about getting me made up to play Boo. The makeup people used just pancake makeup on me. Because my lashes are light, I also had Maybelline mascara that I put on myself. Other than that, I didn't have any other makeup while shooting the film. And I wore big sweaters—Sloppy Joes,

IS IT LOVE?: As Boo Brinker to Robert Montgomery's Carey Jackson in
June Bride *(1948). Photo courtesy of Surry Arts Council.*

they used to call them—and little pleated skirts and things like
that. I was supposed to be younger than I actually was.

Bette and Bob Montgomery did not get along, and it got pretty
tense at times. Later, Bette told me, "He rolled his big blue eyes. He
tried to steal scenes from me."

When I saw Bob in New York years later, he took me to lunch at
Rockefeller Center, and we watched the skaters and everything. It

AN AUGUST MOMENT: With Jimmy Stewart while working on the Lux *Radio Theatre presentation of* June Bride, *an adaptation that also starred Bette Davis and that was originally broadcast on August 29, 1949, thereby making for a swell twenty-third birthday present. Photo courtesy of Surry Arts Council.*

was great to see him. He said to me about Bette, "She's crazy. You know she's crazy, don't you?"

Bette and Bob didn't like each other at all. And politically, they were far apart too. It was really funny to see them interact. I liked both of them a lot.

While I was doing *June Bride*, I was sitting in the Warner Bros. commissary one day and having lunch. Seated just a short distance away was Ronald Reagan. He looked over at me and said, "Betty, I wonder if you could babysit my children sometime."

I took him seriously and replied, "Oh, I've never done any baby-sitting."

He looked a little annoyed and said, "I'm referring to the picture you made, *Sitting Pretty*." I had, of course, played a babysitter in that movie, which had been released in April, just a few weeks earlier. That previous role was the last thing on my mind at that moment. I apologized to Ronnie for not getting his joke.

Three years later, I went to see *Payment on Demand*. I was standing outside the theater and about to leave. Ronnie and Nancy Davis (soon to be the second Mrs. Ronald Reagan) came out of the theater with Robert Taylor and Barbara Stanwyck, Robert's wife at the time.

Ronnie looked over at me and said, "Betty that was a wonderful movie." Nancy nodded in agreement. I thought Ronald Reagan was darling. He was a real charmer. Over the years, a lot of voters obviously agreed about his charm.

Speaking of the Reagans, Jane Powell invited Ann Blyth, Joan Leslie, Jane Withers, and some other friends and me to lunch at Hotel Bel-Air in Los Angeles. Nancy Reagan happened to be seated at the table next to us. This was after she had been First Lady. Some of the ladies spoke to her. Later, she came by our table and spoke again. Katie Couric was with her. They had become good friends through the years. I know that some people have an impression of Nancy Reagan as tough and stern. Maybe she was when she needed to be, but I also found her to be gracious and charming. That said, if I were ever playing a game of dodgeball, I would have wanted Nancy Reagan on my side of the court.

Just One Thing After a *Mother*

While I was on the set at Warner Bros. doing *June Bride*, I got a phone call from Al Melnick. He said that my next picture would be back at Twentieth Century-Fox for *Mother Is a Freshman* with Loretta Young, Van Johnson, and Rudy Vallee. I finished *June Bride* at Warner Bros. in July 1948 and we started filming *Mother Is a Freshman* at Fox in August.

The Fox wardrobe people fitted me with some clothes, and the crew did some makeup and hair tests for color. I took my mother with me to see the tests. Loretta Young was in the room, along with

TEXTBOOK PUBLICTY SHOT: Having some fun behind the lens with Robert Arthur on location at the University of Nevada-Reno while filming Mother Is a Freshman *(1949). Photo courtesy of Surry Arts Council.*

some other people, to view the tests. It was dark. When I appeared on screen, there was an "Ahhhh" from the group, because of the way my light coloring stood out onscreen. I definitely had white skin. It was really pretty skin on camera. I never thought of myself as pretty, but my natural skin was very effective when filmed.

After that screen test, they made me up with darker makeup. They said that was necessary in order to work with Loretta, because her skin was darker. That was too bad for me, because nobody ever went, "Ahhhh" again. That was the end of my light-skin days for that movie.

We started filming in Reno on the campus of the university there. I shared a trailer with Barbara Lawrence. She had been under contract at Fox for quite a while. She was a delightful actress if anybody ever was. She was just adorable in *Margie* with Jeanne Crain a couple of years earlier.

I went into the trailer one day, and Mickey Rooney was there with Barbara. I was surprised to see such a big star in our trailer. Barbara introduced us. He was very cute just sitting there at the dressing table with the lights all around him. I had some braiding in my hair to make my own hair look fuller. I removed the braiding and laid it on the table. Mickey picked it up and stuck it under his arm, and we all laughed. He was truly funny. I had always liked Mickey in his movies, but that was the only time I spent any time around him. I can see how he charmed the ladies, including his eight wives.

At one point, Barbara told me that she couldn't understand how I had gotten the part of Susan Abbott, the daughter of Loretta Young's character, because Dickie Sale, one of the writers, had written the part for her.

As it turned out, director Lloyd Bacon also had not wanted me to be in the movie. I'm sure he wanted Barbara to be in his movie because she had been terrific as Marybelle in *Margie*. I have no doubt that she would have been equally great as Susan in *Mother Is a Freshman* too. Like Loretta Young, Barbara was tall and had great big eyes. As I thought about it later, I realized that maybe Loretta also felt that Barbara was too attractive, and would be a little too interesting to be her daughter. My appearance was less distracting.

Barbara asked me, "How did you come to get the part?"

I said, "I don't know. My agent called me when I was at Warner Bros. and said that I would be doing it. If you feel it was written for you, we haven't started yet. You should go up and tell the producers that Susan was meant to be your part and you want to do it. I don't care."

"Oh, I can't do that."

I said, "Sure you can do that. Why not?"

Barbara ultimately didn't go and tell them what she told me. She kept her assigned part of Louise Sharpe, and I kept the part of Susan.

It was kind of a double whammy for me that the part of Susan had been written for Barbara Lawrence and that Lloyd Bacon had wanted Barbara to play the part as well. He seemed disgruntled with me and treated me terribly during the whole shoot. I could barely make it through each day's work. That natural rhythm and pace that films supposedly find? It certainly wasn't happening for me in this production.

Many of the crew members would commiserate with me about how I was being treated. They couldn't understand why Lloyd was being so hard on me. One of his nicknames was Lightning, because he did everything fast. He had a reputation for competently, if not spectacularly, completing his films on time and within budget. Maybe he was just feeling stress, but he didn't take it out on anybody else in the company except me. I was the only one who felt Lightning's thunder.

In contrast, Van Johnson, who was the male lead in the picture, couldn't have been sweeter to me. He was delightful. He suggested to me that I should have my eyelashes dyed. I told him that I would be afraid to do that. Because Van's natural hair color was blond, he had chosen to have his eyelashes dyed. I just kept using my little cake of Maybelline mascara and putting it on with my little bitty brush.

Later in the shoot, the occasion of my birthday got me to thinking again about that whole casting situation with Barbara and me. It happened that I turned twenty-two when we were doing the movie. I wanted to go home as soon as possible in order to be with my mother and grandparents for my birthday, but the crew kept holding me on the set. My work was done for the day, but the crew kept telling me, "No, you can't leave yet." I was getting kind of annoyed because I really wanted to go home. Then I found out why. They threw me kind of a quasi-birthday party with a big cake. All of the crew and cast were there. That was a very nice thing for them to do.

It was at that party that Loretta learned how old I was. She said, "They told me you are seventeen." Evidently, someone with the studio had told Loretta that I was several years younger than I really was.

I said, "Well, Loretta, I've never lied about my age. If they've told you otherwise, that isn't my fault."

Loretta had never played the mother of a grown person before, and it bothered her. Seventeen wouldn't have been too bad. Loretta was thirty-five at the time. I could see why she was concerned. I wondered whether maybe part of the reason I got the role of Loretta's daughter over Barbara was that Loretta thought I seemed younger than I was. Ironically, it was Barbara who was actually several years younger than me.

Birthday parties and age concerns aside, Lloyd Bacon continued to treat me with disdain. He would hardly even look at me, and he was very gruff when he had anything to say to me. We would run the scene, and then he would just turn his back and walk off. I would go home and cry almost every night. I would go back to work the next day and act like nothing was wrong. Still, the way I was being treated by the director really did upset me. Unfortunately for me, a few others started to follow his lead.

Loretta was no shrinking violet either. I really liked Loretta, but she ruled the set with an iron hand in a velvet glove. That was what people said about her. She didn't want any curse words on the set. In those days, there usually weren't that many being said anyway. Very rarely would you hear something inappropriate.

Loretta had a jar that people had to put a quarter in every time they said a curse word. She was going to give the money to charity after the shoot wrapped. That made the crew a little mad, but they couldn't curse about it on the set, or it would just be more money for Loretta's jar. Now and then, Loretta herself would let a curse word slip out. "Oh my goodness," she would say when she realized what she had said. Like everybody else, she would put a quarter in the jar. I wondered if she let her curse words slip on purpose in order to show that her rules applied to her, too. That would've been shrewd crew relations.

Not everything about working with Loretta was as easy to understand as her curse jar. We had been following the script pretty much as written for most of filming, which is normal. You typically learn your lines for the next day's shooting schedule the night before and come prepared to perform them.

For whatever reason, toward the end of the shoot, Loretta started changing things up. I would come to the set each morning—

MAKING A POINT: With Loretta Young in Mother Is a Freshman *(1949). Photo courtesy of Surry Arts Council.*

dressed in wardrobe and ready to go. When I arrived, Loretta would call me over. She had Ruth Roberts, her dialogue coach, with her. Ruth was the sister of famed writer-director George Seaton. He won Oscars for his screenplays for *Miracle on 34th Street* and *The Country Girl*, and had other nominations for writing and directing. He also had been one of the writers and also our director for *Apartment for Peggy*. Over the years, I've wondered whether the sister of the Oscar-winning screenwriter might have been trying her hand at writing with Loretta, because my part for each day's shoot was totally rewritten. It didn't matter that I had spent the night before learning other lines.

Even though Ruth was a lovely lady, what was not lovely was that, through some combination of inspiration and teamwork between Ruth and Loretta, my lines were being rewritten—virtually all of them. Just in case Loretta didn't do any rewrites for the next day, I would still need to learn the script as written each night. I had to be prepared. I would then arrive on set in the morning, and, without fail, Loretta would have most of my lines rewritten for me to learn anew.

Then, as we were shooting, Loretta would also say things to me, such as, "Now, I have a line here, but I'm skipping that." I just had to keep up. It was rough, but I did it.

I would make it through one day, and then the same thing would happen the next day and for the rest of the shoot. Loretta would say, "Now, come over here, Betty. Get your script and write all this down." She would read all of the new lines to me. Sometimes, I would end up with a brand new monologue that was a page-and-a-half long. I would think, *How in the world am I possibly going to learn all of these new lines the day of the shoot?*

I was panic-stricken on a daily basis that there was simply no way I could do it. Maybe it was just a combination of youthful resilience and sheer determination, but I somehow learned the lines and performed them well enough to get through each day. It was an exhausting way to work.

I don't know why Loretta, with encouragement from her muse, did that or why she suddenly thought that the lines she wrote were better than what was already written, but she did. Then again, maybe she knew what she was doing. She certainly knew more about making movies than I did, especially at that point. It was only my fourth film.

At first, I thought that this was just the kind of thing that people with power did to people all the time, but I soon concluded that it was not typical. No one ever did that to me before or after. Bette Davis never did anything like that. She just slapped me.

To this day, I don't know what was going on with Loretta and the rewrites. Her Hollywood career began in silent films. Maybe they made script changes like that back then. Maybe it wasn't even specifically about me, but rather some other ax that Loretta needed to grind.

The frustrating thing was that I liked Loretta on a personal level. I respected her and was very fond of her. Other than her behavior toward me in that one situation, I had great admiration for Loretta. I always have and I always will.

TURNING HEADS: Strolling on campus in a scene with Robert Arthur in Mother Is a Freshman *(1949). Photo courtesy of Surry Arts Council.*

Eventually—finally!—the shoot was over. I loved making movies, but I must say that I was glad to have that one over with. On the plus side, the movie turned out to be decent. It wasn't destined to be a classic, but it was well done and entertaining.

Fast-forward several years to 1955. I was at a party at the home of Ann Blyth, who to this day is a dear friend, and her husband, Jim McNulty. They had gotten married just a couple of years earlier. Well, who should be at the party but Lloyd Bacon, who lived across the street from Ann and Jim. He seemed delighted to see me. He told me that he had a script that he thought I would be perfect for, and he wanted to send it to me. I could have fallen over. I wanted to say, "Oh, come on. Give me a break." What I said instead was, "Well, that's lovely."

I later told Ann, "I can't believe this. When I worked with him, he was not very nice to me at all." I wondered if he even remembered me. Or maybe he had mistaken me for someone else. I couldn't figure it out, and I never would, because, sadly, he died just a few months later.

Even though *Mother Is a Freshman* was a trying shoot in many ways, there was time to relax. Most of the cast and some of the crew went to dinner one night at the Sky Room at the top of the Mapes Hotel, which was a new tower hotel in Reno and quite swanky for the time. Rudy Vallee, our fellow cast member, was the entertainer that night. He had a ventriloquist dummy and was trying to throw his voice. I can't say that Rudy and the dummy quite worked as an act, but it was a fun night on the town.

Another positive thing for me from the whole experience of making *Mother Is a Freshman* was that my performance received excellent reviews. That's one thing I tell young people who are going into the business: Go ahead and get a press agent so that at least people in the business will know your name. That's who you have to impress. In the end, publicity isn't for the public, not really. It's the decision-makers in the business who need to know who you are.

When I was just starting out at Fox, independent press agents would come to me all the time and say things like, "Betty, you won't have to pay me anything. If I ever get you anything that you get money from, then you can pay me something, but otherwise I'll do all the publicity for free." I guess it's a lot like lawyers today who work on contingency fees.

I mentioned the idea of retaining a personal press agent to Harry Brand, the head of publicity at Fox, and he said, "No, no, no. If we want you to be a star, we'll build you up. Don't hire anybody. Please don't do that on your own." So, I never did. Everybody else had a press agent, but I was so naïve. And besides, Fox was paying me. I felt I needed to follow their program. I think, as much as anything, the studio publicists simply didn't want to have to deal with having to wrangle all the additional publicists for each individual star and contract player. I might have been the only actor foolish enough to take their advice. The result was that virtually nobody knew when I was working except for the people I was currently working with.

Looking back, I think my career could have greatly benefited from my having had a press agent. I advise young people to get a publicist if they can. Social media has changed the playing field to

HAPPY NEW YEAR!: After having an initial three movies released in 1948 and with Mother Is a Freshman *ready for release in the spring, there was a lot to celebrate heading into 1949. This photo was no doubt the idea of a Fox publicist! Photo courtesy of Surry Arts Council.*

some extent, but I think there's still no substitute for having a professional, well-connected publicist in your corner.

What It Was, Was Football

My next film was *Father Was a Fullback*, which starred Fred Mac-Murray and Maureen O'Hara. I played their older daughter, Connie Cooper. There were some other very fine actors and performers in the film, including Thelma Ritter, Rudy Vallee, Jim Backus, and Natalie Wood, who played my younger sister. Natalie was not quite eleven years old, but had already been in several pictures, including *Miracle on 34th Street*. When I think of her and her tragic death, I want to cry. She was darling. I loved everybody on that picture. They all were outstanding actors.

We were all set to start filming when production was suddenly held up because the director we thought we were going to have and who had already been on the set working with us, had disappeared. He had gone off to San Francisco and simply vanished. He evidently had a problem. The studio finally sent somebody up to San Francisco to try to find him and bring him back.

In the meantime, the producers hired John Stahl to direct the film. Maureen said, "Oh, he's very serious." She had worked with him twice before, including on *The Foxes of Harrow*, a drama with Rex Harrison just a couple of years earlier. She was nervous about him because this picture was supposed to be a lighthearted thing. It wasn't the type of movie that you would naturally think of John Stahl directing, but he was very nice. The production went smoothly, and the film turned out fine.

John Stahl did, however, do one thing that was surprising. He didn't know that I was as old as I was, and he would slap me on the bottom every now and then. I would walk by, and he'd give me a playful slap on my behind. After doing that for a while, he suddenly came up to me and apologized. He had found out how old I was. Embarrassed, he said, "Betty, I wish to apologize to you. I had no idea. I thought you were just a little girl."

I said, "Mr. Stahl, that's all right. That didn't bother me at all." We continued to have a fine working relationship.

I loved Maureen O'Hara. She was a beautiful lady in every way. She was fun, but she was also quite careful about her work. Many years ago, I attended an event honoring Maureen. It was a wonderful evening. I got to sit and visit with her a little bit after the show. She didn't want to have her picture taken by anybody who happened to have a camera. She would walk out of places if people started taking random pictures of her.

FAMILY HUDDLE: With Fred MacMurray, Maureen O'Hara, and young Natalie Wood in Father Was a Fullback *(1949). Photo courtesy of Surry Arts Council.*

Maureen told me that she had once gotten some unapproved photos in the mail that people wanted her to sign. She was furious. She was very aware of how beautiful she was. She wasn't about to let photographers snap pictures of her that didn't look great. She was adamant about that. We all had to hide her as we walked out of the hotel that night. We were putting our hands up and doing things to distract people so they couldn't easily snap pictures of her.

I remember a similar situation with Jane Cowl, a splendid actress. In early 1950, she and I worked together on *Payment on Demand*. Jane was a Broadway legend and a beauty in her day. She had played Juliet in *Romeo and Juliet* on Broadway in the 1920s. Jane had beautiful bone structure in her face just like Maureen O'Hara and Greta Garbo.

Because Jane had been known for being this great beauty and was still a very attractive woman, she was always attentive to how her looks were presented. She had screens put up around her so that

BATTER UP!: On deck at a celebrity baseball game in 1949 with Victor Mature and Gloria DeHaven. Photo courtesy of TAGSRWC Archives.

people not involved in the scene being filmed couldn't watch her from the sidelines when she was acting. It was rare that Jane would even do a movie. *Payment on Demand* would be her last film. In fact, she died before the film was released in 1951.

When Jane had the screens put up, Bette Davis, the female lead in *Payment on Demand*, said to me in the dressing room one day, "Boo, she was known as this great beauty all of her life and she's very conscious of that." Bette added, "That's one thing you and I don't have to worry about—not ever having been great beauties ourselves."

I said, "Well, you are *still* a great beauty, Bette, and I have seen pictures of you when you were young. You were a knockout. So don't put me in your class." It is true, though, that being known for great beauty is tough on these ladies. They don't look old. Their bone structure keeps everything in place, I guess. Maureen O'Hara still looked wonderful as she aged, and I have other friends who look wonderful. I age, but everybody else looks pretty young. Oh,

TOUCHING SCENE: With Bette Davis in Payment on Demand *(1951).*
Photo courtesy of Surry Arts Council.

well. Better than the alternative, as they say. I've earned every wrinkle. Even my trademark freckles have wrinkles!

Back to our football movie: We filmed *Father Was a Fullback* in
the spring of 1949, and Twentieth Century-Fox had it in theaters

THREE ON A COUCH: With Maureen O'Hara and Paul Douglas relaxing backstage before a Lux Radio Theatre *broadcast of* Father Was a Fullback *on March 20, 1950. Photo courtesy of TAGSRWC Archives.*

in time for football season that fall. It had a few fumbles, but it scored some points.

Cheaper by the Dozen

I loved my next picture, *Cheaper by the Dozen*. I really enjoyed working with Clifton Webb. I adored him. He was such a genuinely charming man. I had just a short dance scene with him in the movie. He told me that the dance we did was the toddle. He had been a dancer on Broadway, and he was a marvelous actor. Spoiler alert: Whenever I see *Cheaper by the Dozen*, I don't want him to die in it. I always cry at the end.

Clifton gave me a simple performing tip that I used often when I worked. He said, "Before the camera rolls or you go on, stand there and lower your head down. That makes the blood rush to your brain." I've tried to remember that when I perform. I think doing that also helps add that little bit of extra color to your face for that first impression. Clifton was so sweet to me. I was lucky to work with him.

DESIGNING WOMAN: Looking over a script (or at least pretending to) on the set of Cheaper by the Dozen *(1950). Check out the blouse with the unusual pattern consisting of mathematical terms, charts, and graphs— literally a graphic design. Photo courtesy of Surry Arts Council.*

BUT WHAT ABOUT THE FRECKLES?: It's time for just a touchup in the makeup area on the set of Cheaper by the Dozen. *In the background, makeup artist Ben Nye helps Patti Brady have just the right look for her role as Martha Gilbreth. Photo courtesy of Surry Arts Council.*

It was also great fun working with Jeanne Crain in that film. She was a lovely lady. She was simply beautiful. Once again, we had just a short scene together, which was first with Jeanne and then with Clifton. It is a wonderful experience to work with performers when they are at the top of their games, as both Clifton and Jeanne were in *Cheaper by the Dozen*. I think our scene was a nice bit of film. I was happy with it.

A DANCE MEETING: Looking on with Jeanne Crain as Craig Hill (left) comes to grips with Clifton Webb in a scene in Cheaper by the Dozen *(1950). Photo courtesy of Surry Arts Council.*

When I think back on those days—and my career in general, for that matter—I cherish the memories and realize how fortunate I have been.

Don't Miss a Good Bette

My next picture was certainly one of the highlights—*Payment on Demand* and getting to work with Bette Davis again. By that time in early 1950, Bette and I were real friends. Bette called me and told me that she was going to do a picture at RKO and that there was a part in it that she thought I could do. She wanted me to read the script before I decided whether to do it.

TOGETHER AGAIN: With Bette Davis in Payment on Demand *(1951).*
Photo courtesy of Author collection.

I said, "Oh, I don't need to read it."

She said, "No, no. I want you to read it so that you can be sure it's something you want to do. Sherry and I will drive by and give you the script." Sherry was her third husband, William Sherry, whom Bette usually referred to by his last name.

They came by our house, and I said, "Won't you come in?"

Bette said, "Oh, no, no, no. I don't think so." She gave me the script, which was titled *The Story of a Divorce*. That was still the title during the whole time we shot the film. Right before the film was released in 1951, Howard Hughes, who was head of RKO at that time, changed the title to *Payment on Demand*.

I went in the house and started reading the script. There was never a doubt that I would want to do it. To work with Bette again was sure to be a pleasure, and it was a good part. I was to play Martha, the younger daughter of Bette's and Barry Sullivan's characters. After I read the script, I called Bette and told her that I definitely wanted to do the picture.

RKO had to get me on loan from Twentieth Century-Fox, just as Warner Bros. had done for *June Bride*. I don't know which studios came out ahead on those transactions, but I hope my performances were worth it to the studios who borrowed me.

I think that Bette may have had some involvement in the money side of *Payment on Demand* because she asked me straight up, "What are you getting at Fox?"

I said, "Quota." At that time "quota" for the movie studios meant an actor's full quoted rate and a guarantee of no less than a specific number of days of compensation.

"Oh, that much?" Bette asked.

"Yes," I replied. I don't think that was just idle curiosity on her part. However, whatever Fox got for lending me to RKO is what they got. No one told me. I just got my normal paycheck from Fox.

One of the magazines did an interview with me about the fact that Bette wanted me for the part. I shared how happy I was that she asked me to take the role. Many years later, Bette said to me, "You know, I have to give credit where it is due. It was actually Sherry who thought of you for the part, but I agreed with him."

A young lady was chosen to play Diana, my character's older sister in the film. She kind of resembled Bette. Not exactly, but there was a little resemblance. RKO decided they wanted somebody else. The first actress was there for the first day or so, and then they held us up for a week while they got another actress. Peggie Castle got the part. She was a beautiful girl and a very good actress.

A ROSE BETWEEN TWO THORNS: This serene scene in Payment on Demand *shows a happy family before things become bristly between the characters played by Bette Davis and Barry Sullivan. Photo courtesy of TAGSRWC Archives.*

Bette said to me, "Howard Hughes is checking Peggie out." I don't know if that was true or not. Peggie had divorced her first husband. When we were filming, she was engaged to Robert Rains, a very nice man, whom I had known for a long time. He was a publicity man. Peggie and Robert were married right after New Year's 1951, about a month before *Payment on Demand* was released.

We had a whole week that we rehearsed, which rarely happened in those days. We almost never had a real rehearsal. That astounded me when I first started working in movies. You just learned your lines, they checked to be sure you knew them, somebody would run your lines with you, and then you would walk on the set and you would shoot. I thought, *How have they made all these wonderful movies this way?* I couldn't believe it.

Curt Bernhardt was the director and also one of the writers. He was an interesting man. He had made films in Germany in the 1920s and 1930s. He was arrested by the Nazis, but managed to escape to America at the beginning of World War II. He worked first for Warner Bros. and MGM before moving to RKO. *Payment on Demand* was his first picture for RKO. He was a very prepared and assured director. I could just sense that we were in capable hands. With the added bonus of being able to rehearse, I was able to relax much more now than for some of my earlier pictures. Everybody knew what they wanted to do by the time we actually shot. Everything went very smoothly.

After signing on for the film, but before we had started rehearsing and filming, I had a date with Richard (Dick) Anderson, who of course went on to such a marvelous career in films and TV. I suppose he's probably best known across the generations as Oscar Goldman on TV's *The Six Million Dollar Man*. Dick and I came to Hollywood at about the same time and were almost exactly the same age—he was three weeks older. We had first worked together in that production of *Peg O' My Heart* that I did at the Laguna Playhouse back in 1949.

While on our date, I told Dick that Bette Davis had invited me to dinner, and that she said I could bring a beau. I said, "Would you like to go with me?"

He said, "Well . . . ." He was hesitant.

I was wondering to myself, *What is there to think about? You're being invited to dinner at Bette Davis's home!* I said, "Well, you know, do you think you can go or not?"

"Well, yes, I could," he said.

In the car on the way to Bette's for the dinner, Dick said to me, "The reason I was so hesitant earlier about this dinner is that I have an audition tomorrow morning for the part of Peggie Castle's boyfriend in your movie. I feel funny about going to Bette's home."

I said, "Well, why don't we just tell her the truth? When we get there, I'll tell her that you are going to be auditioning to play Peggie's boyfriend and that you feel uncomfortable about coming to dinner, because you don't know whether you will have to see her tomorrow—and that you just aren't sure that it's such a smart move to come with me to dinner." Dick agreed to that plan.

While Dick waited outside, I told Bette, and she said, "Oh, no. I think he would be perfect for the part." Dick came on in the house,

THE EYES HAVE IT: Bette Davis looks on as Peggie Castle and Richard Anderson adoringly gaze at each other in Payment on Demand. *Photo courtesy of TAGSRWC Archives.*

and we had a wonderful dinner. Bette was right. Dick was very good for the part, as he would prove to be in countless roles.

I loved Bette. It's true that she could be volatile, but rarely on the set. Or at least if she was, I didn't see it. In any case, getting to know Bette could be tricky. It got worse as she got older. I think that was especially the case when she came back from living in Maine and being gone from Hollywood for so long. I think she assumed that everybody would be falling all over themselves to be around her—both professionally and socially.

The reality turned out not always to be what she expected. Even during her professional heyday, Bette had never been extremely socially involved, but I'm sure she was hurt that her return didn't make bigger waves in Hollywood's social circles. I always thought it was interesting that having a social life seemed to mean much more to her when she returned than it had to her before.

I would see Bette when she would come to town to do something. Most of the people she had around her were paid to be around. She paid them. They all cared about her. I'm not saying that they didn't.

I think I was about the only one in Los Angeles who was just a friend. I could be useful if, say, her assistant had to be gone for a day or something. Bette was afraid to ever be alone. She would call me. If I were free, I would go and stay with her. I would do things like help her on her lines when she was playing Apple Annie in *Pocketful of Miracles.*

I said, "Now, I'm not going to act when we do this." I never liked it when people "cued me in" when running lines for a script, because I would get their "performance" in my ear. Then, when I got with the actual actor, it would of course be different, which just added unnecessary difficulty. I told Bette, "I'm going to do just a flat reading of the lines of the other characters in your scenes."

We started running the lines. There was one little section that she kept flubbing. I finally said, "Well, listen. Let's just take that section, and we'll do that until you've got it perfect, and then we'll do the whole thing again."

She agreed to this approach. I had her repeat it over and over, and she finally got it perfectly, and then did it perfectly again. I said, "All right. Now, let's just run the whole thing through."

She did, and it was great. We did it a couple of more times. The next day she called me after the scene was filmed. She said, "I want you to know I was letter perfect."

I said, "Of course, you were." She always did whatever it took to get a performance right. She was nominated for a Golden Globe for that performance.

Bette just had that certain allure on screen. No matter what is happening in a scene, you can't take your eyes off her. Even when she isn't saying anything, she grabs your attention. There is just something about her that draws you in. Is it those eyes? I'm sure that's a big part of it.

Bette and I remained friends for many years. One day, she said to me, "Boo, would you mind driving me home?" She had rented a house nearby.

I said, "No, I don't mind."

Once I got her in the car I was scared to death. I thought, *My Lord, what if I do something wrong or something happens while I'm driving*

Bette Davis? I was so frightened. That concern never occurred to Bette.

Not All Work All the Time

With a few films under my belt by early 1950, I had enough money to make a down payment on a house. Mother and I looked around and found a nice Spanish-style ranch house on Tennessee Avenue in the Rancho Park neighborhood southwest of Beverly Hills. It was built in 1928 and was about halfway between the Twentieth Century-Fox studios and St. Timothy Catholic Church, so it was a convenient location for me and for my mother and grandfather, both of whom lived there for the rest of their lives. I lived in that house from 1950 until I moved to Mount Airy, North Carolina, in 2007.

Around the time I bought the Tennessee Avenue house and shortly after we finished shooting *Payment on Demand* in April 1950, I attended the bridal showers and wedding for Elizabeth Taylor's first marriage, which was to Conrad Hilton, Jr. The wedding was held in May at Church of the Good Shepherd in Beverly Hills.

About a year later, I was in New York, and Elizabeth, who by then had divorced Conrad, was dating Michael Wilding. Elizabeth and Michael joined Roddy McDowall and me in going to see Judy Garland perform at the Palace Theatre.

After the show, all of us went backstage to speak to Judy. The others knew her from their work at MGM, but this was the first time I had met her. I was in such awe of Judy after watching her performance that I barely spoke to her that night.

Several years later, I was at a premiere in Hollywood. As I was leaving, I noticed Judy and her husband, Sid Luft, also leaving. From our earlier, brief meeting in New York, I didn't think Judy would remember me at all. I therefore chose not to approach her. About that time, Judy shouted, "Hello, Betty." I was startled. I stopped and spoke. I explained that I didn't expect her even to remember me. I greatly admired Judy Garland, and it meant a lot to me that she knew me and would make a point of saying hello.

FUN TIMES: Enjoying a night at the theater with Roddy McDowall in the 1950s. Photo courtesy of Surry Arts Council.

In 1965, when Liza Minnelli was nineteen years old, she performed at the Cocoanut Grove at the Ambassador Hotel. Mother and I went to see Liza's show. We were very impressed and went backstage and spoke with her afterwards. I told Liza how much I had enjoyed seeing her mother perform at the Palace Theatre years earlier, and that I loved her show as well.

When The TV Land Awards honored *The Andy Griffith Show* in 2004, Liza was seated at one of the tables just in front of the stage. She was sitting up front because she was one of the presenters that night and because, after all, she's Liza. I remember being onstage with others from the *Griffith* show and looking down and making eye contact with Liza. We gave each other a nod of recognition. I was happy to have met both Judy and Liza, who are not only two of our all-time best singers, but also best all-around performers. So much talent!

Fox on the Run

My next movie was *Take Care of My Little Girl*, which would also turn out to be the last picture I did at Fox. It was a story about sororities and how rotten they could be for girls. There was a part in it that I really wanted. It was a girl who gets despondent about not being selected by the sorority. The part had a lot of pathos. Julian Blaustein, the producer, didn't want me for that role, but he wanted me for another part, Marge Colby.

After I read the script, I wasn't sure I wanted to play Marge. Not that it mattered. The studio wouldn't have let me out of my contract. I went to Julian and said, "You have women dancing with each other at formals. I think that looks peculiar, and I don't know if I want to be in this movie." He laughed at me for saying that.

A CALL'S FOR CONCERN: As Marge Colby in Take Care of My Little Girl *(1951). Photo courtesy of Surry Arts Council.*

I said, "Surely, they don't actually do that at sororities, do they?"

He said, "Yes, they do." He thought I was hilarious for being so naïve about sororities, but I still thought it was odd. I didn't want to be in a picture with all these women dancing together, but it turned out to be all right. It wasn't too astounding. Compared to things going on in films and TV shows today, it's downright quaint.

When we were about to start filming, Julian sent me flowers. Of course, he did the same for the other actresses, but it was a thoughtful gesture from a very nice man.

We had another excellent cast for that film as well. Jeanne Crain, Dale Robertson, Jean Peters, Mitzi Gaynor, Jeffrey Hunter, and Natalie Schafer—all were tops. Lenka Peterson, my pal from The Rehearsal Club, was also in the movie. It was great to see her again and to actually get to work with her.

Romanian director Jean Negulesco did a fine job pulling together a thoughtful examination of how social classes can shape life on a college campus. The film didn't get much attention at the box office, but it was a solid film and a good group to work with at the end of my time at Fox.

Even when I had signed my contract with Twentieth Century-Fox "way back" in 1947, the studio had already started making cutbacks. Performers were feeling shaky and uncertain about the future. The atmosphere was the same at the other studios. There was a shift underway. It wasn't an actual earthquake, but it began to feel like one for everybody in the movie industry.

The "studio system" was on its way out. Not only that, but television was making the studios and the theaters nervous.

After *Take Care of My Little Girl* wrapped at the end of 1950, Billy Gordon, who was the casting director, told me, "I feel so bad, but they just don't have anything right now that would be right for you."

I said, "Well, that's all right. I'm just grateful that I've had these four years, so don't feel bad."

Of course, I would have given anything to have kept making movies for Fox. I loved making movies. I also had my family to take care of, and I had a new mortgage to pay. I really could've used the work. I wondered—worried about—what would happen to me and my career. I was only twenty-four.

Chapter 5: After the Fall of the Studios, Humpty Dumpty, and the Rise of Television

While I was anxious about my career when Fox let me go, my mother, on the other hand, had felt an artistic restlessness ever since moving to Los Angeles. Mother had never tried to paint or do sketches or any sort of graphic arts. She didn't think that she had any talent for it. Music had always been her mode of artistic expression. But one morning, Mother literally and dangerously fell into her abilities in the visual arts. She took a terrible tumble down the stairs to our unfinished basement.

She was hurt so badly in the fall that she wanted me to call our priest. She truly thought she was going to die. I called the priest and the hospital. She was severely bruised and generally banged up all over, but she was able to mend in her bed at home. It was just going to take some time for her to heal.

To help Mother pass the time while she was bedridden, I got some pencils and I brought a breadboard from the kitchen to her bed. I thumbtacked some paper to the breadboard, and she just started sketching. She did some angels and crosses and other religious things. They were really quite nice.

She went on from there to develop her talent. She discovered that she truly had a gift. She was an artist. She was a member of the Catholic Women's Club, which met in a building in downtown Los Angeles. A lady taught china painting and oil painting in a studio there. Mother studied both techniques with her and caught on quickly. She got good enough at painting china that she was able to sell some pieces and make a little money. Mother in turn taught me some techniques for painting ceramic tiles.

I started painting tiles in the summer of 1953. I would trace designs of puppies, kittens, lambs, Humpty Dumpty, and similar things onto the tiles and then paint the tiles and have them fired. At first, I intended

A GOOD EGG: One of the surviving painted tiles—so far avoiding nursery-rhyme Humpty's ultimate fate. Photo courtesy of Surry Arts Council.

for the tiles to be gifts that could be used like a coaster for a baby's bottle or as a pad to protect a tabletop from a hot container. Later, I started framing the tiles as decorative art pieces. People liked to use them for decorating a baby's nursery and that kind of thing. I eventually got proficient enough to be able to sell a few. By the summer of 1954, the *Los Angeles Times* even did a profile about me and my tile painting. In truth, I probably gave away more of the tiles as gifts than I sold, but I always enjoyed painting them.

When I moved to Mount Airy more than five decades later, I still had a few of those painted tiles. They survived the move, and I donated some for the local Surry Arts Council to use for fundraisers. The Arts Council also kept a few for a permanent exhibit at the Andy Griffith Museum. During the pandemic in 2020, the Arts Council asked me to do a video tutorial about tile painting that could be used for art classes, including one held during the Mayberry Days festival that year. I never would have guessed that would happen when I first picked up a brush in 1953. I know that my mother would have been pleased to see her only apprentice finally becoming a teacher.

Mother and I had planned for her to help me learn to do oil painting as well, but we never got around to it. In addition to my constantly trying to get acting jobs whenever I could, it seemed as though we always had a family member's illness or some other pressing concern to deal with at home. We simply didn't have a lot of spare time to pursue hobbies.

My mom and I had great times together. She was so wonderful. We talked ourselves to death. We used to say to each other, "Do you realize how we keep talking?" We would never get anything done. We just talked constantly. I'm so grateful for the times I got to spend with her. We didn't always agree on everything, but that didn't matter. My mother had a great sense of humor. We would just laugh and laugh.

Other than my stint with the USO Camp Shows, my time living in New York in 1946 and 1947, and then working in New York for a few weeks or months at a time in the 1950s, Mother and I had always lived together. We were incredibly close—two peas in a pod if ever there were. After several years of declining health that required a lot of care, Mother died on January 27, 1984. For a long time after she died, I would see something, and say to myself, *I've got to tell Mom about this.* Then the reality of her absence would suddenly hit me. It was hard. To this day, I still miss her tremendously.

In addition to my mother's discovered talent, my Uncle George was an artist, and my grandfather was as well. Maybe an artistic bent runs in the Lynn family. My grandfather was a talented woodcarver. It was a skill he developed later in life by taking night classes at a high school in Los Angeles. I suppose it was a talent that was always in him. It finally blossomed. I still have a couple of horse heads that he carved. They're beautiful.

Another hobby I pursued after I had been in Los Angeles for a few years was learning to play the harp. I had always loved the instrument. It has such a beautiful, graceful, soothing sound. I took lessons. My teacher was the same lady who had taught Harpo Marx. Unlike, say, the guitar, the harp is hard to take with you wherever you want to perform. You can't just throw it over your shoulder. Harps also get out of tune very easily. When acting work picked up, I got busy and did not continue the harp lessons. I believe my only chance for getting serious about playing the harp again will be in Heaven.

Later on, when I once again found myself having more idle time, I decided to take up another musical instrument. This time I tried the guitar. I enrolled in a class at Beverly Hills High School. I ended up in a class for Spanish guitar, as opposed to just learning chords. I got to where I was pretty good. I could at least accompany myself when singing to myself, but I recognized that there was no future for me as a guitar player. I practiced less and less. I have not picked

FEELING PLUCKY: Having fun trying out the harp strings in Mount Airy, North Carolina, in 2017, for the first time in many decades. Photo by Ben Currin.

up the guitar since the Northridge earthquake in 1994. There was no connection between the two events—just a coincidence. My guitar-playing definitely was not earth-shattering.

New Medium Rising High

After leaving Fox—or rather, after Fox left me—I was fortunate to stay quite busy, mostly with work in television, throughout the 1950s. Some of the roles were small, but many were pretty meaty. Anthology shows, such as *Chevron Theatre*, which was filmed at Revue Studios (now Universal City) and syndicated by MCA, and *Schlitz Playhouse of Stars*, which aired on CBS, provided steady work once I became established as a dependable, professional performer.

Having reached a dead end in movies, I, like so many others, had turned to television as the best available opportunity to continue making a living in acting. I did quite a bit of live television when I lived in New York, but I did mostly filmed television shows in Los Angeles.

I remember one morning when I came in to work on a new little show of some kind, and the director said, "Before we start the show, there's some wardrobe for you. The wardrobe people will help you in your dressing room. I want you to come in, and I'll just tell you what to do. It'll be totally silent. You don't have to talk or anything, and I'll direct you."

I said, "Oh, all right."

It turned out that the job was doing some little commercials. I didn't have to speak, but I had to act and do various things. For one of them, they put a bow on my head and pulled my hair up and then fixed it up so that I had little bangs. I had a Victrola next to me. I stopped it and turned it off, and then I got up and ran to a door. Next they had me outside throwing my arms around a young soldier—grabbing and holding him. I was instructed by the director to do all of that.

I asked the director, "Why am I doing this?"

He said, "Because Universal contracted for it."

I said, "Oh, O.K."

Before long, I began seeing different parts of what I had done showing up on television. And not just in one commercial or one program. Different parts of what I had done were also being used in other television shows and commercials. I got no money for any of that. The producers and director just reasoned that I was there doing the television show anyway, so why not have me do a few more little things for some commercials. It made me a little miffed. I even spoke to the casting director and said, "I don't think it's fair."

I did four or five of those. I don't remember what the others were, but that one I do remember. Years, even decades, later, I would still see those little bits in things. Every now and then, I would see some of it when I was watching old shows. All of a sudden, there I would be. I was in the background, but I could tell it was me. I would think to myself, *Isn't that odd?* I haven't seen any of them in years, but I suppose they're still out there to see if you happen to flip the channel at the right time and don't blink.

While I was doing some TV work for Paramount, I ran into Carolyn Jones. This was several years before she would become a household name as Morticia Addams on *The Addams Family*. Carolyn and I worked together in an episode of *Studio 57* at the old Republic Studios in North Hollywood. I'm sure the episode is long lost in the dustbin of the early days of live television. So much is gone forever—that is, other than those snippets I did for Universal.

Carolyn said, "My husband, Aaron, would like to meet you."

At that time, Aaron was working as an extra in a movie for Paramount. He was wearing an Arabian costume. He and Carolyn had come up from Texas. They seemed like just kids at the time. She said he was a writer, but he was working as an extra.

I told Carolyn I'd be happy to meet Aaron. The three of us had lunch. Aaron was very cute all dressed in his Arabian outfit. It was funny. Of course, Aaron the Arabian extra soon became known to the world as Aaron Spelling, one of the most prolific and successful writers and producers in Hollywood history. Many years later, I was in a couple of episodes of *The Mod Squad*, which Aaron produced. Still, after that lunch, I saw Aaron only a handful of times over the years. He got very busy.

Coming to You Live—Coast to Coast

When I was doing much of my early work in live television in New York, we generally had plenty of time for necessary rehearsal. But not always. I remember doing *The Freddy Martin Show* in 1951. Freddy Martin was a popular piano player and bandleader of that time, but maybe is not remembered as well as others these days. Be that as it may, he does have a star on the Hollywood Walk of Fame in recognition of his recording career.

Freddy was talented and popular enough to have had his own television show, at least for a season. Merv Griffin was the featured singer in Freddy's orchestra. One night when I was on the show, Roddy McDowall was also a guest performer. We didn't rehearse much, and I also had to be in the commercials, which likewise, had little rehearsal.

I did not get to select which songs I would sing. Perry Lafferty, who was a very nice man and became a big producer in Hollywood, was the director of the show. When I told Perry that I would like to sing such and such a song, he said, "Well, someone did that a couple of weeks ago."

"Well, then how about if I do this other song instead?" I asked.

He said that I couldn't do that song because they had already planned for someone else to sing that song when she came on the show in about a month.

After Perry nixed several more suggestions, he finally just told me which songs I was going to do. They were things I had never sung professionally. One was "The Lady Is a Tramp," which I liked, but I just had never sung it. To top it off, they had me dressed up in this kind of tramp outfit.

I also had to do the commercial for the sponsor, Hazel Bishop lipstick, which was a new innovation that was promoted as the first "no-smear" lipstick. As it turned out, this new lipstick sometimes stained people, but the company eventually worked out the kinks and the lipstick became a very successful brand. Before you knew it, Revlon and everybody else was coming out with no-smear lipsticks to try to compete with Hazel Bishop.

A man who was a senior executive with the Hazel Bishop company was at the studio that night. He was very vocal and no doubt on edge about seeing his flagship product about to be advertised live on national television. Meanwhile, the crew were frantically trying to get me out of my tramp costume and into a more glamorous one to run out and do the lipstick commercial, for which I also had to sing.

I broke out laughing at the whole circus that was going on and ended up laughing through the entire commercial. I still managed to sing everything I was supposed to, but I laughed while singing through the entire spot. The crew had literally thrown me out on the set the second the costume change was complete. I just thought, *Who cares?* I couldn't stop laughing. I'm sure Perry Lafferty had a fit in the control room. And I imagine that the Hazel Bishop executive made a smear when his head hit the ceiling, but at least the commercial was memorable.

Roddy for Fun Times

Mentioning Roddy McDowall earlier reminds me of the many wonderful times we had together. Beginning from our early days in New York and continuing through the decades after both of us had moved to Los Angeles but still worked from time to time in New York, we frequently went to parties together or out for dinner and dancing, or just to the movies. Roddy was so cute and funny. I was very fond of him.

I remember one night in 1950 when Roddy and I went to see a late-night showing in New York of *The Miniver Story,* the sequel to *Mrs. Miniver,* Greer Garson's signature movie. The sequel was a good movie, too, but I remember coming away from it feeling very sad.

After the movie, Roddy and I decided to grab a bite to eat for either a very late supper or very early breakfast. Over at a table for two were Marlene Dietrich and Yule Brynner. Both of them had these faces that were so unusual. It was like watching a movie to see them so intent on each other and their conversation. They were very interesting faces to happen upon at breakfast. That was probably in the early days of what would become a lengthy romantic relationship for the two.

Another time, Roddy and I went to the Photographers Ball in Los Angeles. In addition to being a talented actor, Roddy became a noted photographer. He would have showings of his photographs in galleries. Some appeared in magazines, including as covers. He published several acclaimed books of his photos of celebrities.

For the Photographers Ball, everyone was supposed to dress up as characters. Roddy went as Charlie Chaplin and I was a 1920s-style flapper girl, like Clara Bow, with a short dress. I had my hair curled. We received many compliments on the authenticity of our Roaring Twenties look. We both loved to dance, and it was great fun to dance as those characters.

When we left the ball, we got in Roddy's brand new Studebaker. The windshield was fogged up and Roddy was wiping the inside of the windshield as we were pulling forward out of our parking space. All of a sudden, I screamed, "Roddy, there's a car."

READY TO PARTY LIKE IT'S 1925: Having a roaring good time as fellow redhead Clara Bow to Roddy McDowall's Charlie Chaplin at the Photographers Ball in the 1950s. Photo courtesy of Surry Arts Council.

I was too late. Roddy had crashed his brand new car into a parked car. Roddy also had smashed his head on the steering wheel. (This was in the days before seat belts were regularly used, much less mandatory.) We were on Olympic Avenue, not far from my house on Tennessee Avenue so we just walked to my house and called the auto club. My horrified mother tended to the wound on Roddy's head. The moral of the story is, *Don't drive without a clear windshield, and always buckle up!* The other takeaway is that things were never dull when you were around Roddy.

Break an *Egg*

I was in Los Angeles during the summer of 1952 when CBS called my agent. The network wanted me to replace Pat Kirkland in *The Egg and I*, a live daytime show based in New York City.

As I was rushing around getting ready to go to New York, casting director Ruth Burch called me. Ruth had previously cast me in *Peg O' My Heart* for the Laguna Playhouse in 1949. She would later cast me in both *The Moon Is Blue* in 1954 and *King of Hearts* in 1957 for the Sombrero Playhouse in Phoenix, as well as for a 1963 production of *Come Blow Your Horn* at the La Jolla Playhouse.

Ruth would also cast me in *Where's Raymond?* with Ray Bolger in 1953 and, crucially, *The Andy Griffith Show* in 1960, among many others. Ruth was a great advocate for me for many years. It is a blessing for any actor to have someone like Ruth who believes in you and immediately thinks of you when casting roles.

On this occasion, Ruth wanted me to come in to see about doing something at the La Jolla Playhouse. I went to her office, and she told me to go into another office. I did, and when I opened the door and walked in, who should be standing behind the desk but Gregory Peck! I just spontaneously reacted, "Ahhhh." He was just the most handsome man.

After the initial shock of seeing him, I somewhat regained my composure and said, "Oh, I didn't expect to see you."

He laughed. He asked me to sit down. We visited a while. I mentioned the Barter Theatre in Abingdon, Virginia, where I knew he had gotten his start, as had other stars, including Ernie Borgnine and Patricia Neal. As an icebreaker, I asked him if he knew Frank Gregory, who had done my screen test for Fox and who I knew also had worked at the Barter. We just had a nice chat. I miraculously avoided doing the random babbling that I sometimes did when I was nervous or caught off guard. We concluded our nice visit, and I left.

SOME LIKE IT HOT: Sitting above a radiator backstage at the La Jolla Playhouse while working on Come Blow Your Horn, *Neil Simon's first produced play, during the summer of 1963. (Costar Howard Duff is on the cover of the playbill.) Photo courtesy of Surry Arts Council.*

Soon after that, I was on my way to New York to join *The Egg and I.* Back in Los Angeles a few days later, my mother got a call from Ruth Burch. She was calling to let me know that Gregory Peck and Dorothy McGuire had formed an acting company to do plays at the La Jolla Playhouse, and they wanted me to be a part of it.

Now that I was under contract with CBS for *The Egg and I,* I unfortunately could not accept the offer. Even though I desperately wanted to join the new theater company, there was simply no way I could do so as long as I was under contract for the show in New York. Timing really is everything. In this case, bad timing.

The Egg and I television show was loosely based on the 1947 movie of the same name that starred Fred MacMurray and Claudette Colbert. The movie also included the characters Ma and Pa Kettle, who were played by Marjorie Main and Percy Kilbride. The Kettles were part of the television series as well, but were played by Doris Rich and Frank Tweddell.

Pat Kirkland, who was the daughter of playwright Jack Kirkland and actress Nancy Carroll, had played the role of Betty MacDonald for just a few months. Pat introduced me on my first show. She told the audience that I was taking over her role. Other than that introduction, I got no credit. That didn't bother me at the time. I was just glad to have the work. Looking back at those days now, I care a little more. A replacement deserves credit just the same as anybody else.

In our television version of *The Egg and I*, Bob Craven played my newlywed husband, Jim. Whereas virtually all married couples in early television were shown in separate twin beds, our characters shared a double bed. We were one of the first shows on television with a double bed for a married couple.

In our show, Bob would be crawling out of bed while I was still in it, or I would be getting out of bed while he was in it. This was virtually unheard of at the time. We did have a few love scenes on the bed—fully clothed, of course—but CBS required that at least one of us have at least one foot on the floor whenever both of us were in the bed. As long as one of us had one foot on the floor, I suppose CBS could claim that person technically was not "in bed" with the other character.

The Egg and I was quite popular—one of the top shows in daytime television, but it ended up not lasting long. It was difficult to find sponsors for a live comedy on weekday afternoons.

I stayed in New York for the most part in 1952 and 1953. I did make a point of returning to Los Angeles to vote in the presidential election of 1952. Eisenhower was running, and I wanted to vote for

him. I flew all the way back to L.A. from New York just to be able
to vote. I was thrilled when Ike won. I liked Ike.

Who . . . Me?

As I mentioned earlier, Pat Kirkland was the daughter of Nancy
Carroll, who had been a film star in the late 1920s and early 1930s,
when I was still just a kid and not yet aware of who was who in
Hollywood. Nancy had red hair and kind of a round face like me,
but she had blue eyes. When I first went to New York after being
overseas, cab drivers and people on the street or in shops would ask
me, "Are you Nancy Carroll?"

Finally, I asked someone, "Who is Nancy Carroll? She must have
so many friends in New York."

"Oh, don't you know who she is?" someone responded. "She's a
very famous movie star. She lives here in New York now." I didn't
know.

The Nancy Carroll comparisons continued. Ida Lupino had
directed *Hard, Fast, and Beautiful*, a movie with Claire Trevor and
Sally Forrest about a conflicted young professional tennis player. In
the summer of 1951, the film was having its New York premiere
at Forest Hills. John Springer, who was a publicity man for RKO,
called me and asked if I would like to go to the premiere. I said
that I would. As others had, he mentioned that I looked like Nancy
Carroll.

When John came to pick me up for the premiere, he said, "I have
someone in the limousine downstairs who's anxious to meet you."

I said, "Is it by chance Nancy Carroll?"

He said, "Yes."

I said, "I haven't the nerve to go meet her. If she thinks that people think I'm her, she'll die when she sees me. She'll just die. I can't
go down there."

He said, "Oh, sure you can. It'll be fine. She really wants to meet
you."

We went downstairs and out to the car. I got in the backseat
with her. She looked at me, and she said, "Well, yes, I do see a
resemblance." Of course, what else could she say? Poor soul. I never
was as attractive as she was.

JUST OUR TYPE?: Nancy Carroll and Tom Douglas in a publicity photograph for Paramount's Broken Lullaby *(1932). Photo courtesy of TAGSRWC Archives.*

A few years after that, Bette Davis was making *The Virgin Queen* for Fox. She was playing Queen Elizabeth I. It's a good movie about a lovelorn Sir Walter Raleigh persuading Elizabeth to finance his expedition to America.

One day during filming, Bette invited me to have lunch with her at the studio. When I arrived at the set, I stayed way in the back while Bette was filming a scene with Joan Collins. Charles Brackett, the film's producer, came over to me, took my hand, and kissed it. He said, "I'll never forget Havana."

I said, "Thank you." I didn't know what to say to him. I had never been to Havana.

He walked away. After a few minutes, he came back. He said, "I want to apologize. I thought you were Nancy Carroll."

I should note that Nancy was more than twenty years older than I was. After all, I had replaced her daughter in *The Egg and I*. Either she looked a lot younger than her age or I looked a lot older than mine. Or maybe everybody was just stuck in another time and remembering Nancy from the height of her fame, when she was in her twenties.

Through the years, I got to know Nancy. She was Catholic, as I am, and we went to Mass together one Sunday and then went to Carlos and Mary Montalbán's home for breakfast. Carlos was Ricardo Montalbán's brother. At the breakfast, I told Nancy the story about my encounter with Charles Brackett. I asked her, "What in the world happened in Havana?"

Nancy demurely chuckled and cut her eyes. She said they danced. She wasn't going to say any more than that. I was never very effective at getting folks to reveal gossipy details about themselves. I guess it's a good thing that I didn't ever try to be a Hollywood reporter.

I went through a whole period of people mistaking me for others. One time, I was in Saks Fifth Avenue in New York. I was just walking around and browsing. There was this group of Japanese tourists of all different ages. They kept looking at me and smiling. As I went from one department to another, they followed right after me—at a distance, but clearly following me. I would turn around, and there they were again just looking at me and smiling. I politely smiled back.

A young man in the group eventually got up his nerve to come over and speak to me. Maybe the group drafted him for the task. He asked me, "Are you Shirley Temple?"

I said, "No. I'm an actress, but I'm not Shirley Temple." He was obviously disappointed, but he was polite about it. He then had to break the sad news to the rest of the group.

Especially when I first arrived in Hollywood, it was fairly common for people to mistake me for Shirley Temple. It wasn't so much people in the business who made that mistake, but strangers whom I would encounter when I was out and about. I was in my early twenties at that time, and Shirley was just a couple of years younger. My face wasn't one that people might know as mine, because they hadn't yet seen me in many films, if any. I guess I looked vaguely familiar enough to them that they thought I must be somebody, and Shirley Temple was their best guess.

I don't think I resembled Shirley when we were young children, at the height of her stardom, or later in life. I could, however, see a resemblance when we were in our twenties. Another factor in the confusion might have been that Shirley chose to stop making movies in the late 1940s, which was the same time that my first movies were coming out. Audiences simultaneously seeing less of Shirley and more of me could have contributed to people thinking, after a first glance at me on a movie poster or in person, that they were seeing Shirley.

I met Shirley Temple only a couple of times. The first time, I was with Dick Clayton, who was one of the first people I met in California right after I had signed my contract with Fox. Dick later became an agent for future stars, including James Dean, Tuesday Weld, and Tab Hunter.

When I first knew Dick, he was still acting. He was just a sweetheart, and we remained friends through the years until his death in 2008. When my mother was in the hospital for a couple of months, Dick would go to visit her, which delighted her. I'll never forget how good he was to her. Dick could also be a jokester. He sometimes stood behind me when I was talking to people and would shake his head, as if nothing I said were true.

Dick and I were in the parking area after leaving a premiere one time, and we saw Shirley departing as well. Dick took me over and introduced me to her. I was thrilled. Shirley Temple was no doubt the greatest child actor ever in movies. (I have to leave myself a little wiggle room in my proclamation to allow for Ron Howard's portrayal of Opie on television.) I still love watching Shirley's movies.

Years later, I saw Shirley at NBC Studios in Burbank when she was hosting the *Shirley Temple's Storybook* series for NBC-TV. She was very sweet and seemed to remember me. Her career as an actor was itself worthy of a storybook. The pivot that she made to her second career as a distinguished diplomat was equally remarkable. She was an extraordinary ambassador for the United States. I greatly admired her as an actor, a good citizen, a humanitarian, and a person.

One of the wildest cases of mistaken identity happened in the summer of 1951 and involved Bette Davis, who by then was married to Gary Merrill. They were living in Saint Elizabeth, Maine. Bette and Gary came down to New York for the East Coast premiere of *David and Bathsheba* that August, about a month after I started doing live television work in New York. It was a big film with a stellar cast, including Gregory Peck as David and Susan Hayward as Bathsheba. Bette called me, and said, "Boo, we're at The Plaza. Would you like to come and have dinner with us in the room and then go to the premiere of *David and Bathsheba*?"

I said, "Oh, Bette, I'd love that."

I went over to The Plaza, and we had a lovely dinner in their beautiful suite. After dinner, we went downstairs, where a limousine was waiting to take us to the Rivoli, the beautiful theater just a few blocks away on Broadway at 49th Street. When we arrived, there was a crowd of photographers and excited fans along with the klieg lights, the red carpet going up to the striking Greek Revival façade, and the whole bit. An usher opened the limo door, and Gary got out. Gary then helped Bette out, and then I got out. When people saw me, they immediately started squealing and grabbing at me while screaming, "Susan! Susan! Susan!"

As I was fighting off the crowd, Bette was just standing there and watching the spectacle. Those gorgeous big eyes of hers got bigger and bigger as she observed all the commotion with astonishment. I just kept pushing against the crowd and saying, "No, no, no. I'm not Susan! I'm not Susan!"

After I eventually struggled through the crowd and made it inside to the theater lobby, Bette turned to me and said, "I didn't realize how popular that show you do is." She probably was referring to *The Freddy Martin Show*, which had just started airing that summer and was one of the bigger shows I worked on when I first got to New York.

I said, "No, Bette. They mistook me for Susan Hayward. I think my coloring is what confuses people."

"Oh," she said.

No one even noticed Bette. They were all over me. Susan was starring in the movie, and the crowd was naturally expecting to see her. As it turned out, Susan didn't even attend that premiere. It was obvious that the attention I received, although mistakenly, did not sit well with Bette. It was as if she did not exist.

Bette always did have a competitive nature. Years earlier, Bette had told me that there was a competition—in Bette's mind, anyway—between Katharine Hepburn and her. Bette admired Katharine, but she also felt competitive regarding some of the roles Katharine had done. I don't know if Katharine ever sensed that, or if she would have even cared one way or the other.

Bette also shared with me that one of the few regrets she had regarding her remarkable career was that she had worked with Spencer Tracy only one time very early in both of their film careers and not long after both had come out to Hollywood from Broadway. The film was *20,000 Years in Sing Sing*, which was released in 1932. Bette remembered little about making that movie.

It's no wonder that she didn't remember much about that film, because I've been told that it was just one of a dizzying total of nine movies starring her that were released that year. And it was one of eight films with Spencer Tracy released that same year. I don't think either star ever had more of their pictures released in one year, before or after 1932. I doubt many stars of any era have—maybe some Three Stooges or Shirley Temple shorts, but not full-length features. That is simply a staggering number of feature films for a lead actor in a single year.

Like Bette, I thought it was a shame that she had not worked with Spencer more often. Both were such fantastic actors. I suppose Bette's loss was Katharine Hepburn's gain in that instance.

One of my worst cases of mistaken identity involved Debbie Reynolds and, yet again, Susan Hayward. This particular instance was in the early 1970s, long after I was back in Los Angeles and even after *The Andy Griffith Show*. Debbie and I had been friends since we were in *June Bride*, which was her first film. She had an uncredited role as a friend of my character.

Debbie was getting a whole group of Hollywood folks together at her house to raise interest and money for a museum. Every now and then, she would get on a kick about getting her museum going. She had invited an especially large number of people for this occasion. That's probably why I made the cut for the guest list.

At the time, Debbie was married to Harry Karl, who inherited his father's business, Karl's Shoe Stores, which was one of the biggest chains of shoe stores in the country. Thanks to Debbie's success in the show business and Karl's success in the shoe business, the couple had a lovely home in Beverly Hills, where they raised her children by Eddie Fisher. Her daughter Carrie was still fairly young at that time—maybe sixteen years old and just as cute and charming as she could be.

I remember another party at Debbie's house several years earlier, when Carrie was just a little girl. She was dressed in this darling outfit with a little bonnet. She was very active and talkative. Even as a small child, Carrie was already showing a gift with words that the whole world would one day enjoy through both her acting and her writing.

Anyway, I said to Debbie, "Carrie is so precious. You should have someone paint a portrait of her."

"You think so?"

I said, "Yes, I do. You ought to have a pretty painting of her. She's such an adorable girl." I don't know whether Debbie followed through with the portrait. I hope so.

Back to the later party: Because I was attending the party alone, Debbie had sort of unofficially assigned a young lady who was her assistant to make sure I was kept entertained and had plenty to eat and drink. I went out on the patio to sit while I had a bite to eat. It was kind of dark out there, and I was sitting by myself. Before long, Greer Garson and Buddy Fogelson, her husband, came out on the patio. I happened to look over at them, and they looked at me and immediately came dashing over. Buddy kneeled in front of me and took both of my hands in his. Greer was standing behind him and looking very concerned.

Buddy said to me, "Oh, my dear, what can I say? I'm so sorry." I immediately knew what was going on. Susan Hayward had recently been diagnosed with brain cancer. Though I knew Greer and Buddy's mistake, I was caught off guard and didn't know how to respond.

I should have said to them, "I know who you think I am. I'm not. I know you must realize that by now. Susan's and my coloring are similar, and I've been mistaken for her before. I, too, am concerned for her, and I feel terrible about her condition. I pray very hard for her."

That's what I should have said. Instead, I just said, "Thank you."

Well, word quickly spread that Susan Hayward was at the party. I kept saying thank you to people. That was the only thing I could say. With weak acceptance of people's sympathy, I just kept painting myself more and more into a corner, or digging my hole deeper. Take your pick.

Whenever I think back about that experience, I cringe about how poorly I handled it. I never found a chance, or at least I never found it within myself that day, to say anything to set the record straight with Greer and Buddy or anyone else. I should never have continued with such a dazed response. It was horrible—just awful.

On top of that, I no longer looked like Susan Hayward in *David and Bathsheba*. Two decades later, people now apparently thought that I looked like Susan Hayward with brain cancer.

We all regret things in our lives. That one's a big regret for me. If anyone who talked to me at that party and who wasted their compassion for Susan Hayward on me is still alive, I hope you can forgive my pitiful cowardice fifty years ago.

Being Mistaken for Others—Even in Mayberry

Through the years, the actress I was mistaken for the most was Peggy McCay. Fans of *The Andy Griffith Show* have often told me how much Peggy and I looked alike. That's in part because Peggy appeared in a 1963 episode of the *Griffith* show called "Class Reunion." She played Sharon DeSpain, Andy Taylor's old high school sweetheart.

Though Peggy was a redhead, as I am, she has blond hair in her *Griffith* episode. Quite a few people over the years have thought that was me with a blond wig. I should say that those people were probably the more casual *Griffith* viewers, who maybe just happened to catch that specific episode. The more ardent Mayberry fans have never been confused about Peggy and me. Still, even those fans say that they see a resemblance.

The first time I heard about Peggy was when she was starring in the new soap opera *Love of Life* in New York at the same time that I was doing *The Egg and I.* My makeup woman said to me, "There's another actress whose features are very similar to yours."

I said, "Oh, really?"

I thought to myself, *So who is it* this *time?* She said, "Her name is Peggy McCay."

At that point, I didn't know Peggy and hadn't seen *Love of Life.* I had no idea just how much confusion there was going to be.

Later, after I had moved back to Los Angeles from New York, a few people would pass me and say, "Hello, Peggy." I just assumed they had forgotten my name since I had been gone for a while. I'd say hi and go on. It didn't bother me. I didn't care what they called me.

Peggy apparently did care. I found out that she was upset. I was at a party, and Darryl Hickman was there with Peggy. I had known Darryl for years. He was a few years younger than me, but we crossed paths fairly often in L.A. What a wonderful film career he had—from Academy Award-winning movies, such as *The Grapes of Wrath* as a child and *Network* as an adult, to lots of voice work and character parts later in his career. (Fans will also know his younger brother, Dwayne, best known for his title role in television's *The Many Loves of Dobie Gillis.*) In any case, Darryl and Peggy came

BEWARE OF FAKE ID AT MAYBERRY UNION HIGH: Peggy McCay and Andy Griffith as briefly reunited high school sweethearts in "Class Reunion," a 1963 episode of The Andy Griffith Show. *Photo courtesy of TAGSRWC Archives.*

over to speak to me at the party. Darryl introduced Peggy to me. Peggy said very huffily, "Hello," and turned around and walked off. I thought, *Whoa. Well, O.K. then.*

I told my mother about all the confusion with Peggy and her reaction to meeting me. Mother said, "I don't see a resemblance."

I said, "Well, everybody else seems to."

One day not long after that, I was at NBC's Burbank studios doing *Matinee Theater*. I was in the ladies' room, and in came Peggy. She and I both did several episodes of *Matinee Theater* in the mid-1950s—more than two dozen, in my case—but we had never worked together. Anyway, she hurried about her business in the ladies' room and was ready to get out as fast as possible, but I stopped her. I said, "Peggy, come over here, and let's look in the mirror and see what people see."

She came over, and we looked at ourselves and each other in the mirror. Both of us concluded that we didn't really look alike. She was more delicate than I was. She was tinier and everything. I was taller. She was more petite. There was something that people saw, but I never saw it.

Peggy was a truly nice person and very well respected for her talent and professionalism in the industry. Nevertheless, I sensed that there continued to be some tension about me on her part. I felt her uneasiness might be getting in the way of our friendship. I wanted to get to the bottom of why that was, so I invited her to lunch.

I thought I knew what might be part of the problem. I told Peggy that an actor told me that she had told him that I had followed her from New York to Los Angeles. Also, before that, maybe I had gone to New York and was inadvertently stepping on her potential roles there.

I assured Peggy that I had not been trying to follow in her footsteps and that, actually, I had come to Los Angeles under contract with Fox before she ever came to L.A. I told her, "I did movies long before I did television." It was true that I went to New York after she was already there, but it would have been hard for that not to have been the case, because Peggy was born there, and she was only about a year younger than I was.

When I told Peggy all of that, she said, "Oh. I didn't realize." She didn't know anything about my earlier career at all. She knew that we kept showing up in the same places, and she just thought that I was copying whatever career moves she was making. She really had it in for me, but she got over it once she understood the actual history of my career.

Years later, I persuaded Peggy to do some of the Hollywood autograph shows. I called her, and she enjoyed going. Largely because of her decades of portraying *Days of Our Lives* matriarch Caroline Brady, she was a big draw for fans.

Peggy's one *Griffith* episode was also a big attraction for fans at autograph shows. "Class Reunion" truly was one of the best episodes of the entire series—even if only my doppelgänger and not I was in that episode.

For years, organizers of Mayberry events had been trying to get Peggy to attend some of the reunions, but it had never worked out because of scheduling and other issues. Peggy had to cancel at the last minute several times. Finally, in 2012, she was able to attend Mayberry Days in Mount Airy, North Carolina. She received the Key to the City, and fans loved seeing her. I did, too. I think Peggy had a fun time—so much so, in fact, that she returned to the festival the next year. She was very gracious with the fans and everyone else. Best of all, by that time, no one was mistaking us for each other.

The Live Life

Live television is exciting. It's both scary and enjoyable at the same time. Maybe *exhilarating* is the best word to describe it. My adrenaline surely must've been running near empty from constantly doing so much live television during the 1950s. As I mentioned earlier, for nearly everything I've done, whether for a live audience or filmed or taped, I've tended to get the jitters. Of course, that's the way it is for a lot of performers. Some actors get so nervous that it's part of their performance ritual to throw up before going onstage. Others might have a drink (or two) or follow a specific pre-performance routine as a technique to settle their nerves.

My nervousness was rarely that severe. Even back to my childhood days onstage, I think I always realized that not going on with the show would be worse than actually performing. I would just force myself to get past that initial fright and power through to the part I enjoyed so much—performing for an audience. Once you've done that a few times and realize that you will not literally die doing your performance, it gets easier. Just knowing that you will survive is a real confidence booster. The old cliché that what doesn't kill you makes you stronger is a truth of performing, especially live.

In October of 1952, I did an installment of *The Gulf Playhouse* called "The Rose." It was a live half-hour drama produced in New York for NBC. Frank Telford was the producer and director for my episode. Frank was a prolific writer for radio and television. He likely had a hand in writing "The Rose." It was a good story. An interesting thing about *The Gulf Playhouse* was that it ran for just the last few months of 1952 before being replaced by *The Life of Riley*. The show was retooled and renamed *The Gulf Playhouse: First Person* and was then reintroduced as the summer replacement show for *The Life of Riley* in 1953. The revamped series had all of the characters talk to the camera as if the camera were a character. The idea was to have viewers feel that they were part of the story. That technique didn't catch on, but it was innovative.

As television work was gradually—and sometimes not so gradually—making the move from New York to Los Angeles, I bounced back and forth between the coasts as various jobs came up. In 1953, I bounced to California to work with Lee Marvin, Tom Drake, and Agnes Moorehead on the anthology series *Revlon Mirror Theater* in a production called "Lullaby." We filmed our show at the old Republic Studios in North Hollywood. For its second season, the series had just moved from Tuesday nights on NBC to Saturday nights on CBS.

Agnes Moorehead played the role of a blind woman and I played the role of her caregiver. Tom Drake played her son, who had been away for a while. Tom's character came back, and Lee Marvin played the role of a crook who was with him. In one scene, Lee was supposed to hit me. Felix Feist, the director, had him hit me, take after take. Feist was never satisfied with any of the takes. I finally told him that if he would put the camera in a certain place, the shot should work just fine. I was hoping to minimize any additional takes because Lee was actually hitting me. In frustration, I said to Lee, "Just haul off and hit me as hard as you can. I don't care anymore. Just go ahead and wallop me. I don't give a darn." (I may not have said "darn.")

Lee didn't want to hit me any harder and said, "Felix is a sadist, that son of a bitch. He's a sadist." Lee was right. He thought it was terrible to be doing all these takes. We finally got the shot. Every now and then, you run into someone in the business who is mean like that. I think Feist was enjoying my pain. Even now, that still hurts.

Not the Same Old Song and Dance

I played opposite Ray Bolger in the first season of *Where's Raymond?* beginning in the fall of 1953. I played a character named June. She ran a little coffee shop and was Ray's romantic interest. Ray, who is still best known to audiences today as the Scarecrow in *The Wizard of Oz*, played a big Broadway star named Ray Wallace. We sang and danced together at least once per episode. Sylvia Lewis played Ray's Broadway dance partner. She was also the show's choreographer.

FEELING GOOFY: Ray Bolger looks smitten as he finds himself over a barrel on the set of Where's Raymond? *in 1954. Photo courtesy of Surry Arts Council.*

LET'S MAKE SOME NOISE: A happy pair of partygoers are all set with noisemakers to help Ray Bolger (left) celebrate his fiftieth birthday in 1954. Just in case all the candles on the birthday cake get out of control, Charles Smith, a fellow Where's Raymond? *cast member, is at the ready with his fire chief's hat. Photo courtesy of Surry Arts Council.*

She later choreographed many of our dance scenes for *The Andy Griffith Show,* and she even appeared as a belly dancer in an episode.

Where's Raymond? was shot with one camera at Hollywood's old General Service Studios, which was home to Desilu Studios at that time. There was no audience. We occasionally did three or four numbers that were prerecorded. We often worked sixteen to eighteen hours a day.

After the first season, the producers let me go. They brought in Marjie Millar, a very pretty actress, who then played opposite Ray for the second season, which also turned out to be the final season. I didn't watch the show very often once I was no longer on it, but I did watch it enough to see that Ray was all over Marjie. He wasn't that way with me. I was fond of Ray, but not in that way.

I think men sometimes believe themselves to be these great lovers onscreen, when, in fact, they rarely are. Playing Casanova types was not Ray Bolger's strength. He was a fantastic entertainer. No one could entertain an audience better when he sang and danced. When I saw him kissing all over Marjie, I was glad it wasn't me.

Amazing Gracie—and George, Too

Because I had always loved George Burns and Gracie Allen, I was ecstatic when I was asked to be in an episode of their show in 1954. It was an episode titled "Gracie Gives a Baby Shower for Virginia Beasley." I played Virginia Beasley. The episode was shot at General Service Studios and was directed by Fred de Cordova, who later became best known as the producer of *The Tonight Show Starring Johnny Carson*.

I remember that Gracie Allen had a dressing table right on the set. It had the big mirror and lights and everything. I sat by her to work on my makeup. She was so kind. I said, "If I bother you, let me know. I'm just so thrilled to be around you."

I told her about a time in 1944 when I was in New York to sign my contract for the USO Camp Shows. My mother had come from Kansas City to sign the contract, because I wasn't yet twenty-one. After the contract signing, we went downstairs to get a cup of coffee at Childs Restaurant. Childs had been a popular chain of restaurants in the New York area for decades. There were still several locations around town when I was working in New York in the 1950s.

As we were having our coffee back in 1944, Mother looked across the room, and then excitedly said to me, "There's Gracie Allen sitting with a man in that booth. Why don't you go over there and get her autograph?"

"Oh, I can't do that," I said. I was too shy. I had never been able to approach stars and ask for autographs. I just could never bring myself to do it. But Mother kept after me to go ask for an autograph. The only thing I had with me for Gracie to write on was my contract.

I finally got my courage up and I walked over to Gracie's table. I just stood there. It was probably just a few seconds, but it felt like forever to me. Gracie looked up and smiled. I said, "Miss Allen, would you sign your autograph?" She nodded and said she would.

What else could she do? I handed her my folded contract, and she signed the back.

Fast-forward to a decade later, and there I was actually getting to work with her. As we sat at the dressing table, I told her about our earlier encounter. I said, "You're the only person I've ever asked for an autograph. You signed the back of my USO Camp Shows contract that my mother and I had just signed for me to go overseas in World War II."

Gracie of course had no memory of that chance meeting. Autograph requests from fans probably happened to her several times a day wherever she went. Still, she seemed delighted by the very different circumstances of our two interactions—from my getting her autograph ten years earlier in New York to her now throwing a baby shower for my character on her TV show filming in Los Angeles.

I don't have that contract anymore. It was probably discarded by either Mother or me many decades ago. It likely would have more than just sentimental value now. I doubt there are any other USO Camp Shows contracts signed by Gracie Allen more than seven decades ago that are still floating around.

Episodes of Episodes

There were two *Fireside Theatre* series. One was early in television, from 1949 to 1955. It was produced by Frank Wisbar. I did three of those shows at the old Hal Roach Studios in Culver City in 1954 and 1955. The series later became *Jane Wyman Presents the Fireside Theatre*, and I did a couple of more episodes, which by then were filmed at the old Republic Studios and at the famed Iverson Ranch over in the San Fernando Valley. Jane was the rare woman to host one of the anthology series during that era. She also performed in most episodes.

My first episode with Jane was called "Bamboo Cross," which was directed by the legendary John Ford. Jane and I played nuns at a convent in China.

The next season, I was in an episode called "Let Yesterday Die." It was directed by Don Weis, who would later direct nine of the first ten episodes of *The Andy Griffith Show*, before Bob Sweeney

SISTERS ACT: There was none better to work with than Jane Wyman (left), seen here in "Bamboo Cross," a 1955 episode of Jane Wyman Presents the Fireside Theatre *that also starred James Hong, who remains one of Hollywood's top working actors to this day. Photo courtesy of Surry Arts Council.*

took over for the remainder of the first season and the next two seasons.

In "Let Yesterday Die," Jane wore a white wig and played a lovely older woman whose son had died. I played the woman who had married the son and was mother to his little boy, played by Jimmy

Baird, who was one of the busiest child actors in television and was just adorable. Jane's character initially wanted nothing to do with my character and the little boy, but he eventually softens her heart, and all ends well.

I also did a lot of episodes of *Matinee Theater*, an ambitious anthology series for NBC-TV. They did five episodes every week. I remember a particular episode in the summer of 1956 with Jack Kelly. We had a week of rehearsals and then our dress rehearsal. On the morning of the live performance, we had gone through the show twice. We were waiting in the wings, ready to go on. As I was standing next to Jack, he took hold of me and could tell my body was hot all over from nervousness. He said, "My god, what are you like in bed?"

Well, that just broke me up and totally relaxed me. The show came off great. Ironically, that episode was titled, "But Fear Itself."

In another episode of *Matinee Theater* during the mid-1950s, I played a character who aged from sixteen to sixty-five. The director, a woman, who I believe was directing her first episode of this show, wanted to paint my hair to have it look like I had aged. I suggested they just use a wig instead. I thought it would create a more successful outcome. For whatever reason the director was determined for my hair to be painted. What could I do? I let them paint it.

When I ran into the director after the episode aired, she asked me whether I had seen it. I told her that I had not. She said, "Well, it was the oddest thing. Your hair looked green on film. We had no idea it would turn out like that."

I said, "Oh, I knew it would be terrible." In other words, I told you so. I was now glad that I hadn't seen the episode, and I hoped no one else had either. (Also on the plus side for me was the fact that the vast majority of Americans wouldn't have color TV sets for at least another decade.)

The director apologized. I hope she learned from that experience and then listened the next time an actor balked at having his or her hair painted.

Live television is like doing opening night in theater every time you do it. It's a brand new show every time. There are no do-overs. If you flub a line or miss a cue, then that's it. When I did *The Egg and I*, I had to know everybody's lines because I was in virtually every scene. If anybody forgot a line, I felt that it was my duty to handle it. I would say things like, "Maybe what you really wanted to tell me was . . ." and just carried both sides of the dialogue until the other actor got back on track, which was usually right away, because everyone was professional and prepared. Even for the best actors, sometimes a line will momentarily slip your mind. When that happens in a live performance, you hope you can depend on your fellow performers to carry you past your lapse.

One of the funny things that happened on *Matinee Theater* was in an episode called "The Reverberator," based on the Henry James story. It was about a month after the episode I did with Jack Kelly. Jacques Sernas played my fiancé. Jacques' character wanted to get into the house where I was. He ended up crashing through a window. It was one of those windows with the fake break-away glass made of sugar. I had my back to the camera, and I couldn't help but laugh because the crashing sound was so outrageously loud that it was comical.

Sometimes something like that would happen and my professional composure would crack as easily as sugar glass. At times like that, you hope you quickly recover your composure. Either that or hope that you're in a sketch with Carol Burnett, Vicki Lawrence, Tim Conway, and Harvey Korman, where their cracking each other up was always half the fun.

Au Revoir or Adieu?

Thinking back on working with Jacques Sernas makes me think about how sometimes it is in show business that you'll work with someone once, maybe even memorably, and then literally never see them again. I believe not long after we worked together, Jacques ended up going back to Europe, where he had grown up. He worked mostly in European films and television, a totally different orbit from Hollywood and my work. Some actors are constantly in your orbit. Some come and go and come back again after many years, like Halley's Comet. Others, like Jacques Sernas, fly by and then go on their way to another stardom. Who knows? Maybe Jacques thought I was the one who simply vanished.

After all my years living and working in Los Angeles, Hollywood was definitely my primary orbit, my stomping grounds. A few years after I moved to Mount Airy, North Carolina, in 2007, the Screen Actors Guild informed me that I needed to change my affiliation to the Florida branch of the guild. This was around the time of the SAG-AFTRA merger. After sixty-plus years of being affiliated with SAG in Hollywood, I didn't like the idea of joining the Florida branch. I have nothing against Florida. Other than a stopover there before heading overseas with the USO Camp Shows during World War II, I've never even been to Florida. I protested SAG's changing my affiliation, and the SAG officials agreed to leave me with the Hollywood branch. They probably figured that it was a moot point, because I was officially retired. It still mattered to me.

There's . . . Jimmy!

Sometimes my orbit crossed other people's orbits in unexpected ways. One night during my later years living in Los Angeles, I had been out shopping for a good while. It was late and I was exhausted. After all the shopping, I had worked up quite an appetite, but I had a lot of packages. I got a taxi and had the driver stop by my house, where I left the packages. I was then trying to think of where I could go to get a bite to eat. In L.A., it's peculiar. Sometimes there's no place to go to eat when it's late. I told the taxi driver that I needed to find someplace that was still open. The driver said, "Well, why don't you go to the Beverly Hills Hotel?"

I said, "Oh, I hadn't thought of that. O.K. Let's try it." It wasn't far from my house.

The driver dropped me off, and I went inside to the Polo Lounge. I had been there often for lunch with all my girlfriends. We took turns buying lunch for the group. When it was my turn to buy, I would usually suggest the Polo Lounge. On this night, I saw the maître d', and I said, "I know it's late, but I'm starving and I don't know where to go at this hour. I just want to get a bite to eat."

He led me to a table toward the back of the lounge. On the way, we passed a young man, in about his early thirties, seated at a table. He looked up and smiled at me. I said hello, and he said hello, and I went over and sat down at a table nearby that the maître d' had selected for me. About that time, the lounge's piano player started playing a new song. The young fellow looked over at me and said, "Do you know what the name of that piece is?"

Because of all my years singing, it turned out that I did indeed know. Many of the songs I once sang in shows were now mainstays for piano players in swanky Beverly Hills lounges. I told him what it was. We got to talking back and forth about first one thing and then another. He was just as nice and cute as he could be. I didn't know who he was, but I thought maybe he was an actor. He came by my table to say goodbye on the way out. I finished my hamburger and cup of coffee. When I asked for my check, the waiter told me that the young man had paid for my dinner. I was concerned that I didn't have any way to thank him. I didn't even know his name. The waiter said, "His name is Jimmy Fallon."

I guess I can chalk that one up to my ignorance. Of course, I doubt Jimmy knew who I was either. We were just two people grabbing a bite to eat by ourselves late one night. We had fun chatting back and forth—talking and giggling and carrying on. He was being very kind and sweet talking to a fellow late-night eater.

That encounter was probably around 2005, after Jimmy was on *Saturday Night Live* and before I moved from Los Angeles in 2007, and also before Jimmy started hosting *Late Night* and then *The Tonight Show*. He was probably in L.A. to work on a movie or something—maybe even to be a guest on *The Tonight Show with Jay Leno*. In any case, I know all about Jimmy now! I watch him, and he's so funny. He's a darling, very talented man.

I wanted to find a way to send Jimmy a thank-you note, but I doubted whether anything I might send would actually get through to him. Years later, after he started to do his "thank-you notes" routine as a regular part of his show, I thought how especially fun and appropriate it would have been to have sent a similar note of thanks to him, of all people. He obviously appreciates gratitude, as we all do. I'm just grateful for that lovely encounter. And for the hamburger and coffee!

Best in the West

Back to the Fifties: After doing a string of live shows in New York for a few years, I came back to Los Angeles on a more permanent basis in 1956. It took me a while to get fully reconnected in Hollywood. My agent had me making the rounds.

ON GUARD: Having a serious discussion with Ed Kemmer (perhaps best known as Cmdr. Buzz Corry in the popular Space Patrol *TV series of the early 1950s) in* Behind the High Wall *(1956). Photo courtesy of Surry Arts Council.*

I landed small roles in three films released in 1956: *Meet Me in Las Vegas* for MGM and *Behind the High Wall* and *Gun for a Coward*, both for Universal Pictures. Those were to be my last feature films made by major studios for release in theaters. Work in television was now decisively my bread and butter and would remain so for the rest of my career.

I was cast in a lot of different TV Westerns, from *Wagon Train* and *Bronco* to *Sugarfoot* and *Tales of Wells Fargo*. It was steady work and I was thankful for it, but they were all guest roles. That is, until my agent called about a job opportunity with Walt Disney.

One interview my agent arranged for me was at Twentieth Century-Fox. I was really pleased about that. *Imagine that*, I thought— *Fox, the studio that had originally brought me out to L.A. a decade earlier and had paid me for four years, now was interested in me once again.* I thought, *Gee, this is great.* I went to the studio, and they ushered me into a large office.

There was a group of men seated there. I noticed Walter Lang, who had directed me in both *Sitting Pretty* and *Cheaper by the Dozen*. I went over and spoke to him, but I didn't know who the other men were. I was kind of nervous, and I didn't look at them too much. Then, I happened to look over in the corner, and there, sitting as pretty as you please, was Katharine Hepburn. I thought, *Oh, my gosh. This is an even bigger moment than I thought.* I suddenly got very chatty, just from being so nervous.

One of the men asked me, "What have you been doing?" And then came my big mistake.

I said, "Oh, I've been doing live television in New York."

Everybody froze and just sat there and stared at me. I just kept talking. I had no idea that the movie bigwigs hated television because it was taking audience time away from them. Of course, time really is money, especially in show business. People were staying home and watching *I Love Lucy* and whatever else instead of going to the movies.

As usual, naïve Betty didn't fully comprehend that there was this terrible thing going on and that movie producers passionately hated television. Even in some of the movies at that time, characters would mention things that were derogatory about television. Later, of

DAILEY DEVOTION: Dan Dailey (center) visits with the young bride and groom (George Chakiris) in Meet Me in Las Vegas *(1956). Photo courtesy of Surry Arts Council.*

NOT EVERYTHING STAYS IN VEGAS: This scene with the bride and groom (George Chakiris) dancing in Meet Me in Las Vegas *(1956) was cut from the original theatrical release in order to allow more time for the film's enormous number of cameos. The sequence, choreographed by the legendary Hermes Pan, is, however, available as a restored scene with the version on DVD. Photo courtesy of Surry Arts Council.*

course, the movie studios got into television, right up to their necks, and their doing so saved some of them. Even Katharine Hepburn, along with Jimmy Stewart, Henry Fonda, John Wayne, and most of the big movie stars, later appeared on television and were thankful for the opportunity.

Meanwhile, I just kept chattering away. I asked Ms. Hepburn if she had done any live television, and she politely said that she hadn't. Oblivious of the reactions I was getting from her and everyone else in the room, I said, "Oh, I think you'd like live television. It's a lot like theater. It's really exciting to do." I'm sure everyone in the room was about fit to be tied and hoping that I would just stop blabbering. Or better yet, that I would just disappear from their presence altogether.

AW, BIG AIN'T THE WORD FOR IT: With Yvonne De Carlo (left) and Ann Blyth at the West Coast premiere of Giant *at Grauman's Chinese Theatre on October 17, 1956. Photo courtesy of TAGSRWC Archives.*

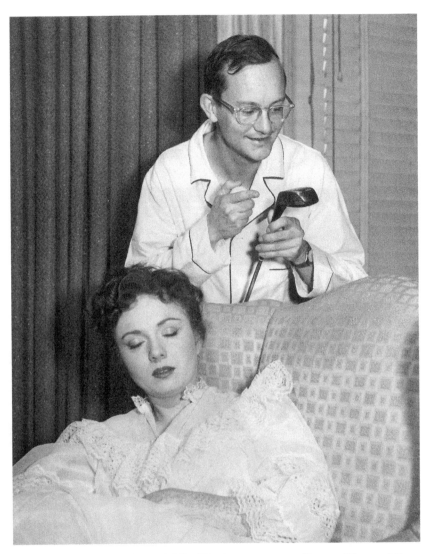

THE CLUB HOUSEHOLD: Having a snooze as Emmy Chase while golf-obsessed husband Vernon (Wally Cox) has only one driving force in "The Nineteenth Hole," a 1957 episode of Matinee Theater. *Photo courtesy of Surry Arts Council.*

Indeed, soon enough, I was thanked for coming and was directed out of the room. In yet another example of my recurring foot-in-mouth disease, I didn't get that job, which turned out to be a role in *Desk Set*, which was another hit for Hepburn and Tracy. That brief interview was the only time I ever met Katharine Hepburn, whose

VESTED IN THE WEST: One on one as Viola, the second mate for Tom Tryon's John Slaughter, in Disney's Texas John Slaughter. *Photo courtesy of Surry Arts Council.*

work I loved. I thought she was such a wonderful actor. Of course, everyone did and still does.

Though I missed out on that particular *Desk* job, I did find steady work in Hollywood during the mid- to late Fifties. *Matinee Theater* provided my steadiest work. The pay was good, typically $500 per episode, but there was also the expectation that there likely would be several full days of rehearsal included in that compensation.

The West World of Disney

From late 1959 to early 1961, I worked on *Texas John Slaughter,* which was one of the series that was part of the *Magical World of Disney* anthology. Texas John Slaughter was a real person. He was a Texas Ranger who became the first sheriff of Tombstone, Arizona. Walt Disney had purchased the rights to his life story. Tom Tryon played Slaughter in the series.

The *Texas John Slaughter* series had already been on for a season when I joined the show. Norma Moore, an excellent actress, had played John Slaughter's first wife, Adeline, who died in childbirth. Slaughter later met my character, Viola Howell, and married her. I played Viola in nine episodes in the second and third seasons.

I really enjoyed working on *Texas John Slaughter.* That's despite my getting injured working on one episode. There was a scene in which Viola had to chase John Slaughter. Tom Tryon was riding his horse at a pretty fast giddy-up. I was wearing a long dress, petticoat, and boots. I had to run in this really squishy dirt and sand, catch Tom, and pull him down off the horse. We had to shoot the sequence several times. I ended up with severe charley horses in both legs. The next day, we had to do some of the scene again. The pain was so terribly excruciating that I really didn't know how I would be able to finish shooting the scene. I somehow got through it. It was rare that I ever did a scene that was that physically demanding. I guess I was fortunate in that respect.

Other than that one scene, I had a great experience on the series. I was very fond of Tom. He was a generous actor and very good to me. We enjoyed attending premieres and other social events together for a time. He had been married to actress Ann Noyes, but they had divorced after just a few years. He expressed interest in our having a more serious, romantic relationship, but I felt our lifestyles weren't compatible. We just remained good friends. He was a very sweet man.

Walt Disney would visit our set every once in a while. We would talk about our memories of Kansas City. He grew up in Marceline,

HOWELL—THE WEST WAS WON: Here's the first page of the original 1959 contract to play Viola Howell (later to be Viola Slaughter) on Disney's Texas John Slaughter *series. Photo courtesy of Surry Arts Council.*

FEELING LIKE A DISNEY PRINCESS: Wearing wardrobe for Viola and obviously delighted to have a visit with Walt Disney and to be working on the Texas John Slaughter *series. Photo courtesy of Surry Arts Council.*

Missouri, about a two-hour drive from Kansas City. I told him one time, "L.A. should've hired you to design their city. Then it could've looked like Kansas City with all its beautiful fountains." And that's true. Kansas City has gorgeous fountains—more than Paris, so I'm told, and more working fountains than even Rome.

Chapter 6: Finding My Place in Mayberry

THELMA WHO?: Often considered to be the quintessential "Thelma Lou" portrait and also the most popular solo photograph among Mayberry fans seeking autographs, this image is technically not of Thelma Lou, but instead was a headshot used by Hollywood agents. Maybe so, but it'll always be classic Thelma Lou to many fans. Photo courtesy of TAGSRWC Archives.

While we were on hiatus with *Texas John Slaughter* at the end of 1960, I got a call from Ruth Burch, who was handling casting for *The Andy Griffith Show*. I had seen this brand new show twice, and both times I had seen Don Knotts with two different actresses playing Barney Fife's girlfriend. The first was Amzie Strickland, a wonderful character actress. She played Miss Rosemary. Just a few episodes later, Florence MacMichael played a new girlfriend, Hilda May.

Both times I watched the show, I thought it was simply wonderful. I laughed so hard when I watched it. I was watching all alone and I could hear that laughter. I couldn't figure out where it was coming from, and then I realized that it was me. I was laughing out loud. I don't usually laugh out loud at shows, but I thought it was such a truly funny show, and Don Knotts was just great.

I was asked to come to Ruth's office to see about a part, but she didn't mention what show it was for. When I got to her office, Ruth gave me the script. I looked at it, and I said, "Well, this is very similar to what I just saw."

She said, "You've seen the show?"

I said, "Yes. I saw it twice. I loved it."

Ruth was encouraged by my response and arranged for me to go over to meet producer Aaron Ruben at his office at Desilu Studios on Cahuenga Boulevard, which is where the *Griffith* show was filmed. I read for Aaron and Bob Sweeney, who was the director. When I finished, I thought it had gone pretty well. They must have thought so, too, because Aaron said that they would like for me to play this part. I told them that I was under contract with Disney for a series that I was doing, but maybe something could be worked out.

Aaron Ruben had an incredible instinct for producing a show and for what a story needed in order to really work. When you take Aaron's immense skill for crafting a good story and Bob Sweeney's natural touch as a director and combine them with Sheldon Leonard overseeing everything and Andy Griffith's own sense of a good story and his commitment to getting things right, that's creative leadership that couldn't be beat. Add a carefully selected cast that also was devoted to doing the best work possible every day, and it's no surprise that magic happened.

I remember that Aaron used to take steam baths. When he'd come on the set, he had the complexion of a baby. His skin would be absolutely beautiful. Steam will take wrinkles out of clothes. I guess it probably takes wrinkles out of people, too. I've never had a steam bath. Every once in a while, I think I might like to try one. Lord knows that I'd get my money's worth per wrinkle at this point. But I don't like heat too much, so I probably wouldn't enjoy a hot steam bath. So, wrinkles, you're safe. As with Aunt Bee's home-made pickles, those "kerosene cucumbers," as Barney called them, I just learn to love 'em.

At any rate, what ended up being the thing that worked out for my being able to work on the *Griffith* show was that Disney made the decision to cancel *Texas John Slaughter*. They dropped my contract at the same time. Disney did one more movie with Tom Tryon, and then they dropped his contract too.

The timing of my transition between shows worked out perfectly, at least for me. As it turned out, my last two episodes of *Texas John Slaughter* aired after "Cyrano Andy," my first episode as Thelma Lou, aired. And my third-to-last episode of *Slaughter* aired the night before my debut as Thelma Lou. So, I was Viola Slaughter, wife of the Sheriff of Tombstone, on Sunday night, and then I was introduced as Thelma Lou, girlfriend of the Deputy Sheriff of Mayberry, on Monday night. That was fun.

Before I joined the series, the *Griffith* show had already finished one more episode with the Hilda May character. It would end up airing two weeks before my first episode aired. However, a couple of months before that last episode with Hilda May aired, the writers had already written the "Cyrano Andy" script, which introduced Thelma Lou as Barney's girlfriend. From what I understand, even before Christmas 1960, the writers had completed a draft of "Cyrano Andy."

I think it was probably late December or maybe early January that I went in to read for the part of Thelma Lou. I believe it was then only two or three weeks from the time that I was cast until we filmed "Cyrano Andy." Things might have moved at a slow pace in Mayberry, but once Mayberry Enterprises, the show's production company, decided to cast me as Thelma Lou, filming of my first episode happened quickly.

I was excited to be a part of the show. I couldn't wait to start. At the time, some might have thought that going from the wife of the Sheriff of Tombstone to the girlfriend of the Deputy Sheriff of Mayberry was a demotion, but it didn't feel that way to me. I believe I was right.

Before I knew it, there I was working with Andy Griffith, Don Knotts, Frances Bavier, Elinor Donahue, and adorable Ronny Howard. There was nothing not to love about that. We were lucky to have such a great cast on the *Griffith* show. Actually, it wasn't just luck. Ruth Burch had a superb intuition for which actors could best fit specific roles.

Like Miss Rosemary before her, Hilda May just disappeared. Florence MacMichael had no trouble finding other roles. In fact, within a couple of years, she was a regular on *Mister Ed*. She obviously had better luck working around horses than I did. I doubt she got any charley horses on that show. Amzie Strickland went on to play other characters on the *Griffith* show through the years, not to mention her distinguished, long career as a character actor both before and after her time in Mayberry. I never felt that I had taken away work from anybody else. Goodness knows I had my own share of roles lost or missed, before and after my years in Mayberry.

At least initially, Amzie may not have been pleased about her exit and my subsequent arrival on the *Griffith* show. I was at a party where Amzie was also a guest. Amzie said to me, "You took my part," and she seemed angry. I was very upset by this. Amzie later told me that she was kidding, but I had believed her. Upon later reflection, I think she had indeed been kidding. After all, it actually had been Hilda May, not Thelma Lou, who had replaced Miss Rosemary as Barney's girlfriend.

I'm not sure there was necessarily any grand plan for Thelma Lou at the time I was hired. Thelma Lou could very well have been just one more woman in a constantly revolving door of love interests for Barney Fife. The character of Barney was still in the early stages of being fleshed out, by both Don Knotts and the writers. His character had started as an afterthought, then had become

CIDER PRESS: Barney offers Thelma Lou some apple cider in "Up in Barney's Room," a 1963 episode of The Andy Griffith Show. *Photo courtesy of TAGSRWC Archives.*

Andy's sidekick, and then eventually a focus of the comedy. During that first season, Andy and Ellie were the featured romance, to the extent that romance was much of a focus at all. The writers were just beginning to come up with bigger plans for Barney when I arrived. I'm just so thankful that I ended up being a lasting part of those plans.

Another part of the blueprint for Barney's love life, as well as Thelma Lou's biggest rival for Barney's affections, was someone that the audience never sees—Juanita, the waitress at the diner. Like Sarah, the telephone operator, we never see Juanita. What those characters look like is left entirely to the imaginations of the audience, as well as us actors.

Despite Juanita's tempting Barney and his affections, everybody always knew Thelma Lou was Barney's true love. We all hoped that things would one day work out for them. Of course, that's exactly what eventually happened. It just took a few more years than expected. Anyway, take that, Juanita, you little floozy! That's all I have to say about her.

When my agent was first negotiating with the *Griffith* show, the show's producers were talking about possibly signing me to a contract as a regular cast member. Once I was free of my Disney contract, however, I suppose the *Griffith* folks felt less concerned that I might not be available whenever they needed me, and they never signed me to a contract as a regular. Instead, they just called me whenever Thelma Lou had been written into a script. That ended up being a total of twenty-six episodes, during the first six seasons, from 1961 to 1966.

My part of the process for filming an episode would start on Thursdays. We would gather around a big table in the show's office at Desilu to read through the script. If I also had a large enough part in the episode scheduled for filming in two weeks, I might come in earlier that morning to do an initial read-through of that script as well. However, that was not typical for me. I believe I had back-to-back weeks of filming the *Griffith* show only eight times, and I don't recall that many of those occasions required me to come in early for the additional script reading.

For the script to be filmed the next week, we would usually start at ten o'clock. It would be Andy, Don, Frances, and Ronny, plus Aaron Ruben and Bob Sweeney or whoever the director was that week, but it was always Bob for my episodes—at least for the first three seasons, before Bob left to do another series. Bruce Bilson, or whoever the assistant director might be that week, would also be there, and sometimes Frank Myers, the production manager, but Frank usually was at only the more preliminary meetings. Any guest actors, like me, would also be there. I was a frequently recurring guest, but contractually still a guest.

We would start reading the script, and all of us would be laughing and giggling all the way through. The stories were so funny. Of course, Don and Andy had already given significant input and knew when all the funny things were coming, but they would be laughing, too. You couldn't help yourself. They were such funny stories. We had wonderful writers.

BREAKING THE HABIT: The cigarettes are sometimes airbrushed out of published versions of this photograph with Andy Griffith, which was taken during a break while filming The Andy Griffith Show *on location at the Forty Acres lot in Culver City. Both avid smokers eventually quit smoking and wished that they had done so much sooner. Photo courtesy of Surry Arts Council.*

That process would take all day Thursday. Andy and Aaron and sometimes Don might work on rewrites into the night until they were completely happy. The next morning we would all be back to read through the script again. By that point, there were few additional changes being made to the script. We would break for lunch and then come back in the afternoon. With scripts in hand, all the actors would be on the soundstage and we would start blocking the scenes, which is the process of going through the action for each scene while the director and the crew work out the camera positions, lighting, and other technical details—making sure that things work as smoothly on the set and for the camera as on paper.

By the end of Friday, things would have come together. When everybody was satisfied that any major wrinkles had been ironed out, Bob Sweeney would call it a day. All the actors then had the weekend to learn our lines and be ready to start filming on Monday morning.

We filmed on Monday, Tuesday, and Wednesday. Depending on which scenes I was in, I might not work all three days. Sometimes I might even work just one. The interiors at Desilu Cahuenga were usually shot on one or two days, and the exteriors would be filmed at Forty Acres, the old MGM (and later RKO) backlot in Culver City, where the streets of Mayberry were.

In some episodes, we needed to go to other locations to shoot a lake scene—or in my case, maybe that always intriguing Duck Pond! The shooting schedule and locations would be arranged to most efficiently complete filming in the allotted three days. The scenes shot at Forty Acres and other locations were often scheduled for Monday. That allowed for switching the filming of those scenes to Tuesday or Wednesday if there were inclement weather on Monday.

Each episode was a full week's work. I was paid $250 per day of filming, or $750 for most episodes. By the time the mandatory one-percent fee for the Motion Picture Retirement Fund, an allotment for my permanent charities, and the federal and state taxes were taken out and my agent got his ten percent, my take-home pay was about $500 for those episodes requiring three days of filming. In the early 1960s, that was still considered good money. Disney had paid me a thousand dollars a week to play Viola Slaughter, but that was for an hour-long show with more filming days per week.

For the *Griffith* show, actors received residuals for only the original broadcast and the first five reruns. That was the standard deal

MAYBERRY COURTIN' HOUSE: A tender moment in the swing on Thelma Lou's front porch in "Man in the Middle," a favorite episode from the fifth season of The Andy Griffith Show. *Photo courtesy of TAGSRWC Archives.*

back then. The first couple of reruns of an episode paid over a hundred dollars, but I generally received fifty dollars, before taxes and commissions, for the subsequent reruns. That was it.

For me, there was also the catch that the most episodes of the *Griffith* show I did in a single season was six. When you play a character like Thelma Lou in a high-profile show, such as the *Griffith* show, people assume that you are busier than you actually are, and they therefore assume that you're not available for other work. That was even somewhat true of my own frame of mind. I hesitated to take other acting jobs, except ones that I knew to be limited in scope and time commitment. I always wanted to be available whenever the *Griffith* show might call.

My biggest window of opportunity to accept other work was during the hiatus between TV network seasons. From mid-spring through mid-July, I could fit in a short-run play, as I did in 1963 with *Come Blow Your Horn* at the La Jolla Playhouse.

ACTORS TELEVISION MOTION PICTURE
MINIMUM THREE-DAY CONTRACT

Continuous Employment—Three-day Basis—Three-day Salary—Three-day Minimum Employment

THIS AGREEMENT made this 18th day of OCTOBER , 19 63 , between MAYBERRY ENTERPRISES , a corporation, hereinafter called "Producer," and BETTY LYNN , hereinafter called "Player,"

WITNESSETH:

1. *Photoplay; Role and Guarantee.* Producer hereby engages Player to render service as such in the role of "THELMA LOU" , in a photoplay produced primarily for exhibition over free television, the working title of which is now "BARNEY & THE CAVE RESCUE" #14-D (109) Player accepts such engagement upon the terms herein specified. Producer guarantees that it will furnish Player not less than 3 day's employment. (If this blank is not filled, the guarantee shall be three days.)

2. *Salary and Advances.* The Producer will pay to the Player, and the Player agrees to accept for three (3) days (and pro rata for each additional day beyond three (3) days) compensation as follows:

Three-day salary ($ 750.00)
*Advance for television re-runs ($)
*Advance for theatrical use ($)

Three-day Total (including advances) ($ 750.00)

3. Producer shall have the unlimited right throughout the world to rerun the motion picture on television and exhibit it theatrically.

4. If the motion picture is rerun on television in the United States or Canada and contains any of the results and proceeds of the Player's services, the Player will be paid the amounts entered in the blanks in this paragraph plus an amount equal to one-third (1/3rd) thereof for each day of employment in excess of three (3) days and if the blanks are not filled the Player will be paid the minimum additional compensation prescribed therefor by the 1960 Screen Actors Guild Television Agreement below mentioned, and the amount, if any, designated in Paragraph 2 as an advance for reruns shall be applied against the additional compensation for reruns payable under this Paragraph 4.

2nd run	3rd run	4th run	5th run	6th and all succeeding runs

5. If the motion picture is exhibited theatrically anywhere in the world and contains any of the results and proceeds of the Player's services, the Player will be paid $ plus an amount equal to one-third thereof for each day of employment in excess of three (3) days (but in any event the total shall not be less than the minimum required by the 1960 Screen Actors Guild Television Agreement). If this blank is not filled in, the Player will be paid the applicable minimum additional compensation to which he would be entitled under such Television Agreement, and the amount, if any, designated in Paragraph 2 as an advance for theatrical use shall be applied against the additional compensation for theatrical use payable under this Paragraph 5.

6. *Term.* The term of employment hereunder shall begin on OCTOBER 18, 1963 , on or about** and shall continue thereafter until the completion of the photography and recordation of said role.

7. *Basic Contract.* Reference is made to the 1960 Screen Actors Guild Television Agreement and to the applicable provisions set forth in such Agreement. Player's employment shall include performance in non-commercial openings, closings, bridges, etc., and no added compensation shall be payable to Player so long as such are used in the role and episode covered hereunder and in which Player appears; for other use, Player shall be paid the added minimum compensation, if any, required under the provisions of the Screen Actors Guild Agreements with Producer. Player's employment shall be upon the terms, conditions and exceptions of the provisions applicable to the rate of salary and guarantee specified in Paragraphs 1 and 2 hereof.

8. *Player's Address.* All notices which the Producer is required or may desire to give to the Player may be given either by mailing the same addressed to the Player at 10424 TENNESSEE AVE., L.A., 64 , Los Angeles, California, or such notice may be given to the Player personally, either orally or in writing.

9. *Player's Telephone.* The Player must keep the Producer's casting office or the assistant director of said photoplay advised as to where the Player may be reached by telephone without unreasonable delay. The current telephone number of the Player is GR. 79321 .

10. *Motion Picture Relief Fund.* The Player (does) (does not) hereby authorize the Producer to deduct from the compensation and advances hereinabove specified an amount equal to 1% of each installment of compensation and advances due the Player hereunder and payable during the employment, and to pay the amount so deducted to the Motion Picture Relief Fund of America, Inc.

11. *Furnishing of Wardrobe.* The Player agrees to furnish all modern wardrobe and wearing apparel reasonably necessary for the portrayal of said role; it being agreed, however, that should so-called "character" or "period" costumes be required, the Producer shall supply the same.

12. *Next Starting Date.* The starting date of Player's next engagement is

13. Reference is hereby made to Section 508 of the Federal Communications Act, making it a criminal offense for any person in connection with the production or preparation of any television program to accept or agree to accept, or pay or agree to pay, any money, service or other valuable consideration for the inclusion of any matter as a part of such program without disclosing the fact of such acceptance, payment or agreement. Player hereby acknowledges that Player is familiar with the requirements of said Act. Player hereby represents and agrees that Player has not and will not accept or agree to accept, or pay or agree to pay, any money, service or other valuable consideration, other than the compensation payable hereunder, for the inclusion of any matter, including but not by way of limitation the name of any person, product, service, trademark or brand name, as a part of any program in connection with which Player's services are rendered hereunder.

IN WITNESS WHEREOF, the parties have executed this agreement on the day and year first above written.

MAYBERRY ENTERPRISES
By Jack J. Engelhardt
Producer

Betty Lynn
Player

*No advance for re-runs or theatrical use may be made unless the three day salary prescribed above is at least $1500.00.
**The "on or about clause" may only be used when the contract is delivered to the Player at least seven (7) days before the starting date.
(The Player may not waive any provision of the foregoing contract without the written consent of Screen Actors Guild, Inc.)

STATIONERY EXCHANGE, MADISON 6-8121 • FORM 515

GOING TO BATS WITH BARNEY: The first page of the contract for "Barney and the Cave Rescue," a fourth-season episode of The Andy Griffith Show *that was filmed in October 1963 and was first broadcast in early January 1964. Photo courtesy of Surry Arts Council.*

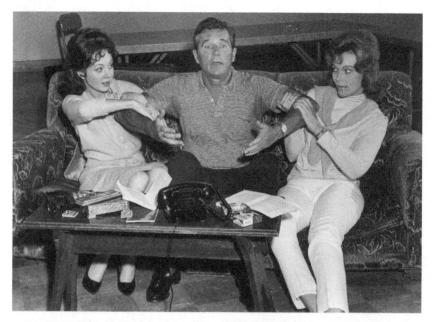

MAN HANDLED: In rehearsal with Howard Duff and Peggy Evans for the La Jolla Playhouse's production of Come Blow Your Horn *during the summer of 1963. The cast also featured Henry Corden, Alice Reinheart, and Alan Reed, Jr. Photo courtesy of Surry Arts Council.*

Even though I was not officially under contract, everyone acted as if I were, and I tended to feel that way as well. I must say that the *Griffith* show was good about consistently using me for five or six episodes during the four complete seasons that I portrayed Thelma Lou, the second through fifth seasons. I was in two episodes the first season, which I had joined late, and in just one in the sixth season, when Barney and Thelma Lou separately returned to Mayberry for their class reunion. More about that later!

After I started working on the *Griffith* show, whenever somebody else did think of me for a role, it tended to be for backwoods women and that sort of thing. They just assumed everything about the *Griffith* show was country and hick, and that none of us could do anything else. It took a long time for Hollywood to clue in to the fact that the *Griffith* show was a lot more sophisticated about what it was doing than people at first appreciated.

A lot of us were typecast because of our Mayberry roles—probably no one more so than Andy. Well, maybe that's not true. George

Lindsey was Goober for the rest of his life, bless his heart. George eventually made his peace with that. He made a good living from it too. If you can't beat 'em, join 'em, right? Or as Goober liked to say, "Yo!"

Despite what the critics or folks in Hollywood might have concluded, the *Griffith* show was a top-notch production. All of us working on it knew that it was. The viewing audience got what we were doing too. I think the test of time has validated the show as well. We knew it was special and we loved every minute of working on it.

Make Room for Ladies

When I was working on *Texas John Slaughter*, Disney had a beautiful dressing room for me on the lot. Because we were on location so much, I could rarely use it, but on location I had my own trailer. On the *Griffith* show, on the other hand, I dressed in the public bathroom. I had no dressing room until Aneta Corsaut joined the cast. Even then, the two of us shared a space that was just a makeshift area with burlap hung over the entrance instead of an actual door. It wasn't so much a room as an area with a burlap privacy shield. It was filthy. It had one couch in it. Because she played opposite Andy, Aneta worked more than I did. So, we just shared the "room" when I came in. At least I had somewhere to hang my clothes. Before that, I had to put my clothes in the prop department.

I furnished all my clothes for the show. I was always afraid that if I wore the same dress on another show, the two shows might air the same week and there I would be in the same dress. They sometimes asked if I could show them something else, but I didn't have the money to go out and buy an extensive wardrobe. Aneta was under contract, which meant that the show provided her wardrobe. Elinor Donahue also had an arrangement with a local dress shop to provide her wardrobe. The store even got a plug on its own card in the closing credits: Miss Donahue's Fashions / Mr. Burt's of Encino.

After being on the show for about four years, I asked my agent to ask for fifty dollars more per show. After speaking with the producers, he called back and informed me that rather than give me a raise, they would replace me. I later told Don Knotts about it. He said they would not have replaced me. I reminded him that

MAN IN THE MIDDLE—With Andy Griffith and Aneta Corsaut in
a favorite publicity shot for The Andy Griffith Show. *Photo courtesy of*
TAGSRWC Archives.

Amzie Strickland and Florence MacMichael had played Barney's
girlfriend before me, and I felt the producers would have replaced
me just as they had them.

The irony is that Danny Thomas was a partner in the *Griffith*
show, and I was donating something every month to St. Jude
Children's Hospital, which Danny founded. It is a wonderful
hospital, and I was glad to donate to it, but I couldn't keep doing

that forever. I finally had to stop because I didn't have the money to continue. There were a lot of charities that I cared about, including my own church. My permanent charities got one and a half percent of everything I earned, and the Motion Picture Retirement Fund also got one percent. So that took two and a half percent of my earnings right off the top. I eventually had to reduce the amount to one percent each because I wasn't working that much. I tried to give back when I could, but it wasn't always possible to do as much as I would have liked.

Happy Years

When we were working on the *Return to Mayberry* reunion movie in 1986, Andy Griffith said that the eight seasons on the old *Griffith* show, especially the first five when Don was still a regular, were the happiest years of his professional life. I have to say that they were the happiest of my career too. I can't think of a thing I ever did that meant as much to me as doing *The Andy Griffith Show* and playing Thelma Lou opposite Don Knotts.

Don was just so superb in everything he did as Barney. People always say, "Oh, Don must've been a riot on the set." He was actually quite the opposite. He was a quiet man. He would often sit by himself. I knew his mind was whirling away, and he was thinking of things he would do as Barney. Don saved every ounce of energy he could for Barney. When the director, said, "Action," then—boom! Barney exploded to life right before your eyes. Don was just brilliant. To be right there working with him and to be a participant with him was extraordinary. It also made me want to make sure I carried my share of the scene. Anybody doing a scene with Don couldn't help but want to deliver their very best performance.

It was the same way working with Andy. Everybody knew how deeply he cared about every aspect of the show—starting with the scripts and right on through the performances. You were expected to be prepared, and I always made certain that I was.

As much chemistry as there was between Barney and Thelma Lou, everybody knew that the true dynamic duo of Mayberry were Andy and Barney. Andy Griffith and Don Knotts were an amazing team. You felt like they could almost read each other's minds. They

APPETITE FOR ADVENTURE?: A happy scene from "Barney and the Cave Rescue" with Aneta Corsaut, Andy Griffith, and Don Knotts. Photo courtesy of TAGSRWC Archives.

were totally in sync. They were like brothers. Don told me that he and Andy talked every day. That tradition continued as the years went by, even long after the show ended. Their bond was truly special and touching.

Andy was a terrible tease, but in a good way. He would tease me about things all the time. His teasing sometimes made me angry, but deep down I knew it was just his way of letting me know that I was one of the gang. Andy called Don "Jess" or "Jesse" because that was Don's actual first name (Donald was his middle name), and Andy knew Don hated it. So, of course, once Andy knew that, he affectionately needled Don by calling him Jesse all the time.

I remember the last season that I was a semi-regular, the fifth season, Andy began using a nickname for George Lindsey. He called him Grover. I never knew why. I think maybe Andy heard somebody mistakenly call George that one time and saw that it bothered George. That's all it took for that to become Andy's pet name for George. Even though being called Grover bothered George at first,

I think he came to understand that, for Andy, an annoying nickname was a term of endearment. If Don could be Jesse, George could be Grover.

Even though Andy didn't have a nickname for me, I have to admit that I had a big crush on him when I first worked on the show. But Andy was married, so I made sure I got over that crush in a hurry. I wasn't going to allow that line of thinking to continue.

Most of us who worked on the *Griffith* show didn't socialize with each other much when we weren't working. It's not like we were all a bunch of introverts, though I think in fact many of us were. It was just that when we worked, our focus was on our jobs. When we weren't working, we had our families and all the other non-work aspects of our lives to tend to, just the same as most other people have a separation between work and home life.

I never intruded on people's lives or thought just because I worked with them that they were my buddies. I never did that. By the same token, people knew where they could reach me if they ever wanted to. I never felt that I had to carry on a relationship with people I worked with unless they wanted to. In that case, I would gladly be friends. It was just not in my nature to be pushy and force a friendship.

The Fine Folks of Mayberry

Elinor Donahue was always delightful to be around, and we're still very good friends. She and I were in only one *Griffith* episode together, "Cyrano Andy," my first episode, but we had met before the *Griffith* show. Elinor had been on the *Where's Raymond?* television show with Ray Bolger when she was sixteen. In early 1954, we did an episode together called "Find the Dog." I played opposite Ray at the time. Elinor's mother was with her. Like me, Elinor had started in show business as a singer at a very young age. Also like me at that age, her mother accompanied her to all her acting jobs. Our similar show-business experiences meant we had a lot in common—even more than actors in general do. She's an extremely nice person. I'm really happy that we've remained good friends through the years.

After Elinor left at the end of the first season, Andy tried different girlfriends on the show. Julie Adams and Sue Ane Langdon

MAYBERRY STANDOFF: It's no fun for Andy and Barney when Helen and Thelma Lou confront them about spending time with Mt. Pilot "fun girls" Daphne and Skippy. This publicity photograph was taken at the Forty Acres lot in Culver City during the filming of "Fun Girls," a 1964 episode of The Andy Griffith Show *that was the only one in the series that included both Gomer Pyle and Goober Pyle. Photo courtesy of TAGSRWC Archives.*

were in one episode each. Joanna Moore was in four episodes. All three were county nurses. We all thought Joanna might be the one. In the end, I think all three might have been too sexy for Sheriff Taylor—and maybe for Andy Griffith. Andy was the first to admit that he was awkward with any kind of on-camera romantic scene. He had difficulty with that chemistry. I think that's at least part of the reason Elinor Donahue left the show. Andy struggled with romance, and the writers, at least in the early days, found it a challenge to write the romantic, non-comedy scenes for Andy and his girlfriends.

That all changed when Aneta Corsaut arrived as Helen Crump, Opie's new schoolteacher in the fourth season. Aneta was a girlfriend of Jim Fritzell, one of the brilliant writers on the show. Andy and many of the others on the production team already knew Aneta and were used to being around her. Aneta was a very pretty lady, but she wasn't as voluptuous as some of the other actresses. She could easily fit in as Opie's schoolteacher. She wasn't exactly the Old Lady Crump, as Opie and his pals once dubbed her, but her beauty was not so overly disarming as to be intimidating or distracting. I liked Aneta a great deal. We all did. She was instantly part of the gang.

There again, even though we were great pals while working together, Aneta and I didn't socialize much away from work. Years later, after *Return to Mayberry*, in the 1990s when she was sick with breast cancer, I would call to check on her. I would say, "Now, when you feel like it, I can come out to the Valley and we can go to lunch." She unfortunately never got to where she really felt like it.

I think Aneta had quite a few friends from her days at Northwestern University. A whole bunch of them came out to Los Angeles to live around the same time. I think they would all get together when they could. In those last few years before she died in 1995, I would send Aneta flowers from time to time—just hoping they might be cheery. I once asked her if she could still eat candy. She said, "Oh yes!"

I sent her some candies from See's, which, especially in California, is a beloved candy company. It has been around forever. Even though I haven't lived in California since 2007, I still send See's candies to people. I think it's delicious.

One day I received the sweetest note from Aneta. This was after she had been sick for a while. I think everybody, including Aneta, had the sense that she probably wouldn't recover. In her note to me, she wrote, "You know, Betty, I've always been fond of you, but you've grown so dear to me this last year, and I want you to know how much you've meant to me." It still makes me cry when I think about the tenderness and emotion of that note. It wasn't exactly a final goodbye, but it was close.

When we went to Aneta's funeral in November 1995, I was seated next to Everett Greenbaum. He and Jim Fritzell, his late writing partner, had written some of the very best *Griffith* scripts. Their scripts introduced beloved characters such as Gomer Pyle, the Darling family, and Ernest T. Bass. Jim had dated Aneta for many years.

At the funeral, Everett, who was Jewish, said something to me that he had never mentioned before. He was upset that through the years I had sent him Christmas cards with the Blessed Mother and the Baby Jesus on them.

I said, "Oh dear, Ev, I never intended for that to be offensive. It's a little Jewish mother with her Jewish baby. It never occurred to me that it could offend you."

He said, "Well, you know, I never thought of it that way before."

I said, "Well, Christ was born a Jew and died a Jew." And it's true. I didn't mean to be offensive.

He said, "I just never thought of it that way."

I said, "Well, please think of it that way, Ev."

It was just a few years later that I saw Ev, who had begun doing a little bit of acting in his later years, in a television commercial for Hallmark—for Christmas cards! He played a grandfather. It was a wonderful commercial. Maybe I helped him be able to enjoy the Christmas season more.

Ev was a sweet man, and very bright. And obviously very funny. He wrote with a lot of heart. We were really fortunate on the *Griffith* show to have such great writers. Sheldon Leonard and Aaron Ruben worked hard to recruit the best comedy writers they could find. After the series was established as a hit and was recognized in Hollywood for being more than just a hick show, writers competed for the chance to be assigned to write a script for the show. Whether you were a writer or an actor, you were always delighted to get a call to work on the *Griffith* show. I didn't meet every writer, but I really enjoyed all their scripts.

ENGAGING CONVERSATION: Andy helps Gomer and Thelma Lou sort out a love triangle that has a decidedly obtuse angle in 1964's "Barney and Thelma Lou, Phffft." Photo courtesy of TAGSRWC Archives.

I didn't get to see all of the episodes when they were originally broadcast, because I might have been out and about when an episode aired, and I would miss it. In those ancient times, we didn't yet have streaming or even VCRs. If you missed an episode, you missed it and that was that unless you happened to catch the episode in a rerun later on.

Andy got upset with me one time when I told him that I hadn't seen a particular episode. One of his very favorite episodes, he said, was "Man in a Hurry," a classic written by Jim Fritzell and Everett Greenbaum. It is a truly wonderful show—one of the most iconic of the entire series—but at that time, I had never seen it.

I said, "Gee, I haven't seen that one, Andy."

"You haven't seen it?" he repeated. He was astounded.

I said, "No. I haven't seen it. After all, sometimes somebody might invite me to go out to dinner or to go dancing, and I would go. So, every now and then on a Monday night, I miss a show."

He said, "Oh." He still didn't seem too pleased after that—no matter what I said. But it's true. Even as much as I watch the shows now, I'm sure there are still a few I haven't seen. They'll be nice surprises when I see them for the first time.

For the record, I don't know where I was on the night of Monday, January 14, 1963, but apparently I wasn't at home, because that's the night "Man in a Hurry" was originally broadcast on CBS, and I didn't see it that night. I don't think I would have been watching either *Hollywood and the Stars* on NBC or *Wagon Train* on ABC. That is, unless maybe *Wagon Train* that night had been a rerun of my 1958 episode, and I very much doubt that was the case.

In any event, I now have not only seen "Man in a Hurry" many times and have loved it each time, but I also know that it was the first episode filmed with Jim Nabors as Gomer Pyle. Jim was such a good-natured person. It made you happy just to be around him.

Everybody's Aunt Bee

Frances Bavier was the perfect Aunt Bee. What a marvelous actor she was. While she was in most of the episodes that I was in, we didn't have a lot of scenes together. Those few scenes we did have together didn't have a lot of direct dialogue between us. Most of the activity in my scenes was generally centered around Barney or interactions involving Andy and Helen and dating.

After Elinor Donahue left the *Griffith* show, basically just as I was joining the show, and before Aneta Corsaut joined us, Frances and I (and to some degree Hope Summers as Aunt Bee's best friend, Clara) were the only actresses who were in more than a handful of episodes. There was a special bond between us. We looked out for each other.

At times, Frances could be difficult with Andy and some of the others in the cast and crew. They had to be careful not to say or do anything that might offend or upset her. Lee Greenway, our wonderful makeup man, was usually the one called upon to appease Frances. Frances adored Lee. We all did, but he was the Frances whisperer. Frances was likewise always very supportive of me. We always got along. And boy, did she ever create an iconic character!

A MAYBERRY FAMILY PORTRAIT: Surrounded by a loving cast (clockwise from the top): Don Knotts, Andy Griffith, Aneta Corsaut, Ron Howard, and Frances Bavier. Photo courtesy of TAGSRWC Archives.

In our respective retirement years, Frances and I also had another thing in common—both of us moved to North Carolina. She moved to Siler City, and I moved to Mount Airy. Each of us was seeking to get away from the hustle and bustle (and in my case, the crime) of Los Angeles. We came to North Carolina looking for tranquility and perhaps a version of Mayberry. I certainly found it, and I hope, in her own way, that Frances did too. She was very private and largely kept to herself. Thelma Lou may have been "the cat's" in Mayberry, but it was Aunt Bee who literally had the cats in Siler City—a couple of dozen or more from what I've heard. She was a dear lady.

My Fellow Redhead with Freckles

One of the things people tell me all the time is that Andy Taylor's parenting of Opie reminds them so much of their own fathers. Or sometimes they'll say they wish that they had a father like Andy, or that they try to pattern their own parenting on how Andy handled things with Opie. I believe the fact that Rance Howard, Ronny's father, was such a presence on the set was a factor in that. More than once, Andy mentioned that he very much admired how Rance handled things with Ronny.

We all marveled at what a great kid Ronny was. Of course, Jean Howard, Ronny's mom, was there some, too, especially during the years when Rance was away in Florida filming the *Gentle Ben* series with Clint, Ronny's younger brother. Rance and Jean were delightful people as well as wonderful parents. They raised two fine sons. It has been fun that Clint has taken part in so many of our Mayberry reunions. He was in several *Griffith* episodes as Leon, the little cowboy who never talks but just silently offers everybody a bite of his peanut butter and jelly sandwich. Clint was such an adorable little boy in that cowboy outfit.

When Ronny was a little boy, he was just precious. Because he was only six when the *Griffith* show started and he couldn't yet read, his parents taught him his lines by reading them to him. I don't know how Ronny did it, but he did his lines perfectly. I thought then and still believe that Ronny was the most natural child actor I've ever seen. I just loved him.

Memorable Moments

One of my favorite scenes of the *Griffith* show was toward the end of our fourth season in an episode called "Barney and Thelma Lou, Phfftt." There's a scene where Barney and Thelma Lou are

WINDOW SHOPPING: A favorite scene with Don Knotts as the happy couple contemplates their future together in "Barney and Thelma Lou, Phfft" (1964). Photo courtesy of TAGSRWC Archives.

looking at furniture in a store window and picturing in their minds how their future home might be decorated. It suddenly dawns on Barney that their discussion sounds too much like a commitment that he's not yet ready to make. He starts backpedaling and saying "if" this and "if" that. It's a very touching scene. It was always a special scene to me, and for years I assumed that it was special only to me. Then I began talking with *Griffith* fans, and many of them mentioned that it was one of their favorites too.

The scene is also memorable to me for other reasons. We were originally scheduled to shoot it outside at Forty Acres. Shooting there could be really hot, particularly with all the reflectors for the sunlight and even when shooting a night scene in the day, or "day for night" as I suppose it's still called. Especially when you're trying to do a tender scene, all the glare and dusty dry air can make your eyes water and can be difficult.

Because I wanted it to be a really nice scene between Don and me, I thought about how I would like to do this scene inside instead of outside. I asked Coby Ruskin, the episode's director, "Would you do me a favor and shoot this inside?" He instantly agreed. I was shocked. My opinions and desires didn't always carry much sway on film sets, but this time I got my way. I think Coby saw that it was a practical request and not unreasonable. I don't know that the scene would've been as intimate and effective if we had filmed it outside. I'm grateful that we moved inside. That choice and that scene still mean a lot to me.

Another reason that scene is special to me is that the day we filmed it was the only time my mother came on the set. I had asked permission for her to visit. Other actors had come on the set with their girlfriends and boyfriends and even their dogs. I had asked permission to bring my mother. Mother came and sat in a chair, and she got to watch that scene. That really pleased me.

My mother and my grandparents never said much of anything about my work. It was as if I just went to work in the morning, did my job, and came home. They would never see one of my films or television shows and say, "Gee, you did a great job in that." It just wasn't our way. I guess it was our Midwestern stoicism or something.

I have an actress friend who said it hurt her feelings that her family didn't tell her how great she was and everything. I finally said, "Well, no one ever said it to me either." I never expected that praise from my family. Only because my friend brought it up did I even think about it.

That said, I am glad that Mother got to see me work at least that one day on the *Griffith* show. She never said so, but I think it had to be fun for her. I hope so. I really do.

On the *Griffith* show, we had to be perfect. I have to admit that sometimes that perfectionism could drive me a little crazy. For example, if somebody missed just a little tiny word, the script girl would catch it and let us know that the scene had to be done again. It had to be exact. There was no ad-libbing.

Of course, it was usually the same way with movies I worked on earlier in my career. You did not make mistakes. You were costing the movie studio thousands of dollars, according to them, if you wasted a minute of their time. You had to be perfect at everything. It could be a terrible pressure.

With the *Griffith* show, it wasn't so much about wasting money. It was just about getting a scene right. The writers and Andy and Aaron Ruben—and others, too, but Andy and Aaron in particular—devoted a lot of time to getting the scripts just like they wanted them, and they didn't want us performers spontaneously thinking that we had better words to use. They also weren't going to settle for a slightly flubbed line. Nor should they have. A few flubs slipped by over the years, but it was a very few.

In comedy, things oftentimes need time to build beyond just a series of jokes. A certain amount of structure is required to get the story's payoff to be where it's supposed to be. Actors don't always have that ability. In fact, more often than not, they don't. Even the ones who do usually can't be on top of tracking the comedy and the storytelling every minute while also delivering their best performance.

Now, Andy and Don could do some changes on the set. They were the exception. They worked so well together that they could make changes while we were shooting. For things like the front-porch scenes when Andy and Barney are just shooting the breeze about going to the drugstore and getting ice cream for later and things like that, Andy and Don would spend time working out all of the mannerisms and timing. They would do that together—perhaps with input from the director. There again, though, the dialogue was all scripted, and Andy and Don would have all the nuances of their performances worked out before any filming started.

As the line producer and head writer, Aaron Ruben was always on the set too. He could make a fix if some part of a scene simply wasn't working out during rehearsal the way it had been intended in the script. Those kinds of hiccups were almost always caught during rehearsal, not while filming.

The fact that we used one camera, as most movies do, instead of three—or now, often four—cameras, as most sitcoms do, also meant that we needed finer precision in what we did. A typical scene required a master shot (the broadest shot) and then a shot closer in with just a couple or maybe a few characters, and then various close-ups of individual characters or occasionally of objects, such as something that a character is holding in her hands. It would be very hard to match all those shots with a lot of improvisation going on.

Nowadays, so I gather, many productions are keen on having more improvisation from their actors. That method apparently works for them. I can see where that could work if you are going more for punch lines and wanting to try different things to see what gets the biggest laugh from an audience. I don't think that would have worked as well for the approach to the character-driven humor and stories we did for the *Griffith* show.

One of the most famous and hilarious scenes of the entire series was in "Opie's Ill-Gotten Gain" when Barney is totally incompetent at trying to demonstrate to Andy how he has memorized the *Preamble to the U.S. Constitution*. I'm not in that episode, but it's one of my favorites. That scene demonstrates the importance of what I was saying about the difficulty of matching up different takes.

That was the second *Griffith* episode directed by Jeff Hayden, a fine director who directed several memorable episodes during our fourth season—including "Up in Barney's Room," the episode with the classic scene where Barney has Thelma Lou's lipstick smeared all over his face. I've signed more publicity photos of that lipstick scene than any other, by far.

In the *Preamble* scene, Barney musses up his hair in frustration as he struggles to remember each individual word. It was hard for Don to muss up his hair in exactly the same way every time, and Jeff didn't get full coverage of all the different appearances of Barney's hair throughout the scene. Jeff assumed the editor would stay in for the close-up of Barney's mussed up hair, but he didn't. Barney's hair goes back and forth between mussed and not mussed when pulling out to the broadest shot.

That's a rare case of an obvious technical slip on the *Griffith* show. The fact that there weren't many more instances of glaring goofs demonstrates why it was so important not to throw any unnecessary wrenches into a one-camera show. Even once you are aware of its editing irregularities, that *Preamble* scene is still hilarious. Most viewers probably never notice that mistake until they've seen the episode several times. Many may never have been aware of it—that is, at least not until now.

One of the times when the crew was really hoping we would get a scene right on the first take was in "Barney's First Car," a classic episode from our third season and one of the last to be directed by Bob Sweeney. The prop guys had rigged the steering wheel of Barney's new car so that the column of the steering wheel would snake its way up toward Barney as he was proudly taking five of us for a drive. Bob told us, "Now, listen. We've got it all set up. We can do this only once."

So, we were all ready to go. I was in the front seat between Andy and Don. In the back seat were Jim Nabors, Ronny, and Frances. We get all set and we're rolling along. The column then slowly came out of the steering wheel, and we all broke up laughing. We couldn't help it. It was simply too hilarious. None of us had been prepared for just how funny it was going to be to see that thing coming up toward Don.

Once we all cracked up, there was no choice but to do the scene again. The prop guys likely weren't thrilled about having to re-rig the steering wheel, but I think they were also probably pretty tickled that their prop gag had worked so incredibly well. I think we got that scene on the second take. I had a particularly startled scream in reaction to the steering wheel. I think that was in part to keep from laughing again. It was probably as much a laugh as a scream.

I would be hard-pressed to think of another *Griffith* scene that I was in where we had to reshoot because of that sort of thing. I know there were instances where Howard McNear as Floyd the Barber would crack up Don Knotts. And a scene with the Darling family all snoring famously made the whole cast and crew have so much uncontrollable contagious laughter that Bob Sweeney had to call an early break for lunch, and then try the scene again later.

Generally speaking, at least for the episodes I was in, we weren't fooling around—especially during filming. We had a ball filming, but all of us in both the cast and the crew were very serious about doing our jobs. You'll never see a blooper reel from *The Andy Griffith Show*. I feel certain that Andy made sure that any footage that didn't make it into the actual episode was not saved for posterity. But honestly, there just weren't that many bloopers to begin with.

THE WHEEL DEAL: Barney has a car full of shock absorbers as he comes to grips with the steering column of his recent purchase in "Barney's First Car," a third-season episode of The Andy Griffith Show *that Andy Griffith often said was his favorite. Photo courtesy of TAGSRWC Archives.*

Chapter 7: Leaving Mayberry

In the late winter of 1965, toward the end of our fifth season, we were filming on location at Forty Acres, the old backlot in Culver City that we used for the Mayberry exterior scenes. That's when I first found out from Andy Griffith that Don Knotts was leaving the *Griffith* show. I believe we were filming "The Arrest of the Fun Girls," which turned out to be my last episode as a semi-regular character in the black-and-white episodes. I would return for one more, traumatic episode the following season, the first season filmed in color.

No one had told me that Don was leaving, and all of a sudden, Andy casually mentioned something to me about Don leaving the show, and I said, "What are you talking about?"

Andy said, "Didn't you know Don's leaving?"

I said, "No." I was truly stunned. I was always the last one to know everything.

As much as I was devastated by this crushing news, both personally and professionally, I could understand Don's reasons. He had been offered a contract to do movies for Universal and had accepted the deal. He had not yet officially signed, but he had made a verbal commitment.

Don said later that, if he had known that Andy was going to continue with the show, he would have stayed. Andy had always said that he would not do more than five seasons. Andy wanted to get back to doing movies. When he didn't get the offers he expected, Andy agreed to a very lucrative deal with CBS to do three more seasons of the *Griffith* show. Meanwhile, I think Don was dying to do movies. I don't blame him. He had the chance to grab the brass ring and become an actual movie star. It was the right career move for him.

In a sense, it was like when Hollywood scouts first discovered me when I was doing shows in New York. People would tell me that

STRETCH AND SHAKE: Helping Barney gain a few pounds as he also works to increase his height in "Barney's Physical," an episode of The Andy Griffith Show *that was first broadcast in September 1964, early in the fifth season. Photo courtesy of TAGSRWC Archives.*

I ought to stay in New York, where people were paying attention to me. But all of the studios in Hollywood wanted to test me, and I realized that I might never have that opportunity again. Even if taking a chance in Hollywood maybe wasn't as safe as sticking to Broadway, I loved the idea of being in movies. Though it meant leaving the security of a hit television series, Don probably felt the same way about taking the plunge into movies.

I truly loved playing Thelma Lou. Andy and Aaron Ruben even mentioned that maybe I could stay on after Don left, but I couldn't see Thelma Lou still being around without Barney. I always thought that being Barney's girlfriend was her whole purpose. What would she have done on the show without him? They said maybe she could have a beauty shop. I thought, I don't think so. I just didn't think it could possibly work out. So, I said no. I was sorry to leave because I loved everybody. Maybe it would have been nice to continue, but I couldn't see a good reason for Thelma Lou to remain in the show. Her whole life revolved around Barney Fife. I guess Barney was right after all when he said that he had Thelma Lou in his hip pocket.

Mayberry's Burns—Ouch!

I wasn't the only actor who had a disappointing Mayberry experience to deal with that year. During the summer of 1965, a few months after my time as a semi-regular on the *Griffith* show had abruptly ended, I was on the Desilu Cahuenga lot on a day when the show was filming an episode for the upcoming season, the first to be in color. I think on this particular day I was on the lot for an interview for a part on another TV show. I thought, *While I'm here, I'll just go by and say hi to Andy and everybody.*

Andy asked me to come watch the filming of a scene. Jack Burns was playing Andy's new deputy, Warren Ferguson, who was Barney's replacement. After I watched the scene, Andy asked me what I thought about it.

I said, "Andy, you can't replace Don. You had better get another idea. I don't know what you can do, but this won't work. No matter how good an actor might be, you can't replace Don. Don't try to have a new deputy. Do something else. Get a woman in or do something else, but it isn't going to work to replace Barney."

That was the truth. While Jack had a distinctive vocal quality and a pattern of speaking and mannerisms that worked well for certain types of comedy, I didn't think those traits would be a good fit for a regular character on the *Griffith* show. It wasn't Jack's fault. He was great at what he did. What it comes down to is that you just don't replace Don Knotts. There is only one Don Knotts, and that's it. It's as simple as that.

I don't think Andy needed me to tell him all that. I believe, in his gut, Andy already knew that neither Jack nor anybody else could ever be what Don as Barney had been for Mayberry and for the show. Millions of viewers would come to the same conclusion. Jack ended up doing about half a season's worth of episodes. I understand that he was fired at Christmastime, which was unfortunate. It really wasn't his fault.

Jack went on to have a very successful career, just as he had done before the *Griffith* show. He was a brilliant comedy writer, and he continued to act, produce, and do voiceover work. For many years, Jack was the voice of Vince, one of the crash-test dummies in public safety ads on television. In a bit of irony, in a couple of the ads back in the 1990s, there was footage from the *Griffith* show of Barney seemingly pulling the crash-test dummies over to give them a ticket. Poor Jack had already had his Mayberry crash test and hadn't survived. Now, here he was decades later with Barney Fife giving him a ticket for not wearing a seat belt! At least it was still probably a good payday for Jack, and the ads likely saved lives.

Leaving Mayberry . . . Again

One of the guests at a Mayberry reunion we did in 2000 was Barbara Perry, who had appeared in small roles every now and then on the *Griffith* show. This was the first reunion event that Barbara had ever attended. I was backstage when she was onstage doing her bit, and I heard her say, "And then there was this girl that came in the ladies' room, and she broke into tears, and she said, 'That was my last show,' and she was crying. I don't know who she was, but there she was crying when she came off."

When Barbara came off the stage, I told her, "You know what? That girl in the ladies' room was me!" She had no idea.

I filled Barbara in on the whole story. I'll share it once again here.

In the fall of 1965, my agent sent me the script for an episode of *The Andy Griffith Show* titled "The Return of Barney Fife." I read the script. And I hated it. As devoted fans of the *Griffith* show will know, it's the episode where Barney returns to Mayberry for a high school reunion after having moved to Raleigh. Thelma Lou, who has also moved away from Mayberry, comes back to town, too, but with the kicker that she is now married to Gerald Whitfield, who, appropriately, was the foreman for a wrecking crew.

The truth is that it made me angry that the writers would do that to Thelma Lou and to Barney—and that the producers would allow it. I fought over this script and told anyone who would listen that Thelma Lou would never marry anyone but Barney Fife. The producers maintained that she did indeed marry someone else, and that was that. I was still convinced that I was right, but my opinion wasn't going to change any minds.

Having played Thelma Lou for five years, I felt I truly knew her and how she would handle a situation like this reunion. To help myself get into a frame of mind to be able to do the episode, I told myself that Thelma Lou was so hurt when Barney Fife left Mayberry that she soon left town as well. In my mental storyline, Thelma Lou needed a way to attend the reunion without being alone. So, she had come up with the idea of asking a man she worked with to accompany her and pretend to be her husband, which he did. That is how I played the episode's scenario in my mind. I simply couldn't face doing the episode the way it was written. I had to create my own, less crushing rationale. In my mind, Thelma Lou was only pretending to be married.

Given the storyline in the script, I knew this was going to be my last time ever on the *Griffith* show, and it broke my heart. I had kept my composure and said goodbye to everybody, but once I got in the ladies' room, I just fell apart. I was totally heartbroken. That's when Barbara Perry had her encounter with this upset lady crying her eyes out. There was a good reason for those tears—real sorrow and loss.

I was incredibly sad to leave the *Griffith* show. Even though the series continued without me for the rest of that season and two more and continued to score high ratings (finishing as the top-rated show in prime-time for its last season), it truly felt like the end of an era for me. At least up until my last episode, I had loved every single minute of doing the series. I still love the show. I watch it all the time. In North Carolina, where I now live, likely more than anywhere else on Earth, the *Griffith* show seemingly is on all the time.

Chapter 8: After Mayberry

Throughout all my years in Hollywood, I seldom took an extended vacation because I was afraid of missing an acting job. Here's a case in point. After I was officially out of a job with *The Andy Griffith Show*, I had recurring roles as secretaries on both *Family Affair* with Brian Keith and *My Three Sons* with Fred MacMurray. While I was working with him on *My Three Sons*, Fred had told me that he wanted me to have a larger part. He had played my father all those years ago in *Father Was a Fullback*, and, in a way, I guess he was still looking out for me. He planned to have the writers expand my role in the show.

I hadn't been aware that the larger and more frequent part would begin as soon as it did. Mother and I were in Europe on a rare extended vacation for most of May and the first half of June 1971 when my agent, who had our itinerary, called the hotel where we were staying and told me that the *My Three Sons* producers and Fred de Cordova, who directed all of the *My Three Sons* episodes that I was ever in, were ready for me in this bigger role. They were going to start filming soon.

I said, "Well, I'll come back to L.A. I can catch a plane and come back right away."

My agent said, "Oh no. Don't do that. There'll be other things coming up."

My agent was right. During the late 1960s and early 1970s, after my work on the *Griffith* show, I had continued to get guest roles here and there on television shows. Most of the roles were not anything earthshaking, but they were on popular shows, and the jobs helped pay the bills for me and my family.

As it turned out, the upcoming season of *My Three Sons* would be the last one after a nice long run. In the larger scope of life, my decision not to interrupt my unforgettable trip to Europe with my mother in order to return for the expanded role on *My Three Sons* was a good one. Mother and I had an absolutely wonderful trip together—truly the trip of a lifetime, especially because vacations of any sort were such a rarity for us.

I traveled a great deal through the years, but it was almost always for work, whether with the USO Camp Shows during World War II or to be on Broadway or to go to Hollywood. In later years, I traveled a lot to public *Griffith* reunions or events, most of which were in the Midwest and the South. I was also a guest for other celebrity and film festivals, and later for things such as the Missouri Cherry Blossom Festival. More about all that a little later.

My trip to Europe with my mother was purely for sightseeing and personal enjoyment and meaning. With my friend Bill as our tour guide and escort, we flew from Los Angeles to New York City the first Sunday in May. We spent a couple of days in New York and then, late one night, we boarded a beautiful ocean liner, the SS *France*. With the torch of Lady Liberty glowing behind us in New York Harbor, we were on our way for the five-day voyage to England, where we saw all the usual tourist highlights in London, dined at wonderful restaurants, and saw the hit play *Sleuth* in the West End.

I loved England. I thought that someday it would be nice to go over there at Christmastime with all the beautiful decorations. In my mind, I picture everything being so elegantly decorated and festive and fit for a queen. I would have liked to have experienced an English Christmas.

We also visited Ireland. For most of our trip, we traveled by train, including around Ireland. Mother was bound and determined to kiss the Blarney Stone. When we were in Dublin, I went to the tourist bureau where they gave sightseeing advice. I told the nice lady there that I wanted to take my mother to kiss the Blarney Stone. The lady looked at me and shook her head doubtfully as she looked at our itinerary. In the loveliest Dublin brogue, she said, "Oh, I don't think you can get thar from har."

I said, "You've heard of it, haven't you?"

"Oh, yes indeed, but I don't think you can get thar from har."

I said, "What do you mean you can't get thar?"

She said, "Your train doesn't go thar. You need to go through Cork."

I said, "Oh."

I looked on the map. After Dublin on the east coast, our itinerary had us continuing by train back to the west coast and the lakes at Killarney. We were on a train with all of these lovely Irish people who were on vacation. Who knows—with all the Irish heritage in our family, maybe some were even distant relatives of mine! Mother and I had the best time ever during that part of our trip. I thought maybe we could rent a car and drive from Killarney over to Cork. It was only about an hour's drive, but it didn't work out. My poor mother never got to kiss the Blarney Stone—blimey! She had a grand time in Ireland just the same.

The next leg of our trip was a flight to Paris, where we spent several days and enjoyed every gorgeous moment. Notre Dame was a truly moving place to visit for both Mother and me. We next traveled by train through the northeastern part of France on our way to Brussels and then the Netherlands. We boarded the MS *Helvetica* at Rotterdam for a very touristy but fun cruise down the Rhine River through what was then West Germany to Switzerland. We then went by train to Zurich, Lucerne, Geneva, and then into Italy.

We relaxed for a few days in Cernobbio, an enchanting Italian village on Lake Como, before heading south and taking in as much of Italy as we could. I must say that all of Italy was just a splendid place with all its history and charming towns and beautiful countryside.

When in Rome, the highlight for Mother and me, especially with both of us being lifelong Catholics, was being in the general audience one day at the Vatican with the Holy Father, Pope Paul VI. It meant a great deal to both of us. He was the only Pope either of us ever saw in person, and to have the occasion be while we were together and at the Vatican made it extra special.

We were amazed by all the ruins in Rome. There is so much history. We toured the Coliseum, the Forum, the Catacombs, and all the things that I suppose every tourist wants to do. How can ruins be so beautiful! It would take a lifetime to see it all.

Of course, you can see only so much before you work up an appetite. Fortunately, cooking and eating are things Italians do better

WHEN IN ROME: Mother and daughter at the Roman Forum ruins during the unforgettable vacation in 1971. Photo courtesy of Surry Arts Council.

than anybody, at least as far as I'm concerned. My apologies to the French, who also create incredible food.

The restaurant in Rome that I remember to this day is Otello. It's at the bottom of the Spanish Steps. I understand it's still in business, which makes me happy. At the time when I was there, they had long tables so that you were seated with lots of people, and they had the best food. I ate spaghetti every day—and practically every meal—when I was in Rome. I dearly love pasta.

Sadly, all great trips must come to an end. We made our way back to Paris for a couple of days to relax before our flight back to the United States. You don't get to see a lot in just a few days at each destination, but we filled every day of our European vacation with as much activity as we could. Both of us loved every moment of the trip. That is, except maybe when Mother fell in a bathtub and fractured some ribs, but even that didn't hinder our fun or break our stride.

For our trip across the Atlantic, we flew to Washington, D.C. Mother had never been there. I had been, but just passing through on the Greyhound bus when returning from the USO tour back in 1945. Mother and I got to see some of the highlights of Washington, but not nearly as much as we would have liked. I wish we could have stayed longer and had the chance to get the full experience. It's such a beautiful city with so much to see. I'm glad Mother at least got an overview of it and could finally say she had been to our nation's capital.

By the time we returned to Los Angeles, *My Three Sons* naturally had given the role to someone else. It turned out to be a nice part for her. If my career had been my top priority, I should have followed my intuition and flown right back to L.A. to take that part instead of following my agent's advice. I believe his agency also represented the actress who got the part, so it was all the same to him whether it was her or me. *Que sera, sera.* I will always treasure the memories of my truly extraordinary trip with my mother. I wouldn't trade those memories for anything.

All in the *Family Affair*

Even though I missed out on some opportunities for larger roles after my time on the *Griffith* show, I stayed busy enough to pay the bills. I particularly enjoyed working on *Family Affair*, another popular family-oriented show of that era. I played Brian Keith's secretary. It was a small part, but a fun show. Brian was such a terrific actor and a joy to work with. I had met Brian in New York in 1952 when I was doing *The Egg and I* at CBS. Brian and Grace Kelly were in New York doing an episode of *Suspense*, another live show that was also performed at the CBS studios. I met both of them that summer.

As I recall, Grace's character in that *Suspense* episode was a dance hall dime-a-dance girl, which seemed funny to me because she was such an elegant and eloquent person—truly living up to her name. It never occurred to me then that Brian and I would one day be working together in Los Angeles. In 1952, we were just two actors working hard at whatever acting jobs we could find in New York. It was no surprise to anyone when Grace became Hollywood royalty and an international movie star, but I don't think any of us working on live television that summer in 1952 ever imagined that she would become actual royalty as the Princess of Monaco. Then again, maybe Grace did.

Because I was the secretary at his character's office, all of my *Family Affair* scenes were with Brian Keith. I didn't have scenes with the kids, but we would visit on the set. They were so cute. Little Anissa Jones with those blond curls was such a darling as Buffy. And Johnny Whitaker was also a curly-headed cutie as Jody. They were just adorable. Years later, after Johnny was all grown up, I would run into him here or there and got to know him better. He grew up to become as nice as a man as he had been when I knew him as a child.

Kathy Garver played Cissy, a teenager who was the oldest of the kids. She was beautiful and very nice. She still is. I would see her sometimes at the Hollywood autograph shows in later years. I learned later that she is a big fan of the *Griffith* show and even has received some of the fan club newsletters and has kept up with what is going on in the Mayberry world.

It was incredibly sad when Anissa died of a drug overdose. No one could believe it. I was devastated when I heard the news. She was only eighteen when she died. What a tragedy. She must have had a lot of struggles in her life, but I just never knew it. I had no idea.

Then, a couple of decades later, in 1997, Brian Keith took his own life. It was, yet again, such a tragic situation. Brian, like so many of us, had been a heavy smoker. He had finally quit smoking, but not in time. The damage was done. He was diagnosed with cancer, and then one of his daughters had died by suicide just a short time before he took his own life. I think it was all just too much for him at that point. I hate that he had so much pain, sadness, and grief after having had such an extraordinary career and life. He was beloved by a lot of people. It was a real shock when he died. The *Family Affair* cast was touched by terrible tragedy twice.

Hanging Out with the Cool Kids

During the same time that I was doing *My Three Sons* and *Family Affair*, I did a couple of episodes of *The Mod Squad*, which starred Michael Cole, Peggy Lipton, and Clarence Williams III. My first episode was in 1969 and was directed by Earl Bellamy, who was a delight to work with. Early in his career he was known for being particularly good at directing Westerns, which was good work, because in the early days of television, there were a *lot* of Westerns. Earl also had the reputation for being a very fast director. He could direct anything with equal ease. He directed sitcoms, dramas, and action with effortless skill.

There weren't a lot of wasted takes or wasted time when Earl was in charge. Because no wasted time meant no wasted money, producers loved to have Earl direct their projects. Earl directed several *Griffith* shows, but none that I was in. As efficient as he was, Earl was still a very easy-going director. If some issue or other came up, his typical response was, "No strain." His temperament reminds me of Ron Howard. I imagine that working on one of Ron's films would be a lot like how it was to work with Earl.

The Mod Squad had lots of *Griffith* connections. Danny Thomas was one of the executive producers, along with Aaron Spelling. Earle Hagen did the music. My other *Mod Squad* episode was directed by Jerry Jameson, who had been an editor on the *Griffith* show after I left. He was also very involved with the *Griffith* spin-offs, *Gomer Pyle, U.S.M.C.* and *Mayberry R.F.D.*

A funny memory I have from *The Mod Squad* shoot was off-camera when Clarence Williams was sitting right in front of me. He had a good-sized Afro hairdo. It was beautiful. As I was admiring it, curiosity got the better of me. I leaned forward and I asked Clarence, "Would you mind if I touched your hair?" This was decades before #MeToo and all that. I can only imagine the blowback from doing something like that now. Or Lord knows, maybe even my telling about it now will incite wrath from all corners! It was innocent admiration on my part. I always liked a beautiful head of hair, whether Shirley Temple's curls, Andy Griffith's and Elvis's wavy pompadours, or Clarence's Afro.

Clarence politely said, "No, I don't mind." Maybe he did mind and was just being gracious. I hope not. He obviously knew he had an enviable head of hair.

It was the softest hair. I expected it to be strong and springy. No. It was just like down. It was so soft. I said, "Oh, my gosh. It's so soft. It's so pretty." He just chuckled.

Later on, he said to me, "My wife's coming to the set this afternoon. I called her to tell her about you, and we would like to take you for a drink after we're done today." I hoped it wasn't because she wanted to meet the crazy hair-toucher!

We went someplace and had a drink together, and they were a lovely couple. His wife at that time was Gloria Foster, the actress who would later become an international icon as the Oracle in the *Matrix* movies. Clarence and Gloria wanted me to stay for dinner with them, but I needed to get home to my family. I appreciated their friendliness to me. I thought it was so sweet that he still wanted his wife to meet me—even after the hair-touching.

I'm Catholic, and we confess our sins. That's why I had to tell that embarrassing story about myself even though it now makes me—and maybe everyone reading it—cringe. I wish I could apologize to Clarence for being so unaware, insensitive, and dumb, but, sadly, Clarence died of colon cancer in June 2021. I just have to find comfort in my belief that all sins and other offenses are forgiven in Heaven, which is where I believe Clarence is now.

I had never worked with Peggy Lipton before *The Mod Squad*, but I had known her before she ever started acting. She was a charming young lady. She had been a model and then had become an excellent actress. She later married legendary music producer Quincy Jones. They had two beautiful daughters, both of whom are having fine careers.

The whole *Mod Squad* experience was fun. The cast was a great group to work with. I had a really good time working with them.

Circus Act

Between my two episodes of *The Mod Squad* and amid my occasional work with my recurring role on *My Three Sons*, I worked on two other TV projects. The first one would turn out to be my last time working for Disney. It was *The Boy Who Stole the Elephant*, a good little movie that was shown in two parts on *The Magical World of Disney* in 1970. It had a really interesting cast—including several familiar faces from the *Griffith* show. Hal Smith even had a small part as the town drunk!

The movie was about a traveling circus around the late 1890s. Doris Singleton and I played sisters who were trapeze artists. I was Lottie Ladare and she was Lizzie Ladare. Doris was such a lovely and talented person. She had a long and busy career. She played various roles in almost every show that Lucille Ball ever did for television. Doris is likely best remembered as Carolyn Appleby, a frenemy of Lucy Ricardo's on *I Love Lucy*. Later in life, she made personal appearances at all the *Lucy* reunion events, much as I have done for the *Griffith* reunions.

Doris was in her early fifties when we made *The Boy Who Stole the Elephant*. I was well into my forties by then as well, and yet, there we were playing trapeze artists. They had us doing some scenes that were pretty high up. We would hang upside down on a swing and things like that. I was never particularly limber. I could hold my own on a dance floor, but that's a lot different than being an aerial acrobat.

A man trained us to do the basic body movements of a trapeze artist, but the producers brought in real trapeze artists for the actual flying and catching. The wardrobe and makeup crew couldn't find a wig to match my hair for the stunt woman, so instead they had me wear a brown wig that could match one worn by my double.

I was wearing that wig on the set one day when my old *Griffith* pal Hal Smith passed by. I said, "Hello, Hal. How are you?"

Hal, who was always very cordial, politely but very generically replied, "Hello. How are you?" and just kept walking. He didn't recognize me in the wig. Years later, I told Hal about that encounter. He had no recollection of it at all. There would have been no reason for him to have remembered a little moment like that, but I thought it was funny that my unintentional disguise had fooled him.

That movie was also where I learned that I had a fractured vertebra in my neck. There was a scene where I had to hang upside down on the trapeze and clasp Doris's arms as she hung below me.

I suppose my being upside down changed the weight load on the fracture just enough for it to finally cause me some real pain. I've been dealing with sometimes excruciating neck and shoulder pain off and on ever since that day.

I think I must have hurt my neck somewhere along life's way, but I probably thought it was a pulled muscle or something like that and just rubbed it out and kept on going, only to find out later that it was something a little more serious. Even when I felt the pain on the trapeze, I had to work through it then too. A lot of times, if you let on that you're injured or can't work because of some ache or pain, the production will just replace you, especially if you're not one of the main stars.

The actor who played Davey, the boy who stole the elephant, was Mark Lester. He was an excellent actor. I thought he was super in *Oliver!* a couple of years earlier. He and Michael Jackson were great friends. They were godfathers to each other's children. Mark has been occasionally making tabloid headlines during the last decade or so, because he has admitted to being one of several sperm donors paid by Michael Jackson.

When that story was first hitting the news, Doris Singleton called me. As soon as she identified herself on the call, I said, "I know why you're calling. I just heard the news too." Both of us thought it was such an unexpected thing to be hearing about, and we felt odd having even a vague personal connection to the story.

Mark has hinted that it's possible that he's the biological father of Paris Jackson, Michael's daughter. I don't know anything about all of that except to say it definitely involves a different kind of "magical world" than Disney.

Another Family Show

Not long after completing *The Boy Who Stole the Elephant,* I received a call to work on *The Smith Family,* a new series for ABC-TV starring Henry Fonda. It had been about a decade since Henry had agreed to do more than a guest-star spot in a television series, so it was considered quite the coup for ABC-TV to land such a legendary star as the lead in a weekly series.

Henry made sure he surrounded himself with a capable cast, which included Janet Blair as his wife and Ronny Howard as his son. *The Smith Family* would be Ronny's first series as a cast regular since the *Griffith* show had ended three years earlier.

I didn't have any scenes with Ronny in the episode that I was in, but I did get to visit with him on the set one day, which was a nice reunion. Despite the star power of the cast, the series unfortunately didn't catch on with audiences. The show lasted only two seasons, and that was likely only because Henry Fonda had a two-season guarantee. But things worked out for both Ronny and the network within a couple of years. The abbreviated run of *The Smith Family* meant that Ronny was available to play Richie Cunningham in *Happy Days* beginning in 1974. As for my part on *The Smith Family*, it was a small role, but I didn't care. I finally got to meet and work with Henry Fonda, and I got to see Ronny Howard again.

Going to the Chapel

I have to tell another Ronny Howard story on myself. In the spring of 1975, I heard that Ronny, or Ron as he by then preferred to be called, was getting married in June. Except for saying a quick hello when I worked on *The Smith Family* in 1971, I hadn't seen Ron in about ten years—probably not since we filmed our last *Griffith* episode together, which was in 1965. I kept telling everybody I saw that I thought it was just so wonderful that Ron was getting married and that I wished I could attend the wedding, but that I also was sure he barely remembered working with me. I should have reminded folks that Opie once had a crush on Thelma Lou!

I kept talking so much to everybody about my wanting to attend the wedding that one day I finally got a phone call from a woman who said she had talked to Ron, and he said I could come to the wedding. I wasn't quite a wedding crasher, but I did beg for an invitation. I know it was shameless of me, but it just meant so much to me to be there.

I didn't have a new dress for the wedding, but I went down to Ohrbach's over on Wilshire and Fairfax. I found a little blouse and skirt that matched and that were cheery and appropriate for a June wedding.

At the wedding, Ron and Cheryl, his beautiful bride, looked at me like this stranger who had walked in, but I didn't care. I just loved him, and I wanted to be there. I'm sure it never occurred to Ron that being at his wedding could mean so much to someone he hadn't worked with in a decade, but it did.

It was a lovely wedding at Magnolia Park United Methodist Church in Burbank, near the Howard family's homestead in Toluca Lake. I arrived early at the church and got a seat. I was soon glad that I did. It wasn't a very big church, and it filled to standing room only. I began to understand why an invitation was so hard to come by.

Andy Griffith and Don Knotts were there, as well as several of the cast and crew from *Happy Days*, a couple of whom were in the wedding party. I remember that Ron and the groomsmen all wore powder blue tuxedos. When the ceremony was completed, everyone applauded. The ceremony was followed by a nice reception at the church. The whole occasion was just so joyous and sweet. I was truly grateful that I could be there.

I didn't have a lot of money for a gift, but I got them a Pyrex baking dish that was held in a silver serving tray. It was like something Aunt Bee might use, but I hoped the young couple would have some use for it, too.

I didn't work with Ron again until we did *Return to Mayberry* in 1986. In the movie, I got to repay Ron with the favor of a wedding invitation, when Opie attended Thelma Lou and Barney's wedding. Not only that, but Rance Howard, Ron's dad, played the preacher who performed that ceremony.

After *Return to Mayberry*, I didn't see Ron in person again until the memorial service for Don Knotts just over twenty years later. Our paths would cross one more time after that, in October 2014, when I visited with Ron in Greensboro, North Carolina, about an hour's drive from my home in Mount Airy. Ron was a featured speaker for the Bryan Series, Guilford College's highly regarded program that hosts interesting, prominent people for talks and lectures.

The Bryan Series presentations previously had been held in a large auditorium, but, at the time of Ron's talk, that facility was being torn down to make room for a parking lot. Ron's program

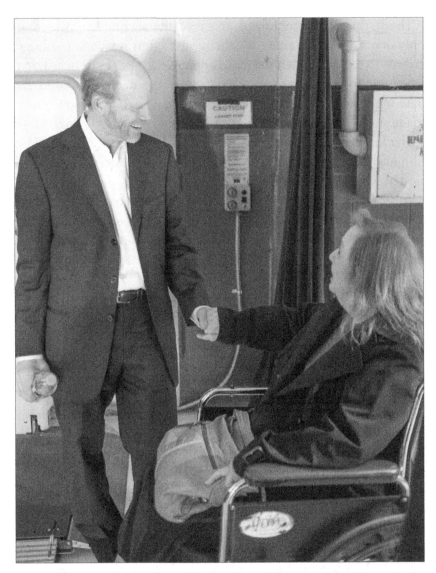

HAPPY GAZE: Meeting with Ron Howard backstage after his presentation at the Greensboro Coliseum on October 23, 2014. Photo by Hobart Jones.

was instead held next door in the Greensboro Coliseum, one of the largest indoor arenas in the region. Elvis performed there at his peak, and it was the site for the NCAA's Final Four in 1974 and more than once for U.S. National Ice Skating Championships. The Greensboro Coliseum has a lot of history.

The Bryan Series organizers arranged the staging in a way that only one side of the arena was being used, but it was still a huge crowd—a sellout. When the main organizer, Ty Buckner, heard that I planned to attend the talk, he made arrangements to accommodate my need to use a wheelchair. Beyond that, he very graciously made sure that I had a seat near the front.

The format of Ron's presentation was for Ron to be interviewed by film historian Leonard Maltin. It was a lively and interesting discussion of Ron's career. The audience was captivated—including me.

After the presentation, I was also really pleased to be able to have a chance to meet privately with Ron. I had traveled with Tanya and Hobart Jones, who is a world-class photographer. Hobart took some photos of Ron and me. The three of us then went to a room backstage where it had been arranged for several dozen members of *The Andy Griffith Show* Rerun Watchers Club (TAGSRWC) to wait for a chance to say hello to Ron. Hobart took some group photos to memorialize the occasion for posterity.

Ron needed to leave soon after the photos were taken, but I stayed and visited with the fans for a while. I knew many of them from all my years of doing Mayberry events, especially Mayberry Days. These fans were some of the most devoted of all. Most were meeting Ron for the first time, and it was a dream come true to do so.

That was a special night for me as well. Unless Ron happens to make it to Mount Airy during my lifetime, I doubt I'll have the occasion to see him again in person. It would be difficult for Ron to attend Mayberry Days. It would probably be pandemonium if he did. It would also be hard for him to quietly sneak into town at another time. Still, I do hope he gets to visit Mount Airy someday and see Andy's hometown and the Andy Griffith Museum. His brother, Clint, has attended Mayberry Days several times. Maybe the two brothers can even visit Mount Airy together sometime. That's a nice thought to hold.

Home on the Range

Let's get back to the Seventies and another adorable person. After my second episode of *The Mod Squad* in 1972, my next notable television job was in 1974. I was in one of the first half dozen episodes of *Little House on the Prairie.* The episode was called "If I Should Wake Before I Die," which I thought was a clever title, because it was about a lady who attends her own wake.

Melissa Gilbert, who starred as Laura Ingalls, was ten years old and delightful. She was a little thing with, yet again, red hair and little freckles. She was just as cute as she could be. She would come up when I was in the makeup department, and she would stay with me and just talk up a storm—lots of nervous energy, I suppose. Or maybe just youthful energy. She was a firecracker. I really enjoyed her. I thought at the time, *This little one is special.* She was outgoing and enthusiastic about everything—very inquisitive.

That series was quite an amazing launch for her career. Someone once told me that when Melissa was about two years old, she had a tiny part in *The Reluctant Astronaut* with Don Knotts, so I guess that was literally her official launch eight years earlier. If I had known that at the time, we could have compared notes about what it was like to work with Don Knotts!

I believe Melissa was the only actor who was in every episode of *Little House,* just as Andy Griffith had been the only actor in every episode of the *Griffith* show. People probably don't realize how difficult that is, especially for a long-running series, as both of those shows were. I imagine that it was doubly difficult for a young kid. Melissa clearly had the fortitude—enough so that, years later, she was elected president of the Screen Actors Guild. She has had an admirable career.

Melissa couldn't have asked for a better acting mentor than Michael Landon. What a sweetheart he was. He was the rock of that show, both on camera and behind the scenes, much as Andy Griffith was on his show. Michael was involved in every aspect. He not only had a starring role as Charles Ingalls, but he was executive producer and also directed and helped write many episodes.

My episode was directed by Victor French, who I thought did a good job. My part didn't have a tremendous amount of dialogue, but there were several shots where I was the focus and needed to express a lot of emotions, ranging from delight and shock to confusion and sadness. My extended scene had a great number of actors in just one fairly small room. There were a lot of logistical details to work out for shooting that.

Victor French was better known as an actor, including lots of episodes of *Little House* and even more on *Highway to Heaven*, again with Michael Landon. They were two nice men, both of whom died far too young. Both died of cancer in their fifties, and smoking cigarettes likely was a factor in both cases. What a shame, and very sad.

After all the years I was in movies and on television shows, *Little House* and *Matlock* are about the only things for which I still receive residuals. Things are different now. Residuals are much better for actors these days. That's thanks to the actors guild and at least in part thanks to folks like Melissa Gilbert for fighting for better compensation for performers and others.

Little House was also one of the few times later in my career that I was asked to audition for a part. For a large span in my career, particularly when I was working in movies, I never had to audition. Folks knew my work and what I could do, and I was under contract with Fox all those years. I never minded when I was asked to come in for an audition, because doing so was an indication that the role was big enough to justify that extra step and additional scrutiny.

Acting Chops

In 1975, my agent called and said that Paramount wanted to see me about a part in *The Legend of Lizzie Borden*, a movie for television that the studio was making for ABC-TV. With the exception of *The Boy Who Stole the Elephant* for Disney, I had never done a movie for television. As it would turn out, *Return to Mayberry* in 1986 would end up being the only other one I ever did.

I first met with casting supervisor Millie Gusse and then the director, Paul Wendkos. They cast me that day as Lizzie Borden's friend. Paul shook my hand and said, "See you on the set."

Millie Gusse had a little office right next to the director's office. I went in her office and signed the contract. The day before I was to go in for wardrobe, I got a call from my agent. He informed me that there was a problem with the movie. He said the director met someone and had a change of heart. He decided he wanted her to have the part that he had given me. I told my agent that I really wanted to work with Elizabeth Montgomery, because I had worked with her father, Robert Montgomery, years earlier, and I really loved Bob. I thought it would be nice to work with Elizabeth, but I told my agent that it was all right. Those things happen. I had been on the positive end of those situations, and this time things just went the other way. That's the movie business.

My agent went on to say that there was a very small part that they still wanted me to do. It would have me in widow's clothes. I told him I did not remember this part in the script. My agent said I should take a look and see if I wanted to bother with such a small part. I was too dumb to know that what I should have done was just say no. It never occurred to me what would happen. I decided to go ahead and take the small role that had a line or two with two other women in a crowd of people.

On the day of filming, I walked in to where the director was, and the girlfriend, my replacement, was there. I thought of leaving, but decided to stay and keep my word, unlike the director. I was in my costume and went on the set, which was outdoors with a lot of people around. The assistant director came up to me and said, "We've cut your lines."

I said, "Oh, well, then I can just go home."

He said, "Oh, no, you can't leave. You'll still be in the scene. You just won't speak."

I wanted to leave the set, and they wouldn't let me. They dropped all but one of my lines: "Not even a tear." They naturally also dropped the money. I thought to myself, *I'm going to end up as an extra in a TV movie.* I was upset and called my agent. I just wanted to die.

A charming, blond-haired woman named Jean Darling was in a black costume like mine. She was thrilled just to be in the movie. She was a friend of Paul Wendkos. I think it was a favor to her to be in this scene. I was sick and wanted to die, and she was happy as a lark. The other actress dressed in black in my scene was Amzie Strickland, who had played Miss Rosemary, Barney Fife's first girlfriend all those years earlier.

I thought, *This is about the worst working experience I've ever had.* I just gritted my teeth and got through it, and then just wanted to forget it. One thing I couldn't forget was a peculiar thing about Paul Wendkos, who was a short man but who had big strong arms, a big head, and lots of dark hair. When he was directing Elizabeth, he flapped his arms as if he were a maestro conducting an orchestra. He's the only film director I've ever seen conduct himself that way.

Years later, I went to read for a part. At this time, I had new agents, and they had decided to put very few credits on the résumé that they prepared for me. They felt that, if they listed everything I had done, directors and producers might think I was too old for a part. One of the things the agents did choose to list was, of all things, *The Legend of Lizzie Borden*. I think they decided to do that because the movie had been well received and garnered several award nominations—including winning a couple of Emmys.

I arrived for the audition with this résumé. The director looked at my résumé and said, "You say you were in this movie?" I explained that I had a very small role.

He then responded in a huff, "I directed that movie. You weren't in it." My old would-be nemesis Paul Wendkos was sure he had caught me in a lie and was very pleased with his "gotcha moment."

As a person who doesn't lie and has never padded her résumé (and had, in fact, had most of her credits removed from her résumé in this instance), I was hurt and very angry. To be honest, I had trouble recognizing this man as the *Lizzie Borden* director from years earlier, because he now had short white hair and he was up on a platform, which made it less obvious that he was short. I was in shock. Under the surprise of that moment, I was having difficulty remembering the precise details about how I had been hired, then replaced, then given a small role with a few lines, and then had my lines chopped, so to speak.

I sat there and tried to think of a way to prove to this man that I had indeed been in his movie. I decided to pray about it. I asked God to help me remember something about that movie that would prove that I was in it and was not a liar—even though for years I had deliberately blocked the entire, terrible experience from my mind.

Then it came to me. I asked Paul if he remembered a pretty blond-haired woman named Jean Darling. He confirmed that he did. I then told him that I remembered that she was thrilled with even the small, uncredited role in his movie. I told him that, after the way I had been treated, I, on the other hand, had wanted to use an ax Lizzie Borden-style on somebody or myself.

I was also upset with this new movie's casting lady, who was very familiar with my entire body of work. I said to her, "You've seen my résumé before and know that many credits were deleted." She nodded in agreement, but clearly didn't want to get in the middle of this spat.

There was no way I was now going to read for a part in his movie. I was simply too upset. By that point, there was also no way I was going to get the part. As I was preparing to leave, Paul was seated and took my hand. I managed to say, "It was very nice to see you again," and, doing my best Rhett Butler at the end of *Gone with the Wind*, I turned and left with my head held high and with a purposeful stride.

A Rocky Time

Later in 1975, I was in one episode of *Police Story*, which was an excellent anthology series. I think just about everybody in Hollywood got to appear in at least one episode. It was sort of the *Law & Order* of its day—a great employer of actors.

My episode was called "The Cutting Edge" and starred Chuck Connors and Mark Stevens. I knew Mark from my years at Fox and also from working on *Lux Radio Theatre*. That was a nice reunion with a friend from that earlier era.

There was another young actor playing a policeman. Members of the crew all wanted me to meet him. "He's got a lot of buzz. You ought to make sure you meet him," they would all say.

I did notice that the young actor was just as handsome as he could be. You might even say he was a knockout. I eventually met him. He said simply, "Hello." He didn't seem at all interested in talking to me. I didn't care whether he did or not, but all the crew had said, "You had better meet him. He's going to go somewhere." And that he did, all right. His name was Sylvester Stallone. Believe it or not, his character's name in our episode, both his and my only episode of *Police Story*, was Rocky. The next year the whole world would be introduced to another character of his with the same name.

Those Seventies Shows

I didn't get a lot of work in television during the 1970s—more during the first part of that decade than the latter part. I probably averaged maybe one role per TV season. That was O.K. because that was a time when I was more focused on taking care of my mother, who's health had declined.

In 1976, I was in one episode of *Gibbsville*, a show on NBC-TV starring Gig Young. For those viewers who sometimes confused me with Peggy McCay, this episode probably either resolved that problem or made it worse for them, because she was a regular on the series.

What I remember most about working on *Gibbsville* is that I played the wife of Alan Young, probably best remembered today as Wilbur on *Mr. Ed*. The producers had us on set all of the first day and then the morning of the next day—just waiting to be called for a scene. Finally, Alan, who lived nearby in the San Fernando Valley, had reached his limit of just sitting around. He turned to me and said, "I'm going home. If they get to us, have them call me, and I'll come back right away."

I said, "That sounds good. I'll tell them that."

When the production assistant eventually came to get us for our scene, I said, "Well, Alan went home. You'll have to call him. He can be here in five or ten minutes." The production assistant called him, and as promised, "of course, of course," Alan promptly returned, and the production didn't miss a beat.

First Thing You Know, Ol' Jed's a Private Eye

Another really nice person I was pleased to get to work with was Buddy Ebsen. In 1978, I got a call to be in an episode of *Barnaby Jones* called "Blind Jeopardy." I played a character named Mrs. Russell. It was not a big part, but it was fun work. Buddy was very pleasant to work with, and Lee Meriwether, his costar, was lovely. The week of work was the first time I had ever met Lee. I didn't see

TRULY THE CAT'S: Prowling the catwalk in a tiger-print dress during a Los Angeles fashion show in 1963. Note a beaming Robert Young in the audience. Photo courtesy of Gilmore–Schwenke Archives.

her in person again until both of us were honored at the TV Land Awards in Los Angeles in 2004. I was there to share in the TV Land Legend Award for *The Andy Griffith Show*, and Lee was there

for a reunion with Julie Newmar and Eartha Kitt. All three had
played Catwoman in the campy *Batman* productions of the 1960s.

After the original *Griffith* show, Lee was also a favorite leading
lady of Andy Griffith's. She played his wife in *Angel in My Pocket*
in 1969. That movie didn't do as well in theaters as either Andy or
Universal Studios had hoped it would. I think the expectation was
that Andy would be as big of a box-office draw as Don Knotts was
proving to be at the time.

Discouraged by his results on the big screen, Andy was enticed
back to television with a show called *Headmaster*. Even with legendary *Griffith* producer Aaron Ruben at the helm, the show about
Andy as the headmaster of a private school never caught on and
was off the air after a half season. It had flunked out.

The New Andy Griffith Show was an effort to totally overhaul
Headmaster. Andy played a man named Andy Sawyer who had
come back to take over as mayor of his small hometown. Lee Meriwether played his wife. In desperation, the producers brought in
Mayberry characters Goober Pyle, Emmett the Fix-It Man, and
even Barney Fife, all with the same actors who had played them on
the *Griffith* show, to appear in an episode, as if Andy Sawyer were
still Andy Taylor and also as if he were still living in Mayberry.
Maybe they should have tried bringing Thelma Lou back, too. On
the other hand, if Miss America of 1955 and Barney Fife couldn't
save a show, I certainly don't think Thelma Lou could have. Probably not even Batman could have saved it. *The New Andy Griffith
Show* didn't last even as long as *Headmaster.*

Chapter 9: *Return to Mayberry* and Elsewhere

Off and on since *The Andy Griffith Show* wrapped in 1968 and *Mayberry R.F.D.* ended in 1971, there had been talk about doing a Mayberry reunion show. By the mid-1980s, the reunion chatter had become more frequent. Different people called me asking, "Have you heard about it? Are you going to be in it?"

I would say, "No, I haven't heard about anything official. I don't know if I'm going to be in anything. I haven't heard anything."

Every now and then, another story would pop up in Liz Smith's column or something, and people would start calling me again. Eventually, I got a call from Andy. It was around Christmastime in 1985, and he was at his home in Manteo, North Carolina. I said, "Is it snowing?"

He said, "Yes." Then he said, "We're going to have a party, and I want to invite you. Do you think you'd like to come?" By "party," he meant the reunion show. Andy said he had agreed to a reunion as a made-for-television movie for NBC.

I said, "Oh, yes. I'd love to, Andy." He was so sweet on the phone.

That call went better than one time a few years earlier, when Andy was in Los Angeles. Andy called me, and I didn't believe it was him, because I hadn't heard him talking on the phone in years. His voice sounded different. I kept saying, "Boy, you're really pretty good. That's a great lingo you've got there. You sound pretty authentic, but you're not Andy Griffith."

"I am, too! I *am* Andy Griffith," he said.

I said, "No, you're not. You're good, though. I have to give you that. You're awfully good, but you aren't Andy." I still didn't think it was him.

Andy was getting really frustrated and angry. He called Cindi, his girlfriend and future wife, to the phone, "Tell her. Tell her it's really me."

Well, I didn't know who Cindi was at that point. Having her get on the phone wouldn't have convinced me of anything. She could have been anybody.

I don't remember what he said that convinced me, but I finally believed him. It turned out that he was having a party at his home, and he was just calling to invite me. After the call, he probably wished he hadn't bothered. In any case, it was a lovely party, and I got to meet Cindi, who was just as nice as she could be.

The call from Andy about doing the *Return to Mayberry* movie went better. Still, I was a little surprised that Andy agreed to do it. Through all the years when people had tried to get Andy to do a reunion, he had always resisted. Andy was very protective of the original show. Because it had been a lot of years—in my case, a full twenty years since I had played Thelma Lou—I, too, wondered whether it was a good idea to try to conjure up the old magic. The original show was perfect as it was. That is, except for that one awful episode that I've already mentioned.

Especially with Andy onboard, I thought, *How can I not say yes to the opportunity to work with so many great friends?* Just the chance to be together again was worth it. I knew I would forever regret it if I turned down the chance.

Aneta Corsaut had seen the movie's script before I received my copy. She called me and she said, "Your part's good in it. You'll like it."

I said, "Great. I'm so thrilled. I can't wait to see it."

When I got my copy of the script, I was so happy—especially about Barney and Thelma Lou finally getting married. Just about all the main characters who were still alive came back to do the movie. Frances Bavier was the only actor who was a central character for more than a season and was still alive who didn't come back. She had been fully retired for a few years and also wasn't in the best health. They ended up doing a tender scene about Aunt Bee having died. They hired someone to do a voiceover of Aunt Bee in flashback.

EVERYONE CAME HOME TO MAYBERRY

—making "RETURN TO MAYBERRY"
the highest rated made-for-TV movie of the season...
and the third most-watched made-for-TV movie in history!*
Anyway you count it, it's *gol-lee* time!

Our thanks to the whole cast and crew! A special hug to Dean Hargrove,
who also did "PERRY MASON RETURNS" and
"DIARY OF A PERFECT MURDER," which did okay too.

NBC ENTERTAINMENT

*Source: NTI average audience (Sunday, April 13, 1986); estimates based on household projections.
Excludes multi-part programs. Subject to qualifications available on request.

EVEN BIGGER THAN THE MONSTER FROM OUT OF TOWN: *This is a print advertisement that was used in selected entertainment-industry trade publications to tout the success of* Return to Mayberry. *Photo courtesy of TAGSRWC Archives.*

Everett Greenbaum and Harvey Bullock, two of our top writers from the original show, returned to write the movie script. Bob Sweeney, our great director, and music director Earle Hagen also returned to work on the movie. Other than them, we largely had a new crew. They were very young. They would say, "We can't get over it. You all hit your marks. You know all your lines." I kept thinking, *Well, who have they been working with?* It was the only way those of us from the "old days" knew how to work.

I had always heard other actors who had done various sorts of reunion shows say, "It was like we left work yesterday and came back to work today. It's true. I felt that. It was just like we picked up where we left off. In our case, we had wonderful actors to work with, and our rapport was very strong. The relationships immediately took hold. There was no strain whatsoever.

For most actors, the actual doing—the acting—is more important than how things turn out. It's the performance itself that's exciting. Of course, you always hope that things come together for a satisfying result. As with the original *Griffith* show, I think the movie turned out to be very good, and the audience was satisfied.

We filmed *Return to Mayberry* in Los Olivos, California, north of Santa Barbara and a drive of a little over two hours from Los Angeles. Virtually all of the shoot was during February. We would all meet at Universal Studios at five o'clock on Monday mornings, and the production company would take us by bus up to Los Olivos. We would film Monday through Friday and then, after the completion of filming each Friday, they would drive us back to L.A. for the weekend.

After we arrived in Los Olivos one Monday, we immediately went to work. Members of the transportation crew had taken all of our luggage by truck to our hotel. When I got to my hotel room later in the day, I opened one of my suitcases, and found a little clear plastic bag that contained some sort of white powder. It looked just like the little bags of cocaine that you see folks getting busted for on cop shows on television. I thought somebody must have planted the bag of powder and was trying to set me up and create a scandal and cause trouble for the movie.

In a panic, I immediately called Aneta Corsaut, who was staying in a different building. I said, "Could you come over here?"

She came over to my room right away. I said, "Look at this. What does this look like to you? Do you think it might be cocaine?"

She said, "Well, I don't know. Have you tasted it?"

I said, "How would I know what it tastes like? I wouldn't know if I tasted it."

"Well," she said, "we'll know if it tastes funny."

I said, "Do you want to try it?"

She agreed to taste it. Just as on the cop shows, she wet a finger, dabbed a little bit of the powder, and tasted it. I did the same. She said, "Well, I can't identify it. I don't know what it is."

I kept kind of tasting my sample. All of a sudden, it hit me. Just before I left to go out to Universal to catch the bus, I had run back in the kitchen and had grabbed a box of Ivory Snow and poured some in a little plastic pouch in case I needed to wash any delicate clothing in the sink in my hotel room while in Los Olivos. I had forgotten all about it, but that's what we were tasting. Ivory Snow. I felt so foolish.

I said, "Aneta, you're going to kill me. I just thought of what it is." Aneta allowed me to live to tell the story, but she was not happy with the unnecessary agitation I had caused.

Fretting about being accused of being a drug queenpin wasn't my only personal drama during the *Return to Mayberry* shoot. We had severe rains both in L.A. and Los Olivos while we were filming. You don't notice it on the screen at all, but we did work on quite a few scenes in the rain.

It was dark, damp, and cold when we returned to Los Angeles one Friday. I turned the heat on in my house. I had an old gravity furnace with a thermostat that had settings of high, medium, and low. A light would go on to indicate that the furnace was on. The light went on. Pretty soon, I noticed the light went off. I thought, *What in the world's wrong with that?* I went in the kitchen, where there was a trap door with stairs leading down to the crawl space where the water heater and furnace were. I pulled up the trap door. With a flashlight, I looked down the stairs. I could see that there was about two feet of water with some wires floating around. It was about nine o'clock on a Friday night, and I didn't know what to do. I called the gas company. The man on the phone kept saying, "Well, go down there and turn off your gas."

I kept saying, "But I don't know how to turn off my gas down there."

I was scared to death that there might be a fire or an explosion. I didn't know what else to do but take a big bucket down there, fill it with water, haul it back up the stairs, and dump it in the sink, dash downstairs again, get more water, and dump it upstairs. I called the fire department at four o'clock Saturday morning, and they came and turned off the gas. I hauled water up those steps all weekend. It just kept raining, and I just kept hauling water.

It turned out that the people who lived next door had built a wall, and they had stopped up all the weep holes, which caused my back yard not to be able to drain, and it flooded. In all the years I had lived there, I had never had a problem, but I did that weekend. All of my neighbors' homes were built on slabs, so they didn't have a flooding problem. They didn't have anything below ground.

When I finally got hold of a plumber who could also work on the furnace, he told me that he couldn't do anything until all the water was gone. I spent that whole weekend trying to get water out of my crawl space by myself. By that point, all my family was dead, and I was all by myself trying to take care of things with no one to even talk to.

I ended up spending about four months without heat or hot water. That's how long it took to get the water out and for somebody to agree to fix my furnace and water heater. I don't know why somebody couldn't or wouldn't just pump the water out for me. The neighbor next door eventually let me come over once a week and take a hot shower at her house. I used cold water the rest of the time during all those months.

I share all of that saga because that's the condition I was in when I went to catch the five o'clock bus to Los Olivos on the following Monday morning, when we were to film Barney and Thelma Lou's wedding first thing. I don't know how I ever did anything that day. I was exhausted and cold from the weekend's ordeal. I'm sure I acted and looked like a total wreck, and I was.

Once I put that wedding dress on and the hair and makeup folks worked their magic, I was suddenly once again transformed from exhausted and waterlogged Betty with major home maintenance troubles into Thelma Lou with nothing more than wedding jitters

THREE'S COMPANY: The Mayberry bride and groom and the best man pose for a wedding photograph during the filming of Return *to* Mayberry *(1986). Photo courtesy of TAGSRWC Archives.*

and the joy of at long last being about to marry the love of her life. That's why Hollywood and Mayberry are magical!

The movie premiered on NBC-TV on Sunday night, April 13, 1986. Golf fans might also remember that as the day that Jack Nicklaus won his sixth Masters Tournament. There was a lot to celebrate that day. When the Nielsen ratings came out, *Return to Mayberry* ranked second for the week. Only *The Cosby Show*, which was having what would turn out to be its highest-rated season, topped us that week. According to some measures, our movie was also the third-most-watched made-for-television movie up until that time.

I was glad the movie was well-received. I was especially happy that Barney and Thelma Lou finally got married! For me, the best part was just being back together and doing work I loved with cherished old friends. I think Andy Taylor's toast at Barney and Thelma Lou's wedding reception beautifully captured the sentiment that all of us who were part of the movie felt about our shared experience:

"There's something about Mayberry and Mayberry folk that never leaves you. No matter where life takes you, you always carry in your heart the memories of old times … and old friends. Here's to all of us … old friends."

Amen to that! What a wonderful experience that movie was.

Next Case on the Docket

After we shot *Return to Mayberry* in early 1986, my agent told me that Dean Hargrove, an executive producer for the movie, had liked my performance. With Andy Griffith's blessing, Dean wanted me to play a part in *Matlock*, Andy's new series, for which Dean was also an executive producer. Dean and Andy wanted me to play Sarah, Ben Matlock's legal secretary. I talked to Andy about my concerns about playing that role. I said, "I've played secretaries, and the parts go nowhere. The main characters were always at home, instead of in the office. The role of the secretary is a dead-end role. In your case, you don't have a home yet, but you will. I'd like to be your housekeeper."

"No, no," Andy said. "You're going to be my secretary."

I pleaded my case, "Please, let me be your housekeeper. Let me wait until you have a home, and I could be your housekeeper like Aunt Bee was in Mayberry. I could use a little Irish accent or something and make it interesting."

"No," Andy insisted. Ben Matlock needed a secretary.

My objection had been overruled, but I was right about Sarah the secretary's prospects. I ended up having a line or two per episode. It was a nothing role. I was almost as invisible as Mayberry's Sarah, the telephone operator whom the audience never sees.

One day I dropped by the *Matlock* set when they were working on an episode that I wasn't in. Roddy McDowall, my dear friend, was a guest star in the episode, and I wanted to say hello. Dick Van Dyke happened to be on the set that day, too, but he wasn't in that episode. He probably had been working nearby and, like me, just came by to say hi.

Andy looked kind of surprised to see me. It wasn't unusual for actors on a series to drop by on days that they weren't working, but Andy seemed uneasy about my being there. I wondered why.

Bob Sweeney, who was directing the episode, eventually came over to me and said, "They're trying to work things out. They're working things out."

I said, "Really?"

I didn't know what he was talking about. Given what Bob said and that I had also just been sent a *Matlock* script with my name on it for an episode that I wasn't in, I called my agent to make sure I had received the correct script and to find out what was going on. The agent hemmed and hawed and finally said, "Well, we were told not to tell you, but you are no longer on the show. The *Matlock* people said that somebody from their office would get in touch with you directly to talk about it."

Stunned, perturbed, and crestfallen all at once, I said, "Well, nobody has ever called me, and you should have told me. You're my agent. They're not paying you—I am. You should have told me."

There I had been on the set and not knowing that I was, literally, an outcast. I'm sure everyone was wondering what the heck I was doing there. Dean Hargrove finally called me and apologized. He said, "I was supposed to call you, and I'm sorry that I didn't."

I said, "Well, you really should have called, because I made a fool of myself. I never would have gone to the set if I had known. I really don't appreciate the fact that you didn't call." I was angry. I felt like such a fool.

And so it was that, after just a few episodes, Sarah the secretary was written out of *Matlock*. My time on *Matlock* was over by Christmas. Just as my case against Sarah had been summarily dismissed, now I, too, had been dismissed.

At that point, I had been working in films for almost forty years. I knew the ropes. I could see where there was potential for a role to grow and where there wasn't. Sometimes other folks have their own ideas, and when they're the decision-makers, I had learned to roll with the punches and hope for the best.

I had been Brian Keith's secretary on *Family Affair*, and he was always home. Every now and then, I would be in a little scene, but really not anything worthwhile. It was the same situation with Fred MacMurray on *My Three Sons*. I was his secretary, but he was always home. I didn't have a meaningful part in the story.

By the time the role of Sarah on *Matlock* came along, I knew from experience where it was headed. Compared to Linda Purl's character as Ben Matlock's daughter and law partner or Kene Holliday's as the investigator, my part was about as interesting as the copy machine. I'd say, "Here's a glass of water," or something like that. Della Street to Perry Mason, I was not.

I remember George Lindsey talking about doing Westerns back when he was still struggling to break through as an actor. He said he never wanted to be in a role where the cowboys ride into town, get off their horses, hand their reins to him, and say, "Here, take our horses to the stable." I balked at those sorts of incidental parts, too, but sometimes you also still have to make a living and you simply take what you can get.

I think I could have been really good as Ben Matlock's housekeeper. The sad thing for me is that, years later, Ben Matlock actually did get a housekeeper. She was played by the veteran character actress Marge Redmond. The producers had finally accepted my idea. Marge was even a redhead like me and she spoke with an Irish accent. It had taken a few years, but my housekeeper idea finally took hold. They just hadn't wanted to use me for the role at the time that I had suggested it. That's life. You don't always get what you want. You just hope for better luck next time.

Some of the cast and crew from the old *Griffith* show were, in fact, luckier with their roles on *Matlock*. Aneta Corsaut and writer-turned-actor Everett Greenbaum were recurring characters, both as judges. Both were excellent in those roles. Jack Dodson, Mayberry's Howard Sprague, also had a featured guest role in an episode. And it was almost like old times when Don Knotts joined the series as Les Calhoun, Ben Matlock's neighbor and slightly frustrating friend. Don was on the show for four seasons until the show moved production to North Carolina. That move made filming easier for Andy, but it also made the commute too difficult for Don and some others, including Marge Redmond, who didn't make the transition to the new filming location.

Of All the Merv

Tradition and transition, whether in roles for actors or in real estate, can be difficult. Merv Griffin bought the Beverly Hilton in Beverly Hills in the late 1980s. He owned the landmark for about fifteen years. One day, after Merv had owned the hotel for a few years, I was there for lunch and saw Merv outside in the garden area with two gentlemen. I went out to speak to him. Merv and I had gone out a few times in New York, and I knew he had a great sense of humor. Merv introduced me to his doctor and to one of the movie-producing King Brothers. I immediately alienated Mr. King by saying something that I thought was funny, but that he did not.

Not deterred by my joke falling flat with one-third of my captive audience, I said, "You know, Merv, you disappoint me in one way. You've had this hotel for a few years now. I thought you, of all people, would have a place where we could dance. Dancing is coming back. I remember being on the Hotel Astor rooftop and dancing with Roddy McDowall. You danced with me there, too. Everybody danced in those days."

I persisted with my point, "There used to be a great place called the Star on the Roof Room on top of this hotel. I used to come here and dance all the time. Freddie Karger and his orchestra were regulars up there. I'm just surprised you haven't revived the rooftop for that."

LADIES OF LEISURE: With Arlene Golonka (left) and Jackie Joseph during a brunch in 1997 at the Beverly Hilton Hotel, a favorite dining spot, in Beverly Hills. Photo courtesy of TAGSRWC Archives.

Merv said, "Betty, that's a good idea." Sure enough, several years later, in 1998, Merv opened The Coconut Club, a supper club with a huge dance floor. It was located in the Beverly Hilton's main ball-room on Friday and Saturday nights. It was kind of a throwback to the legendary Cocoanut Grove at the old Ambassador Hotel, where Merv used to perform early in his career as a singer. A lot of movie stars were invited to the grand opening of The Coconut Club. I was not among those invited, but that was O.K. Even if not on the rooftop, at least dancing was back at the Beverly Hilton, for a while anyway. The Coconut Club closed in 2002, and Merv sold the Beverly Hilton the next year. The dance floor and the transition to a new tradition were no more.

Moving On

Shades of L.A., in late 1990, was officially my last onscreen acting job. The show had an interesting premise. A policeman is shot and dies. He encounters spirits, the so-called shades, who have unfinished earthly business. Until the matters of their earthly life are resolved, the shades are trapped in Purgatory and unable to move on to either Heaven or Hell. After the policeman is resuscitated, he still sees dead people and has to deal with them—sort of like in *The Sixth Sense*.

I played a nun named Sister Clara. I don't know if he had anything to do with casting me in the role, but Bob Sweeney directed my episode. It was fun to work with Bob one last time. We had to re-shoot some of the scenes for my part because Troy Donahue, the actor who originally played the villain, was replaced by Jeff East. I thought Troy was quite good in the role. I don't know what happened, but they recast it. Maybe they wanted someone younger.

I had to come back to reshoot with Jeff the scenes that I had done with Troy. Bob Sweeney didn't direct the reshoot. I suppose Sween, as friends affectionately called him, wasn't available that day. That episode turned out to be the last thing he directed. I think Sween was already fighting the cancer that took his life a year and a half later.

Bob Sweeney was a great actor himself. He could do an impression of anybody. He did Don Knotts to a T. He was such a sweetheart. Of all the directors I worked with through the years—and there were some mighty good ones—Bob was the one that I felt the closest to. His being an actor was a big plus for him and for the actors. He knew what actors needed from a director. I loved Sween, and his dear wife, Beverly. I knew their daughter, Bridget, as well. They were a wonderful family.

And So It Goes

With *Shades of L.A*, my film career came to a quiet end. Unless you were Angela Lansbury or one of the Golden Girls, if you were an actress over sixty, good parts were hard to come by. The same was true of other jobs in the film business. I think back to a period starting around the early 1980s. A lot of younger people came into Hollywood as producers. Many came from the business side of things, more so than from the creative side.

The new kids on the block didn't have any sense for the history and talent of some of the more experienced—that is to say, older—writers. It happened with directors, too, but I think it was often the writers who suffered the most. The kids thought the old warhorses needed to be put out to pasture. They didn't realize how much knowledge could be gained from these older but unbelievably talented writers. A lot of writers complained that they couldn't get work.

While Hollywood's decision-makers didn't always appreciate us old-timers, thankfully at least the fans did.

Chapter 10: Further Returns to Mayberry

Especially after the *Return to Mayberry* movie in 1986 and after we started making lots of public appearances together around 1990, I made an effort, as best I could, to stay connected with both old and new friends from the *Griffith* show. Years had gone by, and I tried not to bother people too much, but after we started making appearances and we got closer, I would call people. Sadly, most of the old crew are now gone. I've been to a lot of funerals—including for Hal Smith, Jack Dodson, Aneta Corsaut, and Howie Morris, as well as services for Don Knotts. And that's just the friends from the *Griffith* show. So many other friends from my movie days and just from daily life are gone.

People used to call me to make sure I had heard the news about the passing of somebody who worked on the *Griffith* show. More

A FUN TIME WITH GREAT FRIENDS: At the Memphis Film Festival in 1990 with Hal Smith and Aneta Corsaut. Photo courtesy of TAGSRWC Archives.

often than not, they would want me to help spread the sad news to others I knew from the show. By default, I had become more or less the matriarch of Mayberry. I would dutifully make the calls to let others know who had died. I finally just had to say, "Please don't call me with the news of people dying anymore. It's just too sad." For a while there, old friends were dying in pretty close succession, and it was a lot to handle emotionally. I said, "You need to get someone younger to be the messenger."

I still hear the news of people dying, and usually pretty quickly, but I now get it in more indirect ways. It makes it easier to absorb the news. I suppose, if you live long enough, eventually most of the people you knew for years and years are gone. One day it will be my turn to be the subject of that sort of call. At least no one will have to worry about calling me when that time comes!

When we had the awful Northridge earthquake in 1994, it scared me to death. My house was the only one on my block that had significant structural damage—maybe because it was older. It was like the devil came up from the ground. I called all of the *Griffith* show people in Los Angeles that I knew how to reach. Hal Smith lived in Santa Monica, which was hit hard, and I called to check on him. Hal died not long after we spoke. I was probably one of the last people to speak with him, if not the last person. He died of a heart attack while sitting in a recliner at his home. I like to believe he died peacefully in his sleep. I've always wondered if the trauma from the earthquake a few days earlier had contributed to Hal's death.

Hal's son, Terry, didn't discover Hal had died until at least several hours after the fact—maybe even longer. As is the custom, the coroner recorded the date of Hal's death as the day he was found, which was January 28. Hal and his lovely wife, Louise, who died a couple of years before Hal, had the cutest little toy poodle, named Nicky. That little dog was so well trained not to go to the bathroom indoors that, after Hal died, he held off doing his business until Terry arrived and could let him outside. Heaven only knows how long Nicky had been waiting to go, but he dutifully stayed by Hal's side until someone arrived.

Mayberry Reunions

We've had many sad losses in Mayberry through the years. We've also had many unforgettable, wonderful times together. The Mayberry reunions have been not only a fun way to visit with fans, but also a chance to see people who worked on the *Griffith* show. Some have been folks I had worked with in my episodes, but the vast majority have been people I never worked with. I knew most of them from their episodes, but getting to know them in person after so many years has been a real pleasure.

Sometimes an actor may have had one line in one episode, or maybe even no lines. Or a director may have directed just one episode. That doesn't matter. If you were in an episode or worked on an episode, then you're officially Mayberry royalty.

I remember for the fiftieth anniversary of the *Griffith* show in 2010, a nice man named Robert Dean attended the annual Mayberry Days in Mount Airy. He had been in the "The Pickle Story," the iconic episode from the second season, in 1961. Bobby, as he was known when he was just a kid back then, had no lines. He was an extra playing one of the observers of the judging of the pickle contest. That was enough to be a celebrated guest at Mayberry Days.

LIVELY MOMENT: Onstage in 1991 with George Lindsey at the Chevrolet Geo Celebrity Theater during the "Mayberry Cast Reunion" show at Opryland in Nashville. Photo by Karen Leonard.

SUPER GROUP: Surrounded by (left to right) Hal Smith, Jack Dodson, George Lindsey, and Howard Morris in a publicity photograph for SuperStation TBS's special celebrating the thirtieth anniversary of The Andy Griffith Show *in 1990. Photo courtesy of TAGSRWC Archives.*

He was a nice and interesting man, and everybody loved meeting him. He had a rare perspective about the *Griffith* show and added another dimension to that year's festival.

Mayberry events started happening in the 1980s, usually with just one actor, such as for Ernest T. Bass Day with Howie Morris in Nashville in 1986 or Otis Campbell Day in 1988, also in Nashville.

SIDE BY SIDE ONCE AGAIN: With Don Knotts in the SuperStation TBS special in 1990. Photo courtesy of TAGSRWC Archives.

I remember Hal making several solo appearances as Otis at events during that time. George Lindsey, who was always in demand as a stand-up comedian, eventually just started dressing in Goober wardrobe for almost all of his performances.

Public Mayberry reunions with multiple stars started in earnest in 1990, for the thirtieth anniversary of the *Griffith* show. In the fall of that year, SuperStation TBS in Atlanta brought several of us—Don Knotts, George Lindsey, Jack Dodson, Hal Smith, Howie Morris, and me—to film a reunion show with a live audience. They showed some clips, had us take questions from the audience, and filmed us just reminiscing about the old show. It was great fun being together again, remembering all the good times we had, and just laughing a lot.

That same fall, there was also a cast reunion in Charlotte, North Carolina. That show was a combination of performances, mostly singing, and panel discussions. We signed autographs for hours. Don wasn't there for that one, but a great group of others were.

MAKING WAVES: Riding down Main Street in Mount Airy in a pink Ford Deluxe during the 2003 Mayberry Days parade. Photo courtesy of TAGSRWC Archives.

Andy Griffith rarely participated in big public reunion events with the large crowds of fans. That was never really Andy's thing. However, Andy did attend the occasional awards show and he did a few Mayberry reunion specials for television with Don, Ron Howard, Jim Nabors, and sometimes George Lindsey.

Some of us have been more like "the regulars" of the Mayberry reunion events. The Dillards (the Darling boys), Maggie Peterson Mancuso (Charlene Darling), Howie Morris, George Lindsey, and I were among the ones who probably did the most. Bernard Fox (Malcolm Merriweather) and Jean Carson (Daphne, the "fun girl") did quite a few, too. Later on, James Best (Jim Lindsey) joined us. Don Knotts often joined us for bigger events. I was also pleased that Aneta Corsaut got to do at least a couple of events, including one with Jack Prince (Rafe Hollister) and writer Everett Greenbaum in the 1980s, before she became too ill to travel. It is always a delight when Elinor Donahue is able to be a part of these gatherings. I know fans would love to see her back at Mayberry Days sometime. I would too!

And it is indeed the Mayberry Days festival in Mount Airy that, year after year, continues to be the biggest Mayberry celebration of all. Sponsored by the local Surry Arts Council, Mayberry Days has been held every year since 1990. Thousands of fans and a good group of people associated with the production of the *Griffith* show participate in the event, which has grown to span the better part of a week. More than three dozen members of the cast and crew have attended Mayberry Days over the years. Many have been guests at the festival at least a dozen times.

A really special thing about Mayberry Days—and most of the Mayberry reunion events, but especially Mayberry Days—is the participation by family members of the *Griffith* cast and crew. Many spouses and significant others accompany the "star" guests. More

STRONG FAMILY TIES: With Karen Knotts at a reception for special guests of Mayberry Days in 2019. Photo by Hobart Jones.

GRAND GREETING: Grand Ole Opry *star Porter Wagoner (far right) offers a warm welcome during a walk-on appearance on the* Opry *in 1991 with Jack Prince (aka Mayberry moonshiner Rafe Hollister, far left) and George Lindsey. Photo by Karen Leonard.*

and more, the children of the stars either accompany their parents or represent their families at Mayberry Days. George Lindsey Jr. has even performed onstage at Mayberry Days while wearing some of the Goober wardrobe that his dad used to wear for live shows and personal appearances. Karen Knotts, who's just delightful and as cute as she can be, has a one-woman show called *Tied Up in Knotts* that she has performed at Mayberry Days and elsewhere for several years. I think it's really terrific that the Mayberry tradition is being maintained through the generations.

Some of the best Mayberry cast reunions we have done over the years were at the Opryland complex in Nashville. The first one was in 1991. We performed four shows at a large outdoor theater in the Opryland USA theme park, appeared on Ralph Emery's popular *Nashville Now* show on The Nashville Network, and made a walk-on appearance on the *Grand Ole Opry.*

In 2001 and again in 2004, many of us returned to the Opryland complex to do more "Mayberry Cast Reunion" shows. Phillip Stegner, a talented musician and conductor, as well as an experienced

STAR-STUDDED STAIRWAY. At the Tennessee Governor's Mansion while in Nashville for the "Mayberry Cast Reunion" at Opryland in June 2001. Pictured in the front row (left to right) are Gov. Don Sundquist, First Lady Martha Sundquist, Rodney Dillard, Howard Morris, Maggie Peterson Mancuso, and Betty Lynn. In the back row (left to right) are Bernard Fox, Doug Dillard, Don Knotts, and George Lindsey. Photo by Jed DeKalb.

director of stage shows, was our director for all of the Opryland reunions. They drew huge crowds of Mayberry fans from all across the country.

Sometimes the fans aren't just fans. They're *adoring* fans! I hear from a lot of young men (and some not so young anymore) who say, "I was in love with you when I was twelve, Thelma Lou." I had no idea how many twelve-year-olds were infatuated with Thelma Lou. Then again, even Opie had a brief crush on Thelma Lou in "The Rivals" episode in our third season. He also had puppy love for his schoolteacher, Miss Crump, in "Opie Loves Helen" a couple of seasons later, so I guess I wasn't the only one getting crushed on.

At one of our cast reunions in Nashville, a whole group of men lined up all in a row to give me a kiss. They all said they had been in love with me when they were twelve years old. It was so cute. It was like a chorus line of formerly smitten fellows. I kept wishing I were a lot younger. It was really sweet.

A DIFFERENT KIND OF CASTING FOR A PART: In show business, they say "break a leg," but maybe they should include a wrist. Still smiling and ready to greet fans after a fall on the dance floor the night before at the "Mayberry Cast Reunion" in Grand Rapids, Michigan, in 1995. Photo by Karen Leonard.

The Mayberry reunion events became bigger and bigger throughout the 1990s and right on into recent years. Most have been held in the Southeast and Midwest, from the Carolinas and Virginia to Ohio and Indiana to Tennessee, Alabama, and Georgia.

During Memorial Day weekend in 1995, a reunion was held in Grand Rapids, Michigan. For me, it was memorable because I tripped and fell while dancing at a reception after one of our shows and broke my left wrist. After a visit to the emergency room and a largely sleepless night, I was back the next day, with my arm in a cast and a sling, ready to participate in a panel discussion and even to sign autographs.

One of the biggest reunions was in Winston-Salem, North Carolina, in the fall of 1995. That was another milestone year for doing our reunions because it marked the thirty-fifth anniversary of the *Griffith* show's first broadcast. The Winston-Salem reunion

BEFORE THE BIG BREAK: The left arm is still intact for this group portrait at the cast reunion in Grand Rapids. Seated next to Jean Carson (Mt. Pilot "fun girl" Daphne) and backed by (left to right) Howard Morris, Maggie Peterson Mancuso, Bernard Fox, and Elinor Donahue. Photo by Karen Leonard.

was organized by Neal Brower, a Methodist minister who taught a continuing-education course on the *Griffith* show. Neal had also spearheaded the reunion in Charlotte in 1990.

An incredibly poignant part of the Winston-Salem weekend for me was when Aneta Corsaut, who, at that point, was far too sick to travel, was able to call in to the live show. She and I had a cheerful phone conversation that the audience was able to listen in on, just like the party line in Mayberry. Everyone was delighted to hear Aneta's voice. We did two shows, one on Saturday night and a matinee on Sunday. Aneta got thunderous standing ovations from the audience both times.

That was the weekend of September 30 and October 1. (Mayberry reunions are often scheduled as closely as possible to October 3, the

"YOU GET A LINE, AND I'LL GET A POLE": Letting Aneta Corsaut (on the other end of the line, from her home in Studio City, California) hear the roar of the standing ovation she's receiving from the sell-out crowd at one of the two performances of the Mayberry cast reunion show, a celebration marking the thirty-fifth anniversary of The Andy Griffith Show, *at Winston-Salem's Stevens Center in 1995. Photo by Steve Keenan.*

date of the broadcast of the first episode in 1960.) Sadly, my friend Aneta passed away just over a month later, on November 6. Like many, if not most, of the adults who worked on the show, Aneta had been a heavy smoker. It was no surprise when her doctors told her that smoking had likely been the biggest factor in her getting cancer.

As a child of North Carolina and tobacco country, Andy Griffith had been as big a smoker as anybody. When Andy quit smoking, he, like so many others who have quit, became outspoken in his opposition to smoking. I think he saw the destruction it was doing to his own health and to those he loved. Don Knotts, no doubt with strong pleading from Andy, finally was able to quit smoking, as did George Lindsey. I eventually quit, too—ironically around the time I moved to Mount Airy, near the heart of tobacco-farming country.

I believe the largest Mayberry reunion we ever did (so far, that is!) was near Birmingham, Alabama, during the weekend of October 7, 2000. A nice man named Joel Laird was running for the Alabama Supreme Court, and the "Mayberry Family Reunion" was sponsored by his election campaign. Already a circuit court judge, Joel was known as the Mayberry Judge, both because of his Andy Taylor-like wisdom on the bench and because he was widely known as a huge fan of the *Griffith* show. The Judge didn't win that election, but he produced a top-notch event.

GAL PALS: *Enjoying some time onstage with Mary Grace Canfield (center) and Elinor Donahue at Judge Joel Laird's "Mayberry Family Reunion" in Pelham, Alabama, on October 7, 2000. Photo by Karen Leonard.*

SARAH, PLEASE CONNECT ME TO 1962: Onstage and on the phone with Don Knotts during the "Mayberry Family Reunion" in Alabama in 2000. Photo by Karen Leonard.

The main event was held in the evening at the Oak Mountain Amphitheater in Pelham, just south of Birmingham. Ordinarily, October in Alabama would be very pleasant, but temperatures that evening were close to freezing. The audience was huddling under blankets. We did the same backstage, but the show went on.

There were other dangers that night. Howie Morris misjudged the front of the stage, and, if not for a quick response and miraculous catch by Allan Newsome, one of the evening's emcees, Howie likely would have completed a really bad tumble and been very seriously injured.

Top Draw

Don Knotts had long toured solo doing stand-up comedy. He had regular routines he liked to do, including "The Weatherman," "The Sportscaster," and "The Baseball Pitcher." They were all brilliant. He had honed the routines to perfection over many decades. They weren't about Mayberry, but they were hilarious and popular with audiences everywhere. For the last portion of his presentations, Don would usually take questions, and inevitably many would be about Barney Fife.

When a Mayberry reunion's budget could afford his hefty fee, Don would join us. The reunions at Opryland were the only ones that ever persuaded Don to wear wardrobe as Barney Fife. He agreed to wear a deputy uniform for the shows in 1991. The crowd went wild.

Then, for the later shows in 2001 and 2004, director Phillip Stegner (aka the Maestro) was once again at the helm and convinced Don to wear one of his original salt and pepper suits to recreate the famous scene with the dead microphone from "Barney and the Choir." Don trusted Phillip to make sure that the scene was staged to his standards. The Maestro delivered. Needless to say, Don and Barney absolutely brought the house down with those performances. Don hadn't worn one of his salt and pepper suits for a performance since *Return to Mayberry*, and I don't think he ever wore one of them again after the 2004 shows. Two of Don's salt and pepper suits are now in the Andy Griffith Museum in Mount Airy.

During the era of doing those reunions with Don, I got to know Francey Yarborough, Don's girlfriend, who would become his third wife. She's a delightful person and very funny. She was always so caring and attentive with Don. She was very protective of him.

The three of us would have dinner from time to time. I would take them out for dinner at a hotel somewhere, and, in turn, they would

HEY, PORTER! REMEMBER US? Looking on with George Lindsey (far left) as Porter Wagoner welcomes Don Knotts and the rest of the stars of the 2001 edition of the "Mayberry Cast Reunion" back to the stage of the Grand Ole Opry. *Photo courtesy of TAGSRWC Archives.*

take me out. The Four Seasons Hotel was a favorite spot for us. At some point, we finally realized we lived very close to each other, and they would come by and pick me up. Francey and I would chatter away and laugh and visit, and Don would just sit and smile and listen to us. Now and then, he would say a few well-chosen words.

In the fall of 1998, Don asked me to go with him and Francey to Warner Bros. for a screening of *Pleasantville*, the new movie that he was in. The film starred Reese Witherspoon and Toby Maguire and had a wonderful cast. Don played the fairly small but pivotal part of a TV repairman who had some of the same bravado and quirks as Barney Fife, which I'm sure Don drew on for the role. I thought he played the TV repairman to great effect. The movie was interesting and entertaining. It got good reviews from critics and audiences, and did well at the box office. It was fun to see Don back on the big screen, and doubly so to be able to watch the movie with Francey and him.

SUIT YOURSELF: With Emmett Forrest, childhood friend of Andy Griffith's and founding curator of the Andy Griffith Museum, proudly displaying two of Don Knotts's trademark salt and pepper suits that were donated to the museum by Francey Knotts, Don's widow. Come to Mount Airy and see them! Photo by Hobart Jones.

The last few times that I talked to Don on the phone, he told me that he wasn't feeling well enough to go out to dinner. I hadn't been feeling the greatest myself at the time. I told him that I understood and that I hoped he would be feeling better soon.

When Don's health took a final turn for the worst, I didn't want to believe how bad off he was. I just thought he would somehow pull through. During his eulogy at Don's memorial service, Andy shared that he was at Don's bedside and kept exhorting Don with his nickname, "Breathe, Jess, breathe." Even while offering Don comfort and encouragement, Andy was still affectionately needling Don with that irritating nickname. That's what friends do.

STARS GAZING: With Andy Griffith and Don Knotts at the dedication ceremony for Don's star on the Hollywood Walk of Fame on January 19, 2000. Photo courtesy of TAGSRWC Archives.

Don died on February 24, 2006. A private service and burial at Westwood Memorial Park was attended by just a few close friends and family. In addition to Francey, both of Don's ex-wives attended, but among those three and myself, I was the only one who could say that she was married to Barney Fife!

A couple of months after Don's funeral, I got a call from a lady who said that Francey wanted me to speak at the memorial service that was planned for the Writers Guild Theater in Beverly Hills on May 4, which was in just a few days. I wasn't sure I could collect my thoughts enough in that short time.

I asked the lady, "How many people are speaking?"

She replied, "About twenty, I think."

With that many people speaking, I didn't think it would be necessary for me to speak, but I asked the lady to talk to Francey and be sure.

A short time later, the lady called me back and said, "Yes, Francey definitely would like for you to speak if you could."

The Writers Guild Theater seats close to five hundred people, and it was packed for Don's memorial service. They had to have attendance be by invitation only. Otherwise, Lord only knows how many thousands of people would have tried to be there. There had been a tremendous outpouring of affection and sadness when Don died.

Ron Howard spoke first, and then Andy Griffith. Those were hard speakers to follow, especially Andy, who was such a close friend with Don for more than fifty years—since *No Time for Sergeants* on Broadway in 1955. A whole parade of people who knew Don then spoke—from Tom Poston to Al Checco and way back to friends from Morgantown. It was really very touching and, at times, funny, which anything involving Don would ultimately have to be.

For my remarks, I told about going to see Don in *On Golden Pond* at the New Theatre & Restaurant in Overland Park, Kansas. Don performed several plays there from the mid-1990s to the early 2000s, including two productions of *On Golden Pond*. I went to see one of the shows in the fall of 2003. I ended up taking roughly forty of my relatives, mostly second and third cousins, to see Don in the play. I knew if I had tried to go see the show by myself, my kinfolk would have killed me for causing them to miss a chance to see Don Knotts perform and possibly to meet him.

I told Don, "You'll have to acknowledge them in some way, because I want my cousins to know that you know they're there."

He said, "Well, just bring them backstage after the show."

I said, "Are you sure that's O.K.?"

"Oh, yeah. Just bring them back."

I brought the group backstage. Some of my cousins and their families had come in from St. Louis. Others came from Tulsa. They were all corralled back in this little hallway. We were practically like cattle in a pen at the Kansas City stockyards. I knocked on the door to Don's dressing room, and Don opened it. I said, "Well, my cousins are all out here, so when you have a minute, would you come out and say hello?"

Out he came. I stood behind him, and I named each of my cousins, some of whom I hardly knew. I named them all. Don graciously shook hands with each one of them. They had no idea how big a deal that was for him to do, because Don was an acknowledged germophobe and hypochondriac.

During remarks when he was accepting an award one time, Don said that he had never realized that he was a hypochondriac until he heard both of his ex-wives interviewed on television. Each mentioned his hypochondria. Only then did he realize that he must be one. That must be a hypochondriac's worst fear—worrying about having the health condition that involves worrying about all the other possible health conditions!

Don looked right at each of my relatives as he shook their hands. They didn't realize that he couldn't see much of anything anymore, because he had macular degeneration. He could see fairly well peripherally, but he couldn't see straight on. You wouldn't know it to look at him. He had those big blue eyes, and he looked right at you. As he shook hands with each of my cousins, I could see their expressions. They were shaking hands with Don Knotts, and they were all just thrilled. I wish Don could've seen their delight, but I'm sure he could at least sense it.

Don shook every hand that was offered and we did some group pictures. After that, I could tell that he was really tired. He had done two performances that day. It was a Saturday, and he had done a matinee and then the evening performance that we attended. We all thanked him profusely, and I did so doubly.

As we were leaving the theater, one of my cousins said to me, "Betty, you'll never have to do another thing for me ever again. That was the most wonderful experience I've ever had." Don was a true trouper to take that time to greet everyone.

When we first started doing public Mayberry reunion events, we would usually have a time for questions from the audience. Someone would inevitably ask me, "Was there something going on between you and Don Knotts?" The news media also haven't been shy about asking that same question.

THE BEST KIND OF RERUN: With Don Knotts, recreating a favorite publicity photograph (the original is on an easel in the background) at a luncheon at the Four Seasons Hotel in Beverly Hills following Don's induction into the Hollywood Walk of Fame in 2000. Photo courtesy of TAGSRWC Archives.

I'd say, "No, of course not. He was a married man." In fact, he was married three times in the time I knew him. At first, I was annoyed by the question. I thought, *How dare they?* As I reflected on the question, I thought, *Wait a minute. I get mad at them, but I shouldn't. It's actually a great compliment.*

In response to the question, I finally started saying, "Don and I were apparently so convincing in our portrayal of the affection between Barney and Thelma Lou that we didn't have to roll around in the sheets half naked in front of the camera for everybody to believe that there must be something going on between us off camera. I guess that means we were pretty good actors."

If Don also happened to be at the event, he would, in his typical fashion, say, "That's right," and not much else. He was almost always a person of few words, and, unlike Barney Fife, he wasn't about to become verbose about his romances.

I loved Don. I truly did. A sweetheart is what he was.

Reading the Lines Between Us

When I was at Mayberry Days in 2001, Tanya Jones, Executive Director of the Surry Arts Council, the organization that sponsors the festival, asked me if I would be interested in performing in a production of *Love Letters* in Mount Airy around Valentine's Day. Without even knowing anything about what *Love Letters* was, I said yes.

As it turned out, all kinds of interesting pairings of couples had been doing productions of the two-person show since the late 1980s, but I didn't know anything about all that. Tanya had the idea of my doing the play with Howie Morris, who had also attended Mayberry Days that year. I thought the play sounded like a lot of fun. I loved Howie. He could be a handful for some people, but he and I always got along great. And what a talented man he was.

Of course, Don Knotts would have been the ultimate pairing with me, particularly for a show in the town that was at least in part the inspiration for Mayberry, but I'm sure Don was far beyond Tanya's budget.

Also, *Love Letters* would have been tough for Don to do at that point. By the early 2000s, he had a lot of vision loss from his macular degeneration. The entire production of *Love Letters* involves reading letters exchanged between the two characters. He would have had to memorize the lines and then pretend to be reading them.

I'm sad that it also never worked out for Don to attend Mayberry Days or even to visit Mount Airy. My feeling is that Don always sort of felt that Mount Airy was Andy Griffith's town, so, out of friendship and respect for Andy, he steered clear.

Both Howie and I agreed to do *Love Letters* in Mount Airy on the Saturday before Valentine's Day 2002. Our production was for one night only. They were going to erect a simple stage for us in the ballroom at the Cross Creek Country Club and make it a dinner-theater production.

A few weeks before the show, I called Howie and suggested we have dinner at the Beverly Hilton and then do a read-through of the play. I booked a room at the hotel for us to use for the read-through after dinner. Howie's son, David, came with him to dinner. We had a nice meal, and then the three of us went up to the room to rehearse. David, who is also a film director, was our audience as Howie and I read the play out loud once through.

Playwright A.R. Gurney had put in his notes that the actors should just read the lines without expression, like reading a tele-phone book. We weren't supposed to do any action or theatrics. Just sit there and read.

I told Howie, "Listen, I don't know about you, but I'm going to do this as a radio show. I'm not doing this like I'm reading a telephone book—not in front of an audience. I'll be darned if I will. I'm going to do it like it's radio."

Howie said, "That sounds fine to me. I'll do the same."

We did our read-through and both of us agreed that the reading went well. I felt that I needed work, but I thought Howie sounded spot on, which was no surprise because he was a master of sponta-neity and working on the fly. The read-through had accomplished what I wanted. At least I now had an idea of how the performance was going to go.

I found it funny that my character was this kind of weird, wild girl, who, shall we say, needed a lot of prayers. I, too, was going to need to pray about some of the language in her dialogue. Meanwhile, Howie, who knew how to really let the expletives fly, played my counterpart, who was a total goody two shoes. Pairing us together was classic casting against type without even meaning to do so.

When we got to Mount Airy, Howie the improviser, said, "I don't want to rehearse."

I had read through the script many times by then and felt comfort-able with what we were going to do, so I said, "That's O.K. with me."

"A ROSE IS A ROSE IS A ROSE IS A ROSE": Visiting with the audience after the sold-out 2002 performance of Love Letters *with Howard Morris in Mount Airy. One performer received a bunch of roses, and the other had to steal his single rose from her bunch. Photo courtesy of TAGSRWC Archives.*

We did the show. For my own comfort and especially knowing that we had a Mayberry audience, we toned down a bit of the profanity for my character. We apparently didn't tone it down quite enough for some folks. A few people were offended and left during the intermission. I later learned that some were relatives of Andy Griffith's. I was sorry that the show had made them uncomfortable.

Fortunately, our performance seemed to be well received by most of the audience, many of whom had traveled from out of state just to see the show. I thought both Howie and I had held up our ends and had done the play justice. It was fun to do. I really enjoyed working with Howie in that manner.

I was very fond of Howie. Thelma Lou and his Ernest T. Bass character had never been in the same *Griffith* episode, but Howie directed "Barney's Physical," an episode in the fifth season, which was my last season as a semi-regular. Both of us were also in the *Return to Mayberry* movie.

Howie and I had become good friends from doing various Mayberry reunion shows. That's not to say that sometimes I didn't get upset with him, because he could be a terrible rascal and even

FUNNY FACE, I LOVE YOU!: Things were never dull when Howard Morris was around. He is seen here during a rehearsal break in Pigeon Forge, Tennessee in 2001. Photo by Bart Boatwright.

downright rude to people. He once told me that he thought people expected him to be that way, but I think sometimes he just got ticked off and liked to give people a hard time. David Morris was really good with his dad. He could generally rein Howie in.

When I lived in Los Angeles, I had one of the old-style tape answering machines that would play back messages through a speaker. I would be afraid to check messages if anybody were with me because I never knew whether Howie might have left me messages that were off-color. He was so funny, though. You couldn't help but love him, no matter what.

Howie died in 2005. I truly missed him after he was gone. His funeral had a lot of laughs. You know it's going to be funny when Carl Reiner gives the eulogy. I still laugh whenever I catch Howie on an old *Griffith* episode or Sid Caesar's show. He was brilliant. Make no mistake, though many people often did—Howie had a heart of gold. A person couldn't have a more loyal friend than Howie Morris.

More Special Gatherings

In March 2004, Andy Griffith took part in the TV Land Awards at the old Hollywood Palladium, when *The Andy Griffith Show* received the Legend Award. A bunch of us were there for that one—just about all of the main cast who were still alive were there, except for Ron Howard, who was busy directing a movie. Rance Howard, Ron's dad, represented the Howard family.

Andy was the ringleader getting everybody onboard to participate in that reunion. Producer Aaron Ruben and Earle Hagen, the *Griffith* show's magnificent music director, were there, along with Harvey Bullock, one of the show's most revered writers. Actors from the show included Don Knotts, Jim Nabors, George Lindsey, Elinor Donahue, Howie Morris, Maggie Peterson Mancuso, and me. It was a special night. Just having such a big group of us together for such a gala event made it memorable.

In September of that year, Andy and Cindi Griffith, for the first time ever, joined a bunch of us who were regulars at Mayberry reunions for the annual Mayberry Days celebration in Mount Airy. Two years earlier, Andy had made his first public appearance in Mount Airy in several decades. That occasion was the dedication of the Andy Griffith Parkway in Mount Airy. An enormous and enthusiastic crowd attended, including the Governor of North Carolina. I think Andy was pleasantly surprised by the incredibly adoring reception he received. I believe he really enjoyed the whole thing and was therefore a little less bashful about returning in 2004. In fact, I think that he was even eager to do so.

The occasion for the second public visit to Mount Airy was the unveiling of the TV Land Landmark, which was a bronze statue of Andy and Opie with their fishing poles. This statue was a replica of one that Andy had helped unveil in Raleigh the previous year. I believe Andy must have pulled some strings to have a second statue placed in his hometown of Mount Airy—thereby making *The Andy Griffith Show* the only TV series to be commemorated with two TV Land Landmark statues.

As with his visit to Mount Airy in 2002, Andy received a hero's welcome in 2004. I know the citizens of Mount Airy were pleased

A DOZEN OF MAYBERRY'S BEST: In 2004, The Andy Griffith Show *was honored with the TV Land Legend Award. On hand to accept the award at the Hollywood Palladium were (left to right) Jim Nabors, George Lindsey, Don Knotts, Aaron Ruben, Elinor Donahue, Howard Morris, Maggie Peterson Mancuso, Harvey Bullock (largely obscured), Andy Griffith, Rance Howard (representing son Ron and the whole Howard family), Earle Hagen, and Betty Lynn. Photo courtesy of TAGSRWC Archives.*

and proud to have Andy return. Fans from all across the country naturally were thrilled. That would turn out to be Andy's last visit to Mount Airy. He had hoped to make it back to see the new Andy Griffith Museum after it opened in 2009, but he was not able to do so. He and Cindi donated some real treasures to the museum, which is a wonderful tribute to his remarkable life.

Sometimes When a Door Closes, It's Locked

One of the places I was asked to perform a few times is Pigeon Forge, Tennessee. I joined several other cast members from the *Griffith* show in participating in reunion events there. During "A Tribute to Mayberry," as a couple of these reunions were called, each of us performed and then met with fans and signed autographs afterwards. Howie Morris and I also joined Don there for

OUTSTANDING CASTING: The second TV Land Landmark for The Andy
Griffith Show *was dedicated in Mount Airy during Mayberry Days, on
September 24, 2004. (An identical statue had been unveiled the previous October
in Raleigh.) Seen here following the Mount Airy unveiling are* Andy Griffith
Show *performers (left to right) George Spence, Andy Griffith, Betty Lynn,
LeRoy McNees, and James Best. The original members of* The Dillards *(Rodney
Dillard, Doug Dillard, Mitch Jayne, and Dean Webb) and Maggie Peterson
Mancuso were also in attendance. Photo courtesy of TAGSRWC Archives.*

"An Evening with Don Knotts," in 2001. So that we could enjoy
some of the beauty of the Great Smoky Mountains during our stay,
Tim McAbee, the producer of the Pigeon Forge events, rented cab-
ins for us.

With no direct flights from Los Angeles to Knoxville, which was
the nearest airport of any size, it took me most of a day to get
to Pigeon Forge. During the summer of 2001, when I arrived on
my second trip to the area, Tim and friend Chris Osborne picked
me up at the airport. It was about 1:00 a.m. They drove me to the
cabin and, after carrying my luggage in, they showed me around. I
decided to step out on the balcony to have a cigarette.

The three of us went outside. By then, it was about 2:00 a.m. Even
though it was pitch black outside, Tim and Chris assured me that
I would have a spectacular view during the day. The cabin was built

THE MAYBERRY STARS ALIGN: Taking audience questions during "A Tribute to Mayberry" in Pigeon Forge, in 2002 are (left to right) Ronnie Schell, Barbara Stuart, Betty Lynn, Jean Carson, Keith Thibodeaux, Howard Morris, and George Lindsey. Photo by Bart Boatwright.

on a hill, and the balcony, supported by huge wooden posts, extended well beyond the hillside and high above the ground below. Once I had finished my cigarette, we started back inside. The door was locked. Tim had left the key on a counter inside. There we stood, high up on the balcony of a cabin in the woods, and locked out.

The cabin had two stories, and there was another smaller balcony above us. Tim decided to climb up to the balcony above and try that door. I was scared to death he would fall. With Chris boosting him up, Tim was able to climb over the railing and onto the upper balcony. We thought it would take just a minute for Tim to go inside, then come downstairs, and let us in. About that time, Tim said, "It's locked!" We had to laugh. What else could we do?

Tim climbed back down onto the lower balcony with Chris and me. Time for Plan B. I thought there must be some people around who would hear us. I called out a few times. No response. I should mention that this was also during a time before everyone carried a cell phone. None of us had one with us.

Tim decided the only other thing to do was to somehow shimmy down one of the wooden supports. The challenge was reaching a support, because they were tucked under the balcony. I refused to let Tim try. I insisted that we at least wait until daybreak in a few hours, when we could see what was below us. The three of us sat on the balcony talking and laughing for the rest of the night. I jokingly said,

"I'M ALWAYS CHASING RAINBOWS": Not just a song during a medley in Pigeon Forge in 2001, but also a general outlook on life. Photo by Bart Boatwright.

"Someday they'll find three skeletons on this balcony and they'll wonder who we were." I still laugh when I think about that night.

At first daylight, Chris lowered Tim over the side, and Tim was able to reach one of the supports and safely climb down. He was then able to open the door for us. Even while the three of us were stranded, we knew it was terribly funny. We just made the best of our situation and had fun talking. When Don Knotts heard what had happened, he deadpanned to Tim, "So, I hear you and Betty spent the night on the balcony."

Love, Connection

The thing that's truly amazing to me is the love all of us who worked on the *Griffith* show get from the fans. It's so heartfelt. I find it incredibly moving. We always knew people liked our show. We knew that just from the ratings. People in the industry would also let us know how much they loved the *Griffith* show. Or somebody at the grocery store would recognize me and that kind of thing. But until we started having the big Mayberry reunions attended by thousands of fans, none of us had any idea just how many fans there are, how enthusiastic they are, and, most of all, how nice they are. It was kind of an epiphany for most of us.

All the fans have been so sweet to me through the years. They really are the kindest, most sincere people. Before the pandemic changed everything, people would want to hug me, kiss me, cry tears of joy, and tell me how much they love the *Griffith* show. Just seeing how much the show means to people makes me cry tears of joy and appreciation too.

Fans will ask me things about the show. They expect me to have inside information that they don't know. The truth is that many of the fans know far more about the show than I ever did—especially about the storylines of all the episodes and the dialogue and all the trivia. I learn more about the *Griffith* show from the fans than they do from me. I may have known Thelma Lou's lines sixty years ago, but fans today are the ones who still know every one of them by heart. They know everybody else's lines too. Fortunately, from visiting with fans and from watching episodes whenever I can catch one, I can deliver enough lines not to embarrass myself or disappoint people too much. Can Barney sing? "Not a lick!"

I think what people are actually hoping for when they encounter any of us who worked on the *Griffith* show is a more personal connection to the magic they feel whenever they watch the show. Fans know that, whether it's Andy Griffith who was in every episode, Betty Lynn in twenty-six episodes, or Bobby Dean carrying a balloon in the background in one scene in "The Pickle Story," we had a firsthand experience, a part in creating the world of Mayberry that they love—that we all love. It helps make the *Griffith* show something more than just entertainment that you watch. It adds another dimension to the experience of enjoying the world of Mayberry, which can feel very real.

Getting to the Heart

Through all the decades, I remain humbled that people have always loved watching the *Griffith* show as much as we enjoyed making it. Many fans really take the characters to heart—sometimes in a way that feels almost like family.

Here's a case in point: I went to a hospital one time for treatment of a burn. I had scalded my right arm with boiling water. I picked up a pan that was too heavy. This was not long after I had broken my left wrist that time in 1995 when I fell on the dance floor at the Mayberry reunion event in Grand Rapids. After I came back home from Michigan and even after I had the cast off, I would sometimes forget that I couldn't lift much weight with that arm anymore. On this occasion, I picked up a big iron skillet with my left hand, and it slipped from my grip and spilled hot liquid all over my right arm. I called the emergency room at St. John's Hospital in Santa Monica and told the nurse who answered the phone what had happened and that I had put an antibacterial ointment on it. I asked her if she thought that would be sufficient treatment.

The nurse said, "No. You had better come on in."

I went down to the ER, but I had to wait several hours to see the doctor, a young guy. He finally came in with a clipboard with all my information in his hand and he thanked me for my patience.

I said, "Well, I do have patience. That's true. But truthfully, Doctor, I don't think I need to see you anymore. A lot of the redness is gone now, and it doesn't hurt quite as bad. I think I can just go home."

He said, "No, no. We should treat it."

He studied my information on the clipboard, and then he glanced at me. Then he looked back at the clipboard again and said, "I love that show."

I'm pretty sure his clipboard didn't have any information that indicated I was on *The Andy Griffith Show*. I think it was just that my name finally registered with him. He looked back at me and said, "When I was interning, I would be so upset. The show was on at eleven-thirty at night in L.A. I would come home all stressed and exhausted. I didn't think I could sleep, but I would turn that show on, and I could laugh and relax and then go right to sleep. That show meant so much to me."

I thought, *Gee, I hope he wasn't sleepy from boredom.* But I knew what he meant. I hear stories like that all the time. People tell me that it's their nightly routine to watch an episode of the *Griffith* show at bedtime and that it's the perfect way to end their day. I'm often right there watching at the same time.

I've heard that, during our recent times with the pandemic, the ratings for the *Griffith* show on streaming services saw one of the biggest increases in viewership of any show. Of course, people watched more television in general when everybody was stuck at home because of the pandemic. Comforting, familiar shows saw particularly large increases in the number of minutes watched. The *Griffith* show was one of the most popular, along with shows such as *Friends* and *The Office*. I suppose folks missed seeing their friends at the office, just as they also felt comforted by Mayberry.

Of course, lots of other television shows—not to mention movies, sports, and any number of other things people are passionate about—have enthusiastic followings. Even so, I think there's something different about the way the *Griffith* show touches not just people's funny bones, but also their hearts.

It's not just meeting people who worked on the show that has helped bring the show to life for its fans. I believe the interaction that the fans have with each other is every bit as special. It's also a two-way street for me and others who worked on the show. Experiencing the joy of the fans in such a direct way reminds us that the work we did all those years ago wasn't just a routine acting job.

BUNCHES OF LOVE: Enthralled with a ninetieth-birthday celebration at the Earle Theatre in downtown Mount Airy in 2016. Photo by Hobart Jones.

None of us who worked on the *Griffith* show ever dreamed we would experience such keen interest in what we had done after our time of making the show was over. We thought that once the work ended, then the interest would also end. Don Knotts moved on to make movies at Universal. Andy Griffith tried different things— trying to move on—but the public and the people writing the checks wouldn't let Andy leave Mayberry. It took Ben Matlock to finally help Andy Griffith get his career out of Andy Taylor's Mayberry handcuffs.

Mayberry had completely ended for me when Don Knotts left the *Griffith* show and Barney moved to Raleigh. That's the way things kind of rolled along for me until Mayberry fans started getting organized in the 1980s. The news media also started observing that there was still a lot of interest in the *Griffith* show. Ted Turner and his SuperStation TBS noticed, too, and carried the *Griffith* show in strong rotation. If the Atlanta Braves broadcasts had a rain delay, TBS would call up the *Griffith* show from the programming bullpen. Then came our *Return to Mayberry* reunion movie and the decades of reunion gatherings that would follow—most notably Mayberry Days. It has all been such a joyful experience for me.

Chapter 11: Ties that Bind—Mayberry and Mount Airy

For years, Andy Griffith was coy about how much Mayberry might be based on Mount Airy. He wanted to stand up for the creativity and talent contributed by everybody who worked on the show, especially the writers. However, in 2002, when he made his first public appearance in Mount Airy in many years, with a twinkle in his eye and a mischievous grin, he finally admitted to the large crowd gathered for the dedication of the Andy Griffith Parkway that indeed Mayberry does feel a lot like Mount Airy.

Andy drew a great deal from his hometown—and not only the names of people and places. You just get a Mayberry vibe all the time when you travel around town. I can see why people come to visit from all over America and even from other countries. Watching Mayberry on TV makes people want to experience Mayberry for themselves. As an appealing little town set among beautiful hills and valleys, Mount Airy is able to deliver an authentic Mayberry experience.

Don Knotts, who grew up in Morgantown, West Virginia, used to say, "Life is hills and valleys." He was speaking metaphorically, of course, but I think growing up among hills and valleys might help form how you view the world. Someone who grew up by an ocean might feel that life ebbs and flows and that experiences come in waves.

When I decided to pick up and move to Mount Airy from California, many of my friends were shocked, including Andy and Cindi Griffith.

I said to Andy, "I hope you don't mind that I moved to your hometown."

"No, not at all," Andy said. "Cindi and I are just amazed."

Andy obviously loved being near the ocean. I think he loved the
Outer Banks of North Carolina from the moment he first went
there in college to perform in *The Lost Colony*, the famous outdoor
drama. As soon as he could, he bought a house there, and it's where
he wanted to be whenever he wasn't working. Even though Andy
dearly loved the Outer Banks, I still think his growing up in a small
town in the North Carolina mountains shaped much of who he
was and what Mayberry became.

I never could have even dreamed that, all these years later, I would
be living in Mount Airy and be regularly greeting fans at the Andy
Griffith Museum. You never know what will happen to you along
life's way. I've been very happy in Mount Airy. The people are so
good to me, and they seem happy to have me here. I hope that the
people in Mount Airy will continue to feel that way and not be
disappointed in me someday. In any case, I'm grateful for all of the
attention and sweetness.

One time, about five years after I moved to Mount Airy, I was in
the waiting room at a doctor's office. A very lovely lady was seated
next to me. She was petite and very ladylike. She turned to me and,
in the wonderfully friendly manner that I had become accustomed
to since moving to the South, she said, "Hello, my name is Juanita."

Without even thinking, I turned to her and blurted back, "You
little hussy! I've been wanting to meet you for a long time." I hadn't
planned the response. It just came out.

Immediately after this mock tirade, I suddenly thought, *Oh, dear,
I hope she knows the show. It would be terrible if she doesn't.*

I also didn't know whether she even recognized me. Though
Mount Airy is a small town and I had been here long enough for
most people to know that I now lived here, it could have been that,
even in Mount Airy, not everyone knew the show, knew who I was,
or knew that Juanita was Thelma Lou's rival for Barney's affections.
Fortunately, Mount Airy's Juanita did know the show and me and
the significance of her name. She responded with a cheerful laugh.
We had a nice chat as we continued to wait.

The first Christmas after I arrived in Mount Airy, another lady
named Juanita called me to ask if I would be willing to be the person who flips the switch to turn on the lights for the city's official

REVEALING MOMENT: The 2007 unveiling in Mount Airy of artist Greg McCormick's portrait (an air-brushed painting on Masonite), which is based on a favorite photograph from the 1950s. Photo by Hobart Jones.

Christmas tree. I was delighted by the offer and said yes. I didn't call her a hussy or anything. I had never before been asked to light a community Christmas tree. I love Christmastime, and I thought the honor of lighting the tree would be a fun way to get into the Christmas spirit in my new hometown.

It turned out that the Christmas tree in Mount Airy is a white ash tree. North Carolina is one of the top Christmas-tree farming states in the country. The farms ship Christmas trees, chiefly Fraser firs, all over the country, but in Mount Airy, the Christmas tree is an ash. It is located at the south end of North Main Street near City Hall and the post office and less than a block from the central business district. It's the perfect setting, and the tree really is beautiful. They light the trunk and all the limbs with little white lights.

I called friends back in Los Angeles and said, "Guess what? I'm going to light the Mount Airy Christmas tree, and it's an ash tree."

They all thought that was the funniest thing, but it really is perfectly beautiful.

Starting in 2015, Mount Airy also introduced its answer to the dropping of the ball in Times Square on New Year's Eve. They constructed a giant lighted Mayberry Sheriff badge, about as tall as Andy Griffith himself. Instead of lowering it from a height, Mount Airy raises the badge to the top of the clock tower that's downtown at the corner of Virginia Street and North Main Street. I think it's a clever and festive idea.

As much as I love living in Mount Airy, I must admit that I do miss a lot about living in Los Angeles. However, I don't miss the crime. That was a big part of my motivation for leaving L.A. I had been robbed three times—twice on the street and once while shopping at a department store. My home was also burglarized twice in the months right before I finally decided that enough was enough. During the second burglary, the culprits really tore everything apart. I suppose that they were looking for valuables. The house was totally ransacked—a real mess. The combination of the destruction and being made to feel so vulnerable made me scared even to be in the house that I had lived in for almost sixty years.

The ironic thing is that, just over three years after I moved to Mount Airy, I was standing outside of Lowe's grocery store on a Sunday afternoon in April when a man sneaked up on me, snatched my wallet right out of my hands, and ran away. The Mount Airy police caught him a short time later, and I got my wallet back with only a few dollars missing. I just had not expected that kind of thing to happen in Mount Airy. Newspaper headline writers naturally made the most of the incident: "Thelma Lou Robbed in Mayberry" and so on. It turned out that the man who robbed me lived across the state line in Virginia. As in Mayberry, my crime troubles in Mount Airy came from out of town. That made me feel a little better.

I do miss seeing my friends in Los Angeles—people such as Joan Leslie and Jane Withers, both of whom, sadly, are gone now, and Ann Blyth. We were all about the same age, within a year or two. We all came up together at Twentieth Century-Fox. Joan, Jane, and I were bridesmaids in Ann Blyth and Jim McNulty's wedding. We remained good friends through the years. I still stay in touch with Ann, though not as often as we used to or as I would like.

I also miss my friends from St. Timothy's, but I've been blessed with wonderful friends and clergy at Holy Angels, my church in Mount Airy. My lifelong Catholic faith continues to be my greatest source of comfort and strength. I feel immensely blessed by that faith.

Likewise, I miss going out to lunch or dinner from time to time with some of the *Griffith* show folks that I kept in touch with. Of course, most of them have passed away now. One of the advantages of Mount Airy and their Mayberry Days festival is that lots of the old *Griffith* cast and crew come to the festival, so I still get to see many of them at least once a year. I always look forward to their visits.

Chapter 12: Positive Signs

Prior to the pandemic, I had been signing autographs at the Andy Griffith Museum in Mount Airy once a month for many years. People come from all over to experience Andy Griffith's hometown, tour the museum, and visit with me. There are these long lines of fans that sometimes go out the entrance to my exhibit area and around the building. I still can't believe it. Some of the fans are so happy to meet me that they cry. Or maybe they're just overtaken with relief when they finally make it through to the head of the line.

I have been told that, at Mayberry cast reunion events and things like Mayberry Days, my autograph lines move slower than just about anybody else's. Having a slow-moving line isn't a ploy to cause there to be a really long line in order to make me look popular. Rather, it's because I like to take my time and visit with people and get to know them a little bit. For many of the fans, I'm somebody who has been in their homes since they were little kids, and they feel they really know me.

Some of the fans are people I have known for years, even decades. I remember them and enjoy learning more about them and what they've been doing since we last saw each other. It can be an emotional experience for them and for me. After more than thirty years of my regularly making personal appearances, both at Mayberry reunion events or just by myself in Mount Airy, it can happen that somebody who was a young person in 1990 has since had children and now maybe even grandchildren, who also are fans of the show and come by to visit.

It's especially fun to see the reactions of the little kids. They have seen the show enough to know who Thelma Lou is, and they come running up to see her. Of course, here I am, this old woman now. I don't look like I did years ago. Either they instantly understand what happens with the aging process, or maybe they've been prepared by their parents or grandparents to meet a much older Thelma Lou. In

LOVING HANDS: *Signing a photograph at the Andy Griffith Museum in April 2018. Photo by Hobart Jones.*

any case, they don't seem to mind. They are as thrilled to meet me as I am to meet them.

It means a lot to me to be able to have those kinds of connections with people, and it's all because of *The Andy Griffith Show*. What a gift that show continues to be for me and so many other people. It just keeps finding new ways to spread joy. Andy often said that, at its heart, the *Griffith* show was about love. I see every day that he was right and probably in ways that even Andy himself never could have imagined.

All that said, as the years go by, I find more and more that there is a certain group of kids who have never watched the *Griffith* show. They were really young when I first met them, but are getting grown up a little by now. The *Griffith* show was always their idea of what Grandma and Grandpa or Mom and Dad would watch, but the kids themselves have never watched the show. Instead, they're busy

READY TO RIDE: Leading the Mayberry Days parade past Mount Airy's Earle Theatre in 2018. Photo by Hobart Jones.

on their cell phones with games, texting, or maybe social media. I think they're missing out on a lot. I tell them, "Now, you be sure to watch this show. You'll be glad if you do." I think all that it would take is getting them to sit still just long enough to watch "Opie the Birdman," and then they would be hooked on Mayberry.

Back when the *Griffith* show was originally on, people would say that kids were going to be ruined by watching too much TV. That was back when there were only three networks and you couldn't carry your own personal screen with you wherever you went. Kids in the 1960s turned out just fine, and today's kids are good too. Even so, I still think kids and, for that matter, all of us are better off when there's more Mayberry in our lives.

For me, as with everyone else who worked on the *Griffith* show, the joy comes from more than just its being a show that we watch and are entertained by. It's something that we were a part of. And it's a part of us. We have memories of the work we did and the friends we made—friends that became people we loved.

It is a bond that has continued to grow stronger over time, especially after we did the reunion movie and then when many of us

NOW AND FOREVER: Touring the Betty Lynn Exhibit during ninetieth-birthday festivities in Mount Airy in August 2016. Note the Shirley Temple doll, a favorite toy from childhood, still sitting pretty in the exhibit case. At far right are the trunk and personal pistol from the USO Camp Shows tour during World War II. Photo by Hobart Jones.

also started doing the reunion events and personal appearances together. We all started having an even greater appreciation of the show and of the sincere passion that fans have for it.

Tourists come to Mount Airy not just for Mayberry Days but pretty much year round. The area has a lot to offer. There's beautiful scenery, a rich history of country music, and, more recently, local wineries have been an added draw. After being in the works for years, the Andy Griffith Museum was established and then received a complete update of its exhibits a few years ago.

The late Emmett Forrest, who was a truly lovely man, grew up with Andy Griffith, and then, as an adult, collected all things Andy. His collection became the core of the museum, which also received many artifacts from others involved with the *Griffith* show and other parts of Andy's career and life, including from Don Knotts, George Lindsey, Ken Berry, and Maggie Peterson Mancuso, as well as from Andy himself and Cindi. It's quite an impressive collection of items related to Andy Griffith and *The Andy Griffith Show*.

I donated some of my *Griffith* scripts to the museum. I was also honored and pleased when the Surry Arts Council wanted to install a permanent exhibit about my life and career. I knew I had kept

FELINE GROOVY: If there were ever any doubt that Thelma Lou is "the cat's," young artist Mackenna Forrester answered that question once and for all with this ninety-fifth birthday card in 2021. Or at the very least, we know that there is a Thelma Lou who is an actual cat. Photo by Hobart Jones.

items from my childhood and from my time with the USO Camp Shows all those years for a reason.

Not All Paths Lead to Mayberry

In 2006, I was pleased to be invited to the first year of the Missouri Cherry Blossom Festival in Marshfield. Nicholas Inman, a Methodist minister, is the driving force behind the festival, which by now has become a tradition. It is held each April. I was fortunate to be able to visit Marshfield several times. The people there were always extremely kind to me. They truly roll out the red carpet for all of their guests, the majority of whom have a connection to Missouri or to American presidents. I was really pleased to be able to meet family members of so many presidents. I was impressed by how many presidents were represented. The festival has only continued to grow through the years. They always have the most fascinating guests. It's quite a feat for that charming little town.

During that first festival I attended, I was honored to be one of the six inaugural members of the Missouri Walk of Fame. The others in that first group of inductees were President Harry S. Truman, astronomer Edwin Hubble, writer Laura Ingalls Wilder, the unsinkable Molly Brown, and Mickey Carroll, one of the Munchkins from *The Wizard of Oz*. All of us, except Laura Ingalls Wilder, were born in Missouri, but she lived much of her life in Missouri and died there. Edwin Hubble was even born in Marshfield. Mickey Carroll and I were the only inductees who were still alive. He was a delightful man. I really enjoyed visiting with him. He was one of the last surviving Munchkins. He died just a couple of years later.

While in Marshfield that year, Nicholas took me to the local Walmart to get some things I needed. I told the manager, a nice man named Tim Slavens, that I thought it would be such fun to be a greeter at Walmart and get to say hello to everyone and make them feel welcome. The next day, when I returned to the store, Tim was ready to outfit me with a blue Walmart vest and a name tag with "Thelma Lou" on it. I immediately put on the vest and went to work greeting customers at the front entrance.

It wasn't long before a lady in a wheelchair entered. When the woman recognized me, she became extremely emotional. I asked her if she was all right. She told me that she had recently been in an automobile accident. Her doctors had told her that they didn't

CHECK IT OUT!: Totally invested, even if just for a short time, in the dream experience of being a greeter at the Walmart in Marshfield, Missouri, in 2006. Photo courtesy of Nicholas Inman.

expect her to be able to walk again. She had been dealing with depression as she struggled to recover at home.

The lady went on to explain that, as a way to fight depression, she had watched episodes of *The Andy Griffith Show*, because it always made her laugh. She said that watching the show had helped get her through some really dark moments. She said this was the first day she had been out of her house since the accident. She took "Thelma Lou" being the first person to greet her as a sign from God that everything was going to be all right.

Both the lady and I spontaneously began to cry, as did everyone in our little group who had heard us talking. She and I hugged and had a very nice conversation. Just as I had always suspected—being a Walmart greeter was the best job ever!

After the festival that year, Nicholas arranged for me to go with him to visit the state capital, Jefferson City, a couple of hours north of Marshfield. We received a tour of the Missouri Governor's Mansion by the gracious first couple, Governor Matt Blunt and First Lady Melanie Blunt. We then went to the Missouri State Capitol, where we visited both the House and the Senate chambers.

I expected that we would just be observing the proceedings and that they might acknowledge us sitting in the gallery or something like that. We did indeed do all of that, but in the Senate chamber they also invited me to come up to the podium and make some remarks. I wasn't sure what I could say that would be interesting or appropriate, so I just talked about being a proud Missourian and thanked them for their good work on behalf of Missouri and for inviting me to speak.

The next year I received the Cherry Blossom Medal at the festival. I'm not sure exactly what that medal signifies, but I think it means that they like you. I appreciated receiving it. I never gave them a medal in return, but I liked the Missouri Cherry Blossom Festival right back. I enjoyed visiting Marshfield so much that one year I even paid my way to be there for the Fourth of July. They put on a terrific parade—pure Americana. They gave me the honor of being the parade's grand marshal. The experience was like a living Norman Rockwell painting or Frank Capra movie. You couldn't help but be filled with patriotic pride and gratitude.

In late May 2007, just a few weeks after the Cherry Blossom Festival, Nicholas Inman made arrangements to pick me up in Mount Airy and join him and his lovely mother, Jeanette Evans, and his beautiful fiancée, Sarah, for the drive to Charlotte, North Carolina, for the dedication of the Billy Graham Library. I'm sure it wasn't easy to get tickets to that event, but Nicholas has a way of getting

AMONG DISTINGUISHED AND ECLECTIC COMPANY: Special guests at 2007's Missouri Cherry Blossom Festival helped one Missouri native (the one seated and wearing a corsage) continue the celebration of her eightieth birthday (August 29th of the previous year). Pictured (left to right) in the back row are Linda Ditzler and Neita Campbell (both members of President James K. Polk's family); Jennifer Harville (great-granddaughter of President Calvin Coolidge); Brad Turner (President Harding's family); George Cleveland (grandson of President Grover Cleveland, and the only one in this group who knew which camera to look at!); Mary Prince (personal assistant of President and Mrs. Jimmy Carter); Dean Webb and Mitch Jayne (members of The Dillards); and Jamie Rupe (Cherry Blossom Queen). In the front row (left to right) are Virginia Roedder (President James K. Polk's family), our birthday girl, Karolyn Grimes (Zuzu Bailey in It's a Wonderful Life*), and Mickey Carroll (a Munchkin in* The Wizard of Oz*). Photo courtesy of Missouri Cherry Blossom Festival.*

difficult things done. It was a grand event with many dignitaries in attendance, including not only the Reverend Billy Graham, but also three former Presidents: Jimmy Carter, George H.W. Bush, and Bill Clinton. I was thrilled just to be a face in the crowd and see that beautiful facility.

O.K., but Many Paths *Do* Lead to Mayberry

Not to be outdone when it comes to saluting stars through pathways, Mount Airy has its own walkway with stars—only their stars look like Mayberry Sheriff badges. The Mount Airy badges are not as official as the Missouri Walk of Fame, but they're seen by lots of visitors. The badges are right outside the entrance to the Andy Griffith Museum. I'm proud to be there with a badge, along with Andy Griffith and others—just a few steps away from Mount Airy's TV Land Landmark statue of Andy and Opie.

As the longtime Executive Director of the Surry Arts Council, Tanya Jones has spearheaded many of the tributes to Andy Griffith and the *Griffith* show in Mount Airy. Tanya instigated Mayberry Days in 1990 and has led the charge for the event every year since then. She has meant the world to the Mayberry Days festival and the legacy of Mayberry.

More than that, Tanya and husband Hobart have been great friends to me. I doubt I ever would have moved to Mount Airy without Tanya's encouragement and support. Without the continued efforts of Tanya, Hobart, the Surry Arts Council staff, and many others in the community, I certainly would not have had such a happy experience during all the years since I made the move to Mount Airy. I'm forever grateful.

Flight of Honor

I had been to Washington, D.C., only twice in my life before what I knew would likely be my final trip there in 2009. The first trip had been in 1945 when I was on the Greyhound bus going from Newport News to New York after my overseas tour with the USO. The second trip was with my Mother on our return from our European vacation in 1971. It was a thrill to see our nation's capital as a tourist the first two times, but it was a deep honor when, for my third trip, I was offered the chance to fly from North Carolina with World War II veterans on the first Triad Flight of Honor to visit the new World War II Memorial.

Rotary groups in the Piedmont Triad area of North Carolina raised money to fly veterans to Washington, D.C., on charter flights. The organizers generously wanted to include me among the veterans and cover the whole cost of my trip, but I felt that I shouldn't fly entirely free. I sent the Rotary organization some money that I hoped would cover at least part of the cost of my seat. It didn't feel right for me to accept a free ride with their funds, which could have been used to pay the way for the men and women who had served in the actual military during the war. It was still a bargain for me, and a tremendous honor.

I guess my wartime experiences were what qualified me for a seat on the Flight of Honor. I had helped with the war effort in my own way by touring overseas with the USO Camp Shows. I had been in some pretty harrowing situations and had seen up close the horrors that war can do to people.

The USO touring I did at home and overseas was about eight months altogether. Of course, I was not an actual war veteran. When my mother was given a blue-star pin because I had served in the USO, I told her, "Mother, I wasn't really a soldier."

She firmly replied, "I know, but you were over there. You were serving your country. That counts for something."

I suppose my mother was right. I'm sure she worried about me while I was overseas as much as parents of those in the actual military worried about their sons and daughters. What I did during the war still could never compare to the sacrifices of all the servicemen and servicewomen. They were the heroes, and we should never forget that. I hope the World War II Memorial helps make sure that future generations continue to remember.

I don't think I ever would have managed the logistics of going to see the memorial without the kind of organization and assistance that the Rotary Club provided. Many of us were needing to use wheelchairs and other assistance devices. The Rotary Club's team of volunteers worked hard to make sure everything was as comfortable as possible for all of us. We made the trip from Greensboro to Washington, D.C., and back to Greensboro in one day, and I never felt rushed. We were treated like royalty from beginning to end.

Our Flight of Honor received a lot of news coverage by local media, especially by television stations, which sent crews to the Greensboro airport for our departure and for our arrival back home. One of the news reporters apparently got word that I liked to be called Thelma Lou. She or whoever told her that about me apparently had not understood that I had played Thelma Lou on the *Griffith* show. She thought I was just some old lady who thought

GRATEFUL TRAVELER: Arriving at the airport in Greensboro, North Carolina, on October 3, 2009 (coincidentally, the forty-ninth anniversary of the broadcast of the first episode of The Andy Griffith Show*), after a thrilling day with war veterans visiting the World War II Memorial in Washington, D.C. The trip was the first Triad Flight of Honor, which was organized by Rotary Club groups in North Carolina's Piedmont Triad area. Photo by Scott MacKenzie.*

she was Thelma Lou and liked to be called Thelma Lou. In other words, "Bless her heart," as I've learned that we in the South say about somebody like that. It gave me a good chuckle that I was on the local news as some random lady who liked the *Griffith* show and liked to be called Thelma Lou.

And you know what? That's just fine. Because I *do* like to watch the *Griffith* show and I *do* like being called Thelma Lou. When I watch the show, I still laugh as though it's the first time I've seen it. No one laughs harder than I do. When we were filming, I was a great audience for Andy and Don, and for everybody else on the show. Because I would have disturbed everybody, I couldn't burst out laughing while we were working, but I can be boisterous when I watch the show now—and I am!

I can still see Don's big blue eyes looking at me. It was really special to be able to watch him work close up and see him become Barney Fife. More than that, of course, it was a thrill to be able to work with him and be a small part of some of those hilarious moments, as well as the tender ones. I still miss him a lot, I really do. I miss them all. Thank God for the memories and the reruns and for the fans who share a love and respect for our creative efforts from so long ago. In a way, the *Griffith* show was its own kind of flight of honor for me. It's a flight that continues to soar.

Happy Trails

As I've said throughout these pages, I feel extremely blessed to have had the chance to work with so many talented performers and to know so many wonderful people. While doing *The Andy Griffith Show* sixty years ago, I never would have dreamed that people would still want to see me at the age I am now. What's more is that I can go onstage and have people come from all over and seem happy to see me and say, "We love you, Thelma Lou!" It's incredibly touching. I don't think that happens with too many shows and performers that are as old as the *Griffith* show and I are.

One of the last public appearances I made before the pandemic lockdowns in 2020 was when North Carolina Governor Roy Cooper came to Mount Airy to tour the Andy Griffith Museum. I was part of a local group that was at the museum to greet him. He is such a nice man. I could tell when I met him that he is a genuine fan of the *Griffith* show. Governor or not, he's a Goober. (That's a high compliment among Mayberry fans!) I think he has been an outstanding governor of North Carolina during incredibly difficult times. I was pleased to be able to meet him and to thank him.

Even as I was working on this book in the summer of 2021, just as the country was trying to come out of restrictions caused by the awful pandemic, who should come to Mount Airy, but Ted Koppel, a journalist whom I have always greatly respected.

MORE THAN JUST A MAYBERRY HANGER-ON: Welcoming North Carolina Governor (and Mayberry Sheriff shirt-toting) Roy Cooper to the Andy Griffith Museum during his visit to Mount Airy in January 2020. Photo by Hobart Jones.

Ted was in Mount Airy doing a story for *CBS News Sunday Morning*. He was basically taking the pulse of rural and small-town Americans about the condition of the country. Where better to do that than Mount Airy and Mayberry?

The day I met Ted was my first day back doing autographs at the Andy Griffith Museum in the many months—well over a year—since pandemic restrictions had first been put in place. The Surry Arts Council had been diligent about its pandemic protocols, and of course, at my age and with a variety of existing health concerns, I was extra cautious too.

As we senior citizens often do, Ted and I mostly just chatted about arthritis and other aches and pains of growing old. I told him how much I admired his work over the years. He and his crew enjoyed seeing the fans who had shown up that day to visit with me and get autographs. The finished story ended up being somewhat controversial among some Mayberry fans and folks in Mount Airy. It wasn't an episode of the *Griffith* show. For my part, though, I had a very pleasant visit with Ted.

That has been a nice benefit to my being in Mount Airy. Though it's nothing like the old days in Los Angeles when I would frequently run into people in show business, having old friends visit Mount Airy—and getting to meet people that I otherwise might never have known—has been a bonus of making the move from Los Angeles.

In addition to all of the *Griffith* show people who come to town, folks like Donna Douglas from *The Beverly Hillbillies* and Nancy Stafford from *Matlock* have visited Mount Airy—all because of Andy Griffith's close association with the area. Except for the fact that I was on the *Griffith* show and happen to live in Mount Airy, I don't think I would have ever had a reason to be interviewed by a nice man like CNN's Tom Foreman, who came to town to do a story about Andy Griffith and Mayberry in 2011.

On June 1, 2012, just a little over a year after CNN's story about Andy Griffith's impact on Mount Airy, I called Andy to wish him a happy birthday. He was very gracious and appreciative. We had a really good chat. He seemed to be in an especially reflective mood.

"Y'ALL COME BACK NOW, YA HEAR?": With Donna Douglas, best known as Elly May Clampett on the Beverly Hillbillies *TV series, during her visit to the Andy Griffith Museum in August 2013. Photo by Hobart Jones.*

I had no idea at the time, but that conversation would be our last. Andy died of a heart attack on July 3.

As I looked back on that conversation and Andy's general tone, I wondered whether maybe Andy sensed that his time in this world was drawing to a close. Of course, for most of us of a certain age—Andy was born about three months before I was—that sense is part of our daily reality, just as it is even for younger people dealing with certain serious health issues and for people in dangerous lines of work. You become keenly aware of your mortality.

In Andy's case, I'm comforted in the knowledge that he was a man of deep Christian faith. I know their shared faith was a source

*SOLEMN COMMEMORATION: Making heartfelt remarks at a special
memorial held for dear friend Andy Griffith during Mayberry Days in
Mount Airy in 2012. Blurred in the background are festival guests (left
to right) George Lindsey, Jr.; Janice McNees; LeRoy McNees; and Peggy
McCay. Photo by Hobart Jones.*

of strength and comfort for both Andy and his wife, Cindi. The
preparations of faith notwithstanding, Andy's sudden passing sent
shock waves across the country, most especially among the legions
of Mayberry fans and in Mount Airy and throughout North Carolina. With the possible exception of Billy Graham, I doubt that
there has ever been a native of the Tar Heel State more beloved than
Andy Griffith. Certainly no one was ever a more ardent booster for
North Carolina than Andy was.

Andy Griffith was truly one of the giants of American entertainment of his time. *The Andy Griffith Show* just might endure for all
time. I think there are few television shows that have meant as much
to as many people as the *Griffith* show. Andy's movies, especially *A
Face in the Crowd* and *No Time for Sergeants*, are also standing the
test of time, as are *Matlock* and his comedy and music recordings.
More than any of that, for me, Andy was a colleague for a time, and
a friend always and foremost. As with Bob Sweeney, Hal Smith,
Aneta Corsaut, Howie Morris, Don Knotts, Jim Nabors, and so
many others before him and since, I really miss Andy.

I often hear fans refer to their fellow Mayberry enthusiasts as their "Mayberry family." I know exactly what they mean. I truly love my Mayberry family too!

On that note, I'll say, "That's a wrap!"

Thank you for reading my story. God bless you.

JUST SIGN HERE: As was the case at the Andy Griffith Museum on the third Friday of most months for many years, the last person waiting in the long line for an autograph on this day in 2015 followed the customary protocol of holding this sign. The sign would be handed to each new arrival until the line had to be cut off. The lucky person who was last in line had to not only hold the sign but also break the bad news to the late arrivals that they had been "nipped in the bud." Photo by Hobart Jones.

Epilogue

After a brief time in hospice care, Betty Lynn died peacefully in Surry County, North Carolina, on October 16, 2021. She was buried near her mother and maternal grandparents at Holy Cross Catholic Cemetery in Culver City, California, on October 27, 2021.

Betty's last public appearance was as grand marshal of the annual Mayberry Days parade in Mount Airy, North Carolina, on September 25, 2021. Ever the trouper, Betty didn't want to disappoint fans. Through sheer determination and the able assistance of devoted caregivers, Betty led the parade down Main Street in the same cream-colored 1953 Buick Skylark convertible as she had for many previous editions of Mayberry Days. The adoring crowd lining Main Street cheered her all along the way. Just being able to catch a glimpse of Betty that day would become a precious memory.

GRAND FINALE: One last public appearance, as grand marshal of the Mayberry Days parade on September 25, 2021. Photo by Hobart Jones.

Many in the crowd no doubt suspected that the parade that morning could be the last time that they would get to see Betty. Betty very likely had that same feeling. Even so, she was at peace. As she had been all of her life, Betty was strong in her religious faith until the end. Regrets? Betty had a few. But just a few. She didn't dwell on them. Rather, she lived her life with grace, true grit, and genuine gratitude.

Friends and fans of Betty will forever cherish the joy that her performances and even just her presence have given to all of us. Barney Fife was right when he declared that Thelma Lou was "the cat's." So, too, was our friend Betty.

—J.C. and T.M.

Acknowledgments

Writing this book has been a labor of love not only for us, but for many others who have helped us along the way.

It was in 2009 that we first mentioned to publisher Ben Ohmart at BearManor Media that we were working on this book. Ben patiently waited for us to submit the manuscript. If Ben didn't understand the meaning of "working at a Mayberry pace" in 2009, he does now! We thank Ben for that. We also thank designer Robbie Adkins, and the whole team at BearManor for helping us produce a book that we believe would have pleased Betty.

We appreciate the efforts of Jay Williams, executor of Betty Lynn's estate, for helping us navigate the legal waters of posthumously publishing Betty's autobiography and for giving his seal of approval for the final manuscript.

Betty would certainly join us in expressing deep appreciation to Tanya Jones for her beautiful Foreword for this book. More than that, Tanya, who has served as Executive Director of the Surry Arts Council for more than three decades, was instrumental in encouraging and facilitating Betty's move from Los Angeles to Mount Airy in 2007. No one was a closer friend of or a better advocate for Betty during the last fifteen years of her life.

Right beside Tanya all that time was Hobart Jones, her husband and an award-winning photographer, who provided many key images for this book. Hobart also assisted Betty in making her final revisions to the manuscript.

Also greatly helping with photographs as well as document research was Abigail Linville. As Director of Collections and Exhibitions for the Surry Arts Council, Abigail is curator of photographs, documents, and other items that Betty donated to the Arts Council and its Andy Griffith Museum, which also includes the Betty Lynn Exhibit. Abigail's efforts provided crucial information and materials for this book.

SHARING THE LOVE: Onstage in Pigeon Forge, Tennessee, in 2000—always ready to greet the world with open arms. Photo by Bart Boatwright.

Betty was very supportive of the Surry Arts Council and its mission. Likewise, Arts Council staff and volunteers, as well as many others throughout the Mount Airy community, assisted Betty with a variety of endeavors during her time living in Mount Airy—all of which was ultimately of great benefit to our completing this book.

We also thank others who directly or indirectly helped with photographs, research, and other elements. Those folks include Ken Beck, Nicholas Inman, Mark Evanier, Terry Dennison, Terri Champney, Lynnette Young, Ben Currin, Ruth Currin, Kenny Hooker, Karen Leonard, Bart Boatwright, Phil Bowling, Jason Gilmore, Steve Keenan, Scott MacKenzie, TAGSRWC Archives, Kellie Highfill, Teresa Neighbors, Robert Collier, Lisa Fulk, Mitzi Ellis, Jeff Sims, Kristine Krueger, Phillip Stegner, and Karen Knotts. And a specific thank-you, on behalf of Betty, to Jimmy Fallon.

Jim especially thanks his wife, Mary, who was one of this project's biggest cheerleaders from start to finish.

Tim wishes to thank his family and friends for their support and encouragement.

Most of all, Betty would want us to be sure to thank all of her fans. She treasured you and became good friends with many through the years. Betty was always humbled both by the long lines of people cheerfully waiting to visit with her when she was signing autographs and by the enthusiastic standing ovations she received at performances and other public appearances. She genuinely loved visiting with and getting to know people.

Though no book can be a substitute for Betty herself, we hope this volume is a fitting stand-in as one final hug from Betty to all of her friends and fans.

—J.C. and T.M.

FAREWELL: What a wonderful ride it has been. Photo courtesy of Surry Arts Council.

Made in the USA
Columbia, SC
20 November 2023

26676952R00183